PENGUIN BOOKS

EXCESS BAGGAGE

Judith Sills, Ph.D., is the author of four books, including the #1 *New York Times* bestseller *Excess Baggage*. A three-year National Science Foundation Fellow, Dr. Sills is a contributing editor to *Family Circle* magazine, and has written for *O: The Oprah Magazine*, *Cosmopolitan*, *Mademoiselle*, and other national magazines. A nationally recognized public speaker and former radio host, she is a clinical psychologist in private practice in Philadelphia.

Judith Sills, Ph.D.

EXCESS BAGGAGE

Getting Out
of Your Own Way

PENGUIN BOOKS

PENGUIN BOOKS
Published by the Penguin Group
Penguin Group (USA) Inc., 375 Hudson Street, New York, New York 10014, U.S.A.
Penguin Books Ltd, 80 Strand, London WC2R 0RL, England
Penguin Books Australia Ltd, 250 Camberwell Road,
    Camberwell, Victoria 3124, Australia
Penguin Books Canada Ltd, 10 Alcorn Avenue, Toronto, Ontario, Canada M4V 3B2
Penguin Books India (P) Ltd, 11 Community Centre,
    Panchsheel Park, New Delhi – 110 017, India
Penguin Books (N.Z.) Ltd, Cnr Rosedale and Airborne Roads,
    Albany, Auckland, New Zealand
Penguin Books (South Africa) (Pty) Ltd, 24 Sturdee Avenue,
    Rosebank, Johannesburg 2196, South Africa

Penguin Books Ltd, Registered Offices:
80 Strand, London WC2R 0RL, England

First published in the United States of America by Viking Penguin,
a division of Penguin Books USA Inc. 1993
Published in Penguin Books 1994
This edition with a preface by the author published 2004

10 9 8 7 6 5 4 3

Grateful acknowledgment is made for permission to reproduce the Calvin and Hobbes
cartoon on page vi. Copyright 1992 Watterson. Distributed by Universal Press Syndicate.
Reprinted with permission. All rights reserved.

THE LIBRARY OF CONGRESS HAS CATALOGED THE HARDCOVER EDITION AS FOLLOWS:
Sills, Judith.
Excess baggage : getting out of your own way / Judith Sills.
p.   cm.
ISBN 0-670-84062-9 (hc.)
ISBN 0 14 20.0419 7 (pbk.)
1. Self-actualization (Psychology).   2. Self-defeating behavior.   I. Title.
BF637.S4S548 1993
158'1—dc20   92-50370

Printed in the United States of America
Set in Garamond Light
Designed by Kathryn Parise

For
Spencer, Lynn, and Mother

■

Pamela Dorman, Susan Schulman, and Denise Logan
and
in memory of Peter and Peter

■

(Love, Work, and a little bit of Glamour)

Contents

■

PREFACE   viii

Chapter One ■ Free Yourself From Yourself   1

Chapter Two ■ The Price You Pay for Being Who You Are   12

   Chart: Excess Baggage at a Glance   26

Chapter Three ■ You Need to Be Right   29

Chapter Four ■ Ain't I Awful? Ain't I Swell?   76

Chapter Five ■ You Dread Rejection   116

Chapter Six ■ You Create Drama   159

Chapter Seven ■ You Cherish Rage   206

Chapter Eight ■ Enough   243

Postscript ■ The Anxiety of Change   249

Acknowledgments   253

Author's Note   254

NOTES   255

BIBLIOGRAPHY   264

INDEX   268

Preface

■

$\int$ elf-awareness can be a real bitch.

This morning I sat with a man who suddenly recognized the damage his critical nitpicking had wreaked on his relationship with his son. "I was only trying to push him to his outer limit," he'd explained to me, over and over. "I was trying to give him the help and encouragement I never got." Then rationalization and justification were swept aside in a tide of clarity and remorse. "Once my son left home, he's never voluntarily sought out my company. Given my laserlike review of his every move, I can't blame him. How could he love me? He can't even breathe around me."

A middle-aged, discarded wife was similarly self-loathing. "I tolerated years of exploitation and emotional abuse. I would have told you then that I did it out of love, that marriage requires forgiveness, that he was only tired or testy, that he loved me underneath. The truth was that I lived with it because I'm weak, because even the thought of conflict makes me sick, because I was pathetically afraid to be alone. Even a starfish would have had the guts to scrape herself off that decaying rock. But not me. I clung. Actually, the rock ended up scraping me off."

A second woman reviewed herself with equally harsh clarity. "I made him buy a large cubic zirconium to replace the measly diamond engagement ring he could afford. That's the kind of person I was, the kind I think I probably still am—even though it cost me that relationship and probably some others. I know it shouldn't matter, but if a man can't give me the best of the very best, I can't keep loving him."

Your need to be right,

Your dread of rejection,

Your sense of superiority,

Your need to create drama, or

Your attachment to an old, burning rage

—these were the five blindspots I was highlighting ten years ago when I wrote *Excess Baggage* and they remain the five I emphasize today. We get in our own way, and I intended to show you a way to get around yourself.

The deepest structures of human nature, if they shift, do so only at a glacial pace. But our individual traits and tics can change, and will, with the leverage of cleverly applied continuous pressure. Showing where to apply your pressure was the point of *Excess Baggage*. I wanted this book to give you a shortcut to yourself, to make it easy for you to see the ways that normal, functional people trip over themselves. I believed if I could help you see yourself, I could help you develop yourself, help you push past the unnecessary drags on your spirit and the struggles in your relationships.

And I wanted to make your seeing gentle, to lighten your self-awareness with humor. In other words, I thought I could help you see without the sting. Now, ten years later, I think I underestimated that.

I tried to minimize the inevitable ego pinch of self-awareness by stressing the point that we are all in this human pickle together. Every one of us has personality baggage, and if you think you don't, it only marks you as one of the blind. It would be impossible for us to be otherwise because, as the book explains, your baggage is the natural outgrowth of your personality's strengths. It is these strengths taken to excess that creates the behaviors that make your life harder that it has to be. When a proud asset is also the source of a problem, how could that be anything but difficult to recognize?

I wanted to write a book that would make self-recognition easier, and, once accomplished, would point out small, definite new choices that could reduce your excess baggage and bring better balance to your life. Ten years later, I still think that was a great goal. It is, after all, the goal of all psychotherapies, in fact of all programs of introspection and execution, whether focused on spiritual or emotional transformations. See through to yourself, spot the block, slowly, doggedly, tiptoe past it.

Excess Baggage worked. Readers loved it. They wrote to me, called me, still get in touch with me ten years later. "How did you know me so well?" they ask. "I'm in every chapter!" Or, "Who told you about my fetish with the staple gun/my standing ovation fantasy/the lies I tell on trains?" They asked these questions with a laugh, or wrote in tones of affection, which suggested that I had been successful in helping people to smile at their own reflections, even when they weren't entirely flattering.

I felt that readers were responding to the book in the same emotional tone in which I had written it—with humorous self-acceptance. Yes, they seemed to be saying, you helped me to see this old self and love this old self, even though I know, and you know, that I could stand to do some work on this old self.

Of course, readers also frequently used the book to spot baggage in the people to whom they are connected. It's generally the baggage of your husband, your girlfriend, your boss, that gets dropped heavily on your feelings and naturally hurts. *Excess Baggage* seemed to have lightened even that load, which was an unexpected benefit of the book. Readers told me it was easier to tolerate a mate's heated outburst over a sloppy laundry pile, to set sensitive limits with an attention-seeking friend, or to be less intimidated by a paranoid boss, when they understood the underpinnings of these frustrating behaviors. Spotting the baggage in other people was not necessarily my goal, but it has its definite rewards.

All this was great as far as it went. But as I reread the book ten years later, there is one point I want to emphasize further. It is still the absolute truth that to get your baggage out of your way, you first have to spot these negative traits in yourself. That initial sighting usually hurts. Ten years later, in this preface, I want to talk to you much more about that bite.

Why is it that we all keep doing what we do, even when it creates problems for us? Because spotting our own flaws is hurtful and scary and changing them is work. That is an emotional truth, no matter how trivial the personal flaw, no matter how small the necessary change.

Ironically, identifying your own personality foibles hurts *because* we have baggage, and that baggage magnifies our flaws into something frightening. For example:

If you need to be right, spotting your baggage means recognizing you are wrong.

If you feel superior, spotting your baggage suggests you are ordinary.

If you dread rejection, spotting your baggage makes you feel unlovable.

If you create drama, spotting your baggage makes you seem merely needy.

If you cherish rage, spotting your baggage feels like blaming the victim.

In every case, spot your baggage and it suggests that you are not as right, as special, as safe, as beloved, or as righteous as you thought you were. That awareness stings.

In fact, everyone's first glimpse of these truths comes with a huge rush of anxiety. Given that feeling, most people will immediately look away. Force yourself to keep focused, and you'll see that your baggage is not nearly as scary as it first seemed. But you'll never get to that awareness if you don't keep looking.

None of us skips that first rush of discomfort when we see through ourselves, because the *baggage blocking your view is there for a purpose.* It is your defense against anxiety, your way of feeling safer in this chaotic, threatening, sometimes overwhelming world in which we all live. Yes, as I point out in the book, your particular baggage developed as an excessive application of your strengths. But we all go to these extremes for a reason. It's our way—however inappropriate, ineffective, or even self-defeating it may be—of defending ourselves against the awful feeling of being scared.

If I'm always right, if I'm really special, if I avoid emotional risks, keep people around me who will take care of me, and never, ever forget who my enemies are, then I'll be safe.

Sneaking past this defense, even though you've seen that it isn't working, is an uncomfortable thing to do. That's why you're unlikely to do it, unless you consciously bear down and push yourself through the anxious feeling till you get to the other side.

The exercises in this book are simple strategies for preventing yourself from doing what you normally do. But try one, taken from a chapter that particularly describes you, and you'll probably find that it requires dogged effort to get yourself to persevere. You will have excellent intentions, but never quite get around to the doing. You will forget, lose interest, get confused, become distracted by something or someone. Each of these is an automatic, even instinctive way of avoiding the wince that will come when you spot your baggage and then actually make the uncomfortable effort of putting it down.

Simply willing yourself not to speak where you always inserted an opinion, or forcing yourself to make a minor decision without consulting a friend, merely stifling the explanation for the stain on your tie or letting someone else choose the movie—these small shifts require concentrated exertion and the ability to tolerate the uncomfortable feeling of doing something different. I can guarantee you that change will not occur without determined effort. But I can also guarantee that the effort will be worth it.

The rewards of small change in a smart direction can be huge. Think of your baggage as a traffic jam on your developmental path, a small highway blockage that has brought you to a standstill. Once you move past that stuck point, the path ahead is suddenly clear and you whiz forward, finally free from whatever held you back. It's the possibility of this huge forward leap that makes pressing through your personality traffic jam worthwhile.

A life that was endlessly burdened with responsibility lightens immeasurably—once you no longer need to be right.

Your wicked self-consciousness eases up—once you've reduced your sense of superiority.

You can escape the awful feeling of being unappreciated, of always giving more than you get—when you've overcome your dread of rejection.

Your needy, attention-seeking self can relax—when you've controlled your impulse to create drama.

And you will increase the possibility of experiencing love and trust—when you have freed yourself of the rage you cherish.

These are not small rewards. But they come at the price of enduring an internal ouch that always accompanies self-recognition. If you don't manage that reflexive wince, it will turn into a whine and then a moan and finally, miserably, a mood of self-flagellation so painful that it can only be avoided by not seeing through to yourself in the first place.

Self-awareness should have just enough personal sting to keep you humble, and not one iota more. How do you mute the voice of your inner critic when it starts to sing and dance? By admiring your ability to change at least as much as you loathe the shortcomings that need changing. By appreciating that we are all on the path, and progress on that path is our purpose. And by recognizing that the point of the path is love, and the object of that love is always some very flawed self. Including your own, baggage and all.

Chapter One

FREE YOURSELF FROM YOURSELF

This book is not about other people and the way they make you crazy. It's about you—you, and me—each of us, and the ways we make ourselves crazy.

We do, you know. We keep getting in our own way, stumbling over the same parts of ourselves. We do it; we notice ourselves doing it. Then, somehow, we do it again. We're making our lives harder and we don't have to.

Maybe you're doing all of the work and having none of the fun. Or maybe you make your life harder by losing things—your wallet, your heart, your sense of humor. You might keep forgetting appointments. Or you could be a slave to your datebook. You might have become everyone's friend and no one's lover, or worse, everyone's lover and no one's beloved. Maybe you keep a mental directory of all your failures, your miscalculations, and every time you're faced with an opportunity, you scare yourself by running through the list.

You don't have to keep making these same mistakes, setting up the same roadblocks. You could go a very long way toward making yourself feel good—if you knew what was getting in your way in the first place. What's getting in the way is your excess baggage.

Here's what I mean by baggage:

You might be that person who is working too hard—not just at a job, at life. You're always on duty, always running an errand, loading a dishwasher, returning a phone call. Frankly, you could do all this while you ran a small country—and sometimes it feels as if you do.

The problem is, you live with someone who doesn't. Doesn't see what needs to be done. Doesn't bother to do it, and doesn't feel bothered when it (whatever *it* is) isn't done. And everything that person doesn't do infuriates you.

You are angry much of the time, or disappointed and depressed. After months or years of this domestic frustration, you are no longer a nice person. Now you are either a nag ("I'm asking you again—get your clothes off this chair so there's somewhere to sit down") or a martyr ("Never mind. I'll do it myself." Sigh. Huff. Cold silence).

You believe the cause of your problem is clear: It's him. Or it's her. It's his laziness, her irresponsibility, or his selfish princely attitude. To a point, you are probably right. Your mate *is* difficult to live with, because of his or her own baggage, namely a sense of superiority. He has a feeling of entitlement that allows him to serenely ignore mundane maintenance, leaving him free for pursuits that merit his interest, like his career or his tennis serve. Basically, he does what he *wants* to do, while you do what you *have* to do. This is an inequity that would infuriate anyone.

But it's only half the story. Yes, he makes your life hard, but your own baggage makes it harder. What's your baggage? It's your need to be right. You need the clothes hung up because you know that's the right way to treat belongings; you know that's the right way to maintain a room; you know that's the right way to *live*. You need to do things the right way, the way they should be done, and you know what that right way is. You get stuck doing what has to be done, partly because you are the one reading from the rule book that says we have to do it. Yes, you are carrying twice the load he carries. But it's not just his laziness that doubles your burden. It's your own baggage weighing you down.

Or you might be a different person, with a different kind of baggage. You might be someone who thinks things are always happening to her. You are the one who had two emotionally wrenching abortions, even though you tried hard to be careful. You got fired once too, although you chalk that up to the despot you worked for. And you've been unlucky in love—one long affair with a married man who broke your heart and several short-lived romances with men who seemed nice enough initially, but turned into bastards by the end.

The pain you've experienced during these episodes is all too clear, but your understanding of what caused them is foggy. Your explanations center around poor luck, few available men, or simply the unfortunate fate of vulnerable women. And you are right, to a point. These outside factors do make your life harder. *But so does your own baggage*—your need to create drama that stirs up crisis after crisis in your life, without your even knowing it's at work.

Here's another possibility. You could be a man or woman anguishing over an empty marriage. You are not necessarily abused, not living with an addict or an alcoholic—just with a person who doesn't love you, isn't interested in you, and isn't nice enough to hide it. You collect examples to prove that she belittles you, neglects you, and exploits you. But you don't leave.

Or you might be playing out this same scenario at a job, suffering because you are demeaned, tyrannized, or just bored to death. Your complaints are accurate, your malaise real. It's a fight to get out of bed in the morning. But you don't quit.

Why not? What makes a man (or woman) stay put when he is so obviously suffocating? He stays, he believes, because he can't afford to leave, because the economy is weak, because he has responsibilities, children, aging parents.

He stays because things are not "all bad." The husband reminds himself that his home is lovely, his children happy, or at least happier than they would be if he left. The employee reminds himself that he has seniority, and excellent benefits. Both men repeat that there is no guarantee of happiness elsewhere, and each sadly reassures himself that "no one is really happy in his marriage or job, anyway." So they stay.

It's true that the financial need is real, the kids are real, the lost benefits are real. Each of these reasons is so real that it's easy to obscure the underlying internal barrier. Yet in the end, men like these stay put because of their own baggage—fear. They are so frightened of risk, of change, of rejection and failure that they will stay in their niche no matter how uncomfortable it becomes. Their baggage keeps them imprisoned, and as long as it's in the way, they can't take their best shot at being happy.

And neither can you.

Baggage is a burden. Yes, some burdens are imposed by the outside world, just because we're grown-ups, just because we have complicated lives, just because we live with, love, and work with other people.

But some burdens are self-imposed, and they are the ones most difficult for any of us to spot.

It's easy to notice how other people trip over their personalities. You know why your anxious single friend never gets to have a first anniversary. You notice how your brother, the eternal rebel, manages to convince his every boss to hate him. You see exactly how your lonely mother is so controlling that she drives away the very company she seeks.

If you are looking, these examples of excess baggage are not difficult to recognize in the people you know well. They are, however, immensely difficult to see in oneself. When it comes to our own baggage, we are nearsighted. Maybe even blind.

Excess Baggage is the story of these blind spots. It's like the table you bump into in the dark every night; you know it's there, but somehow you keep forgetting. It's the story of the way we contribute to our own suffering and create our own obstacles to happiness.

Here's the definition of excess baggage: it's all those things that we can't see about ourselves that keep getting in our way.

Our family and friends probably know what this baggage is. It's what they say about us when we're out of the room ("If only he weren't so insecure . . ." "If only she weren't so picky . . ."). Actually, over the years, they may even say it to us face-to-face—pointing to the same failings time after time. Amazingly, we often agree—we see their point, and yet . . . and yet that critical awareness slips away. Why?

Well, for one thing, we are inside our personalities, so it's very difficult to step back and get a sense of the whole. At best, we are conscious of ourselves as having a quirk. You'll catch yourself bumping up against that psychological table—pressuring your boyfriend after you vowed to back off, avoiding your boss when you swore you'd assert yourself, sniping at your mother-in-law just as you used to with your mom. You'll say, "There I go again . . ." or, "Isn't it just like me . . ." But we don't stop to put that "quirk" into a larger context.

Besides, most of what goes wrong in life really does feel like someone else's fault. We can't see our own baggage because we're preoccupied, looking backward at our parents and the burdens they've saddled us with, or looking around at the jealous colleague, the thoughtless room-mate, the critical spouse, the neurotic friend, and seeing these as the forces in our lives that weigh us down. As, indeed, they are.

Even more, we're blind to our baggage because paying attention makes us anxious. Baggage can be seen as a flaw, a weakness, a failing. It's a threat to our self-image, and to our sense of security. We automatically defend ourselves, pushing the awareness of our baggage out of our minds, easing our anxiety by rationalizing, denying, or blaming away our inner obstacles. When we do, we make our own lives harder.

It doesn't have to be so scary, you know. Many of us worry that if we ever really looked inside, we'd find something awful, something that makes us truly unlovable. Naturally, with this exaggerated fear, we hesitate to look at all.

Well, chances are great that if you do take a searching look inside, you won't find anything frightening. What you'll find is just your excess baggage, your blind spots. You'll find out what you are doing to reduce your chances for love, money, or peace of mind. And you'll be able to stop doing it.

There are five themes at the heart of *Excess Baggage*. Most of what we do to get in the way of our own good time falls into one or more of these five areas:

- We need to be right, and

- We feel superior, and

- We dread rejection, and

- We create drama, and

- We cherish our rage.

Each of these blind spots is defined by a constellation of personality traits, behavior patterns, beliefs, and feelings. The baggage that comes with these personality styles is normal, inevitable. It's also disposable. You don't have to carry it around forever.

What if you had a trait, a habit, or a quality that built a huge barrier between you and happiness? You might be a less attractive candidate for a promotion, less likely to love and marry happily, or riper for illness, disease, or physical injury. Your baggage might make you sad when you don't have to grieve, or anxious when you have nothing to fear. What if you had such an obstacle and you weren't aware of it?

If you're anything like the rest of us, you do.

CLUES IN YOUR DAY-TO-DAY LIFE

It's difficult to spot the ways you defeat yourself. But there are clues: patterns of bad luck or bad feeling that you experience again and again, recurring struggles or disappointments you know cannot be mere chance. These are clues you have been leaving for yourself. Use them as a first step toward identifying your excess baggage:

- You feel bound to finish what you start—a book, a project, a marriage—even when you know it's not worth finishing.

▪ You find it bitterly difficult to be happy with "second best," whether it's a home, a husband, or a seat in a restaurant.

▪ You feel as if you are always the "giver"—to friends, lovers, children—but you never get your fair share in return.

▪ You get accused of flirting when it was the last thing on your mind.

▪ You find yourself paralyzed by an important decision. You can't choose a mate or make a career move without enduring an agony of ambivalence.

▪ You are still angry about something that happened years ago. And you still remind yourself of it on a regular basis.

▪ You long for the loving relationship, the better job, the time to play or learn. But you've stopped trying for it. You've given up.

▪ You say "yes" when you mean "no," simply because you can't stand anyone being mad at you.

▪ You live for "someday, when I'm . . ."

▪ You feel boredom, disappointment, outrage, or apathy more often than you want to.

If any of these thoughts, feelings, or behavior patterns sound like you, you are toting some heavy baggage.

A DEFINITION

The patterns of experience just described point to your blind spots.

Your excess baggage could be a style of thinking, reacting, or perceiving; it could be a fear, an ideology, an old passion. It's excess baggage if it meets one of three criteria:

It Comes Between You and Success

It doesn't matter how you define success. If there is something about you that's stopping you from getting it, it's baggage.

It Comes Between You and Satisfaction—Peace of Mind and a Sense of Well-being

Your excess baggage makes it harder to feel comfortable with yourself, to relax inside yourself, and ultimately, to follow the age-old formula for happiness—"Be yourself."

At the core of much emotional pain is the simple feeling "I don't like myself." It's peculiar, really. It's not as though you're dating and deciding where the relationship is going. Yet the grudging and critical acceptance we bestow on ourselves often has the flavor of a blind date that's limping through dinner. What we refuse to accept about ourselves becomes an emotional albatross that drags at our spirit.

It Makes You Harder to Love

With all the competing ambitions vying for our time and energy, one goal rises to the top, over and over again. We want love. We want to be loved, especially—loved unequivocally, uncritically, and unconditionally. We want people to think we're terrific and love us for it.

Yet if being loved is such a central human need, and it is, why do we make it difficult for other people to love us? Because we can't see the baggage that's getting in our way.

It is perfectly easy to see what other people do that makes it harder for us to love them. We know all about his embarrassing tendency to boast, her hysterical outbursts, his legendary temper, her anxious efforts to please. We've had friendships we allowed to lapse because the friend was too self-destructive to tolerate. We resent parents who refuse to butt out, bosses who have no concept of warmth, sisters who rebel and leave us to pick up the pieces, brothers who are viciously competitive. In all these ways and a thousand more, other people's baggage makes it very hard for us to love them—or at least to love them in the ways they were hoping we would. Unhappily, our own baggage has the same effect on them.

If you think of people from the outside in, you'll see examples of baggage in what they do, in how they think, and in their underlying emotional life. There will probably be a consistency to this baggage in any one person, which points us to the deeper, structural level of personality. *Excess Baggage* paints a portrait at each of these levels, with a special emphasis on personality because that's where the juice is.

First, on the *behavioral level,* our excess baggage includes, among other things, our bad habits—all those guilty pleasures, devastating attachments, and knee-jerk responses that endanger our health, interfere with our productivity, and/or offend the people we'd most like to impress. An all-inclusive list is nearly impossible because part of the magic of being human is our capacity to generate an infinite number of bad habits. The most common struggles, however, occur around drugs, sex, alcohol, cigarettes, food, television, spending, and other gratifications so intensely satisfying at the moment of use that they are unlikely to be used in moderation.

This book does not dwell on these addictions and social problems, though they are frequently symptoms of excess baggage, because so much is already available for the reader on these subjects.

On the *cognitive level,* excess baggage refers to any unexamined values, beliefs, or assumptions that make you sadder, more anxious, more frightened, or generally weaker than you would otherwise have to be. *Belief baggage* is the frame you've outgrown, a personal motto that no longer serves its purpose. For example, "Nice girls don't talk about money" is a belief that worked perfectly well until nice girls joined the work force and were matter-of-factly underpaid. Or take the belief "Men fix things"—a favorite of mine until my husband freed me of it. (Early in our marriage, the bathroom faucet had this irritating little drip. Finally I said: "You know, honey, the bathroom faucet has this little drip . . ." He unzipped his pants, pointed to himself, and said, "Judith, this does not make me a plumber.")

Baggage on the *emotional level* has to do with pieces of your past that interfere with pleasure and productivity in the present. These are old, powerful feelings that intrude on new situations. Our parents are the main focus of these feelings, especially their failings as parents and our own lingering disappointment or rage as a result of these failings. But an ex-spouse can generate an impressive amount of intrusive emotional baggage as well, as can siblings or other family members.

Actually, the biggest source of emotional baggage is the secrets we keep. A secret is more than a truth withheld. A secret is a truth that requires energy to hold back, to guard. It has big-time emotion attached to it—a feeling of guilt or shame, of triumph, of domination or despair. There is an old rule in family therapy: A family is only as sick as its secrets. In the same way, an individual's secrets are an excellent measure of his or her emotional baggage.

The heart of *Excess Baggage* is a description of the way each of these psychological levels—your behaviors, your beliefs, and your emotional freight—has, as its source, a consistent personality style. Given our individual personalities, we are more likely to have one or another kind of baggage. Each personality has its own strong suit. But each has its own blind spot as well.

SELF-HELP?

We are all so exhausted with the idea of self-improvement. Can't we just set ourselves aside and get on with life?

Apparently not. We can't ignore ourselves and get on with living, because we keep getting in our own way.

Understanding how we defeat ourselves is simple self-awareness. Self-awareness is not self-absorption. Self-awareness is what makes our lives work; self-absorption is what we do instead of living.

Understanding your baggage and taking some steps to minimize its effects is not something you do for the sake of your vanity. It's not about chasing a perfectly packaged, perfectly performing, ideal version of yourself. It's about making your life easier, sweeter, and richer in opportunity. And it's about being more resilient when life cannot be made easier, but can only be endured. It's about making love more accessible and making yourself happier because it is. It's about making more of a contribution to the world and getting more back as a result.

Excess Baggage shows you how you weigh yourself down. Then it shows you how to lighten your load—just in case you don't have time to be crazy anymore.

Chapter Two

THE PRICE YOU PAY
FOR BEING WHO YOU ARE

There is a single message in this book: Every one of us has baggage. We trip over it trying to get where we're going. If we could get our defenses and anxieties under control, we'd see the baggage ourselves. Then we'd move it out of the way.

We've mentioned some of the powerful forces that blind us to the problems we generate. But we haven't tackled the greatest of these forces, the central psychological paradox with which we struggle, on some level, our entire lives: *Our greatest weaknesses are always the flip side of our greatest strengths.*

She's always there when you need her . . . because she's too scared to go anywhere else.

She's almost always well informed . . . but she can't admit when she's not.

He's highly organized . . . but the rest of us are a slave to his schedule.

He's marvelously warm and entertaining . . . but he has to be the center of attention.

You can rely on her to set exquisitely high standards . . . and to be disappointed because, of course, we didn't meet them.

Every one of these strengths comes with a weakness—an excess, a problem, a blind spot. These weaknesses are tough for us to perceive, precisely *because* they are shrouded by the strength they accompany.

It is difficult, if not impossible, to accept criticism for something on which you pride yourself. A mother works for weeks planning every detail of a wedding. Two days before the event, her daughter bursts with fury, accusing Mom of "always needing to control everything . . . always needing to get your way." Does this mother feel justifiably accused? No! No! No! She feels vastly unappreciated. The pride Mom takes in a job well done blinds her to the hostility she aroused because she was the one who decided to do the job in the first place. People (especially adult children) may resent being part of a show that's being run by you, even when you are running it superbly, even when you are running it to please them, and even if you are the only one willing to run it.

Strength blinds us in so many situations. One man's capacity for loyalty and depth of feeling makes him a magnificent husband, father, and friend. Unfortunately, he insists on that same show of loyalty in return, requiring that friends and family take his side in any dispute, regardless of their own opinions.

The person who is immensely gracious about advice and guidance can be the same person who resents you when you choose a different course. The most cheerful companion you know is too busy to depress herself with a visit to you in the hospital. Your very generous friend is also the one who often needs to borrow money. The man with the most charm is also the one who can't bring himself to charm only one woman.

Our baggage is not an accidental personality development. *It comes directly out of the personal strengths we've cultivated.* And it is precisely these strengths that make us oblivious to the baggage they engender.

Remember, the fact that there is a downside to your personal style doesn't mean there's something wrong with you. It's normal. In fact, *Excess Baggage* focuses exclusively on normal, functioning people. We are all juggling love and work and trying to feel good about ourselves at the same time. Our baggage simply complicates the juggle by having us do it blindfolded.

You should know that I have a deep professional bias toward viewing people as "well." Where other professionals see clear signs of pathology, I tend to see basically healthy people struggling to do their best. *Excess Baggage* very strongly reflects the bias of this perspective. If, as some of my colleagues would argue, the problems described in each chapter indicate something deeply or fundamentally wrong with you, then nothing short of a major personality restructuring would make a bit of difference. I don't see it that way.

Excess Baggage does not take up the question of the emotional or psychological burdens of those who are deeply disturbed. It does not discuss the frightening emptiness of the sociopath, the bitter self-hatred and helplessness of the seriously depressed, the fragile emotional balance of the borderline, or the flood of chaotic stimuli that clouds the psychotic. These are burdens too serious to be trivialized by the word "baggage."

But the rest of us do have baggage—normal, inevitable, self-imposed, disposable burdens. They are the direct outgrowth of our personal strengths. In this sense, baggage is the price you pay for being who you are. And you could lower the cost.

WHAT CAUSES BAGGAGE?

We've said that baggage comes directly out of all your strengths. Actually, it's your strength run amok.

Here's what that means: As you'll see in each of the chapters that follow, your baggage is not a random character tic, or an isolated piece of irritating or self-defeating behavior. It is an outgrowth of the dominant drives that shape your particular personality.

Each of our personalities is built around a complicated core of motivations, needs, drives, instincts. One way to think about the cause of our baggage is to assume that in everyone's personality, one cluster of these drives tends to predominate.

In this book, that central need is described as your *ruling passions,* meaning a group of core drives, basic motives, around which you've organized a good deal of your personal style. Your ruling passions provide much of the fuel for your personality. Think of them as primary needs you are looking to satisfy, no matter what situation you are in.

Excess Baggage talks about five ruling passions, each associated with a personality style, each likely to create a particular kind of baggage. They are:

- the drive for control
- the drive for self-esteem
- the drive for security
- the drive for attachment
- the drive for justice

Each of these is a perfectly healthy human need, and naturally, we all are motivated to some degree by every one of them. "Ruling passion" only means that one or two of these needs is probably dominant for you. To the extent that your ruling passions dominate, they are likely to help you develop some very clear strengths. Along the way, they also help you develop baggage.

A ruling passion is a need that you feel you *have to* satisfy. It has an urgency behind it, which makes you likely to satisfy that need whether or not it's appropriate or even if it creates a problem for you. In this sense, the dominance of your ruling passions is part of what creates your baggage.

For example, if you are driven by a need for control, it won't matter whether you are on the refreshment committee or running a corporation. You'll need to dominate in both arenas. You will have developed a whole range of take-charge skills and attitudes in order to satisfy your ruling passion. When you apply these well-developed controlling behaviors to running the corporation, they are a tremendous asset. You are successful because of these skills, you're likely to feel good about yourself, and other people respect and admire you for it. But when you automatically apply the *very same* personality traits to choosing the refreshments, they can become a liability. Other people find you bossy, and you exhaust yourself with the never ending burdens of responsibility and decision making.

In the same way, if you are hungry to prove your worth above everything else, your friends, your furniture, your life's work, will all be chosen to establish your superiority rather than to give you pleasure. If you crave security above all else, you can get stuck in an abusive marriage or a dead-end job just because they are safe. A ruling passion can be so urgent, so overwhelming, that we gratify it even at the expense of our own success and satisfaction. We do it automatically; we do it unconsciously. We do it because we are used to doing it, and any other way of responding would feel strange and different and uncomfortable.

Where do our particular passions come from?

We have only theory to explain why any of us developed our own particular package of drives and passions. Like the rest of both our inner dynamics and outward manifestations of personality, our ruling passions are probably the combined product of our genetic and biochemical heredity and our intimate and extended environment. That is, to some degree you were born with them, to some degree you were taught them. Now they're a big part of who you are.

In big ways and small, we function efficiently to satisfy our ruling passions, creating loving relationships and productive work lives in the process. Along the way, because we're not perfect, we overdo—making our lives more work, hurting people we love—all in the service of the very same ruling passion. These negatives are our baggage.

The question of what caused our baggage is always interesting in and of itself. The answer is even helpful in repairing the damage. But the bottom line is always the same. Your heredity and your environment probably created this baggage. But you don't have to be sure of where you got it, in order to put it down.

HOW-TO

Once you begin to get a clear picture of your ruling passions, you'll start to see the baggage created in their wake. But that doesn't necessarily mean you'll want to change. Let's face it—some of us, when confronted with articulate evidence of our baggage, respond simply: *"Take it or leave it."*

The take-it-or-leave-it speech goes like this: You go nine rounds with your wife or girlfriend about how you hate the fact that she's on the phone all evening, every evening, with her girlfriends. You'd like a little peace and quiet; you'd like to sit down with her yourself; there's a mess in the kitchen that still has to be cleared up; and besides, it doesn't seem healthy to you for someone to be so continuously involved in the lives of others. In response, she says, in effect, "That's how I am! Take it or leave it."

"Take it or leave it" might include a defense: "You knew how I was when you met me. Now all of a sudden you want me to change." It might include an attack: "Why should I bend over backward to change?—you'll just find something else about me you don't like. You can't be pleased." Or the speech might be delivered indirectly: "Yeah, sure, honey, I'll be done for the night right after I call Lindy."

"Take it or leave it" is really a prayer and a plea: "Please, don't make me change." I am personally highly sympathetic to this plea because I hate change. I do it, but I hate it. Change is disruptive, uncomfortable, all for an end that is uncertain. Who needs it? I mean, stimulation is fine—new places, new people, new ideas. But change requires loss— loss of the old things, old people, old, comfy ways of doing and being.

I want my old friends around me—the ones it's too late to make a good impression on. I want the string bean casserole at Thanksgiving, and I want the people at the table to love me as I am so I can say, with great conviction, to any new person in my life foolish enough to challenge it, "This is how I am—take it or leave it."

To the part of each of us that pleads or bullies, "This is how I am —take it or leave it," I can only state the obvious as gently as possible. If *how I am* makes you love me less—like me less, trust me less, make love to me less—then I'm foolish to hope you take it instead of leaving it. In the end, the person who stays in a take-it-or-leave-it situation stays grudgingly. You don't want to be on either end of that relationship.

When you assume the position "Take it or leave it," it's quite possible that you are presenting what feels like an honest choice to your partner. Whatever the trait in question, you have decided after thoughtful consideration that it is not a trait on which you either can or will budge. Perhaps it represents a deep personal value ("I will not lie on our income tax form. Take it or leave it"). Perhaps it is symbolic of your autonomy or power ("I go out every Friday night with my friends. Take it or leave it"). Whatever the meaning, you are entitled to your position.

But most often, "Take it or leave it" isn't a decision, it's a defense, a last-ditch effort to avoid the anxieties of self-awareness. It's a defense that takes a lot of energy to maintain. And if you are able to maintain that defense successfully, what you get to be is a person whose baggage is still getting in his or her way.

When you get a glimpse of your baggage, you have two choices. You might say "Take it or leave it." Or you might be willing to change.

Here's how:

To lighten your load of baggage—little by little, bit by bit, you must learn to resist your ruling passions.

This is not easy to do, because a lot of old habits and deeply ingrained expectations will stand in your way. Fortunately, you don't have to make a major change in yourself to see big changes in your life. A small shift in your perspective, a slight increase in your range of possible reactions to a situation—these modest differences are all that is required. As you'll see, the tasks through which you learn to resist your ruling passions are simple—a movie chosen differently, an apology made instead of assumed, a phone unanswered, an opinion stated, an argument turned aside. But the will, the emotional energy, the effort required to react differently, are difficult for all of us.

To make it easier for you, each chapter here is written to help you ease into this change in a three-step process:

Change what you see. Then *change what you think.* And then, with the momentum of these shifts in your view of yourself, *change what you do.*

Change What You See

First, you need to change your perception. Remember, excess baggage is what you don't know about yourself or can't see about yourself that keeps getting in your way. It's a blind spot, a blur, the first stage of a Polaroid you'll need to develop into a clear, focused, and fully rounded self-portrait. Your first change is to spot your baggage in the whole context of your personality, and that is the purpose of the first section of each chapter.

Change What You Think

You need to get a deeper understanding of your ruling passions, of how they drive you, of what might have created them, or both how they pay off and how they create problems for you. That is the purpose of the middle section of each chapter, entitled "The Inner Portrait."

Changing what you think means coming to a deep appreciation of the fact that it hurts you to satisfy your ruling passions all the time. You must come to believe that

- even though these ruling passions are a big part of you,

- even though so much of what's good about you comes out of them, and

- even though it *feels so good to satisfy them,*

you will have to learn to say no to that need *some of the time,* in order to make your life work better.

For example, say you are someone whose ruling passion is a need to feel secure. That's fine. But every time you try to learn something new, you find you feel uncomfortable. You worry—What if I'm not quick enough to catch on to bridge bidding? What if I'm too weak in math to learn navigation? As soon as learning gets hard, and you are threatened with failure, you quit. Immediately you feel better. You aren't anxious anymore. You've satisfied your need for security, and you rationalize your choice by saying, "After all, I was doing this for fun. It stopped being fun, so naturally I quit."

Now you are back in your safe nest, but you are not laughing around a bridge table or you are not enjoying sailing the way you'd hoped. You quit because your baggage, your fear that you'd fail and be rejected, scared you away from the fun. In order to overcome your fear of rejection, you need to resist your ruling passion's impulse to run back to safety. You need to stay out there, even though it's scary and even though you might fail. After all, you might succeed. When you do, you will have made room to satisfy another need—namely, the need for creating self-esteem. You'll be impressed with yourself both because you overcame a fear and because you learned something new. But first you have to resist making yourself feel good by automatically doing what is safe.

Probably nothing short of brain trauma could change your ruling passions. And why would you want to? It's the source of much of your strength. But you can rein it in, redirect it. You can choose when and where to satisfy it, rather than responding automatically and unconsciously.

The main result of consciously choosing whether or not to satisfy a ruling passion is that it will give you a whole new range of behaviors in your emotional repertoire. Now you no longer *have to* be the one who plans the trip, but you can still be the one who decides to. You won't *have to* have a passionate affair with another difficult lover, though you can certainly still choose to. You won't *have to* fight back at your ex, and you won't *have to* feel that you gave in if you didn't.

Along with the freedom that comes with not having to react a certain way, there is a second enormous gain. A lot of what we have to do, because we are driven by our ruling passions, interferes with what other people have to do (or with what they'd like to do, if only we'd let them). And they get mad at us, or love us less, or hurt us more. When we are less driven by our passions, and instead become the thoughtful driver, we tend to crash into other people less frequently.

To rein in your ruling passion, to redirect its enormous energies in a productive way, you need to take the third step. First, change what you see. Second, change what you think. And finally, change what you do.

Change What You Do

Changing what you do is a complicated process. For one thing, it means you have to think about what you do before you do it. For another, it means you have to tolerate some discomfort by doing something unfamiliar, unnatural, actually un-you. Finally, it requires effort. To let go of baggage, you need to stand up to your own very powerful impulses. It can be exhausting. But it can also be exhilarating.

The goal of each exercise in the prescriptive section of this book is to produce behavior that is counter to the trend of your ruling passions. The behavior changes suggested are small, but the goal of these small behavior changes is grand. If you resist your ruling passions:

- You make room to satisfy other needs.

- You make room to satisfy other people, and in so doing, you make your family, your friends, and your colleagues nicer people to be around.

▪ You set yourself free. When you consciously choose to act against a ruling passion, the greatest reward is discovering that you can do it and you'll live. Not only will you survive but you might even enjoy it. There is a sense of being unburdened, a lightening of the spirit, an elation that comes with feeling, *"I don't have to anymore."*

When you try to change what you do, you will probably experience all the feelings that arise when something of central importance has shifted. You may feel a bit silly, embarrassed, even dishonest. Some part of you is lost and an alien is in its place: "I can't say I'm sorry, when I don't think I'm wrong." "I won't call my father and listen to him gloat."

Acting counter to the trend of our ruling passions is clumsy and awkward. But it can also be a kick: "I'd love to see her face when she gets the apology call." "My kids will be shocked if I'm not their old faithful mom." Change is, in part, a joke on other people, a chance to surprise them out of their complacent vision of you. If you can get past your own awkwardness, you can enjoy their reactions immensely.

But whether you're embarrassed, awkward, or gleeful, acting counter to the trend is absolutely guaranteed to make you feel one thing: *anxious.*

After all, what is our baggage anyway if not a giant shield against anxiety? Why hide in the safety of one ill-paying job, but to avoid the anxiety of struggling in the world for a better one? Why hide behind the security of a status watch or a glorious car, but to avoid the anxiety that you wouldn't measure up if you were stripped of it? We wouldn't need to be right if being wrong weren't so frightening. We wouldn't create such an emotional storm if silence didn't leave us so ominously alone. And we wouldn't cling to rage as a banner if peace didn't leave us feeling defenseless.

Going counter to the trend of any core personality dynamic is putting down your shield against anxiety and confronting the fear directly.

It feels awful.

It feels tense, overwhelming. In fact, it may make you physically ill, choking you, cramping your stomach, knotting your neck and back. It might disrupt your sleep and leave you preoccupied with repetitive visions of disaster that won't fade and won't let you concentrate on anything else.

You would do almost anything to get rid of the feeling. Naturally, the simplest thing you can do is to stop trying to buck the trend. Go back to doing what you always did. Your anxiety will disappear. But so will your opportunity to leave your baggage behind.

The exercises in *Excess Baggage* will elicit a certain degree of anxiety. (This is sort of the psychological equivalent of "Good medicine tastes bad.") The postscript at the end of this book includes a list of antianxiety techniques. Most are old standards. Some may be new to you. The thing is, they work if you use them. Don't make life harder on yourself. Use what works for you, to make change possible.

READING *EXCESS BAGGAGE*

Each chapter in *Excess Baggage* defines one central psychological burden. Chapters begin with a portrait of the person, male or female, most likely to have that particular kind of baggage. *This person is described from the outside in—that is, from the most easily observable traits through the layers of personality to his or her underlying themes and unconscious dynamics.*

These personality portraits are, of necessity, paradoxical because they describe real people. It's hard to squash real people into categories. Real people always do one thing, except for the times when they do the opposite. On the one hand, generalizing about different personalities and their probable baggage does help you get a sense of the pattern—a big picture of human beings and how they operate. It gives you a context in which to view yourself. On the other hand, what is wonderful about people is that their individuality leaks, no matter what kind of category a psychologist tries to put them in. So when you read each chapter, be prepared for the parts that don't fit.

By way of overview, each personality portrait includes the following:

■ What are your strengths? Why do we seek you out? What do people rely on you to contribute? What is your likely profession? And why did you probably choose it?

■ What is your greatest psychological obstacle? What can't you bring yourself to do? Why not?

■ What is your particular style of socializing, handling money, and relating to authority, of handling sex, expressing outrage? What are you likely to lie about?

■ What kind of person are you likely to marry? What kind of relationship will the two of you probably create? And what will you fight about?

■ What fantasy situation would make you feel your absolute best? What roles feel most comfortable to you?

■ What is your most likely "belief baggage" (the old rule or personal motto you still try to live by, even though it no longer works in your life)?

■ What is your "secret brag" (the tendency each of us has to admit an ostensible weakness when we're actually presenting an asset)?

Then each chapter moves inward, beginning to grapple with the question of what internal dynamics create your baggage. That question is answered in two ways:

■ What is your "theme song"? This is the semiconscious internal voice that repeats endlessly in your psychic ear, forcing your attention to some single aspect of life. Your theme song focuses your energies so that you are in the best possible position to satisfy your ruling passion.

■ What is your "ruling passion" (the central driving need you *must* satisfy)? How did you get to be this way? Why does it work for you to stay this way?

Finally, each chapter focuses specifically on your baggage. Each answers:

- ▪ What is the baggage likely to be created by this personality, this theme song, this ruling passion?

- ▪ What can you do to polish your rough edges and lighten your load?

Excess Baggage is not like your horoscope. You won't simply find yourself or your baggage in one chapter. Most readers will identify to some degree with each of the chapters. Personality is a symphony, not a solo. A typical response to *Excess Baggage* is, "Oh my God, they're all me!" Good. In general, the more of a mixture you are, the healthier you are. (In fact, if you do find one chapter that fits exactly, it may simply describe the parts of your personality you are most aware of. Chapters describing baggage you have not, as yet, thought much about may give you some surprising information about yourself.)

It's possible to have any of these inner obstacles, in any combination. Some combinations are more likely than others. Quite often, people who need to be right also feel superior. A person who creates drama is often someone who also dreads rejection. And, as you'll see in Chapter 7, any of us might be burdened with rage under certain circumstances. These are the common ways baggage clumps together, but less likely combinations occur too.

Also, each type of baggage has typically been associated with either men or women. Specifically, common wisdom holds that more men need to be right or need to feel superior; women are the ones who create drama or tend to dread rejection; and in the case of anger, women tend to direct it inward and become depressed, while men tend to project it outward and become paranoid. As with most stereotypes, there is enough truth in these generalizations that the tendencies shouldn't be ignored, and there are enough exceptions that they shouldn't be overstated.

There is a logic to the order of the chapters that follow. We begin with the need to be right, which is the price paid by some of the

EXCESS BAGGAGE AT A GLANCE

	YOUR RULING PASSION	YOUR FAVORITE DAYDREAM	IF YOU ARE INVITED TO A PARTY . . .	YOUR MOTTO
You need to be RIGHT.	■ CONTROL	You've updated and filed all your insurance policies.	You want to know what to expect.	"Finish what you start."
You feel SUPERIOR.	■ SELF-ESTEEM	You're rehearsing an acceptance speech.	You want to know if anyone worthwhile will be there.	"I can do anything I want if I put my mind to it."
You dread REJECTION.	■ SECURITY	You're snowed in with everyone you love.	You want to know if you can get out of going.	"If I have to ask for what I want, it's not worth having."
You create DRAMA.	■ ATTACHMENT	You get a standing ovation.	You want to know what to wear.	"If you loved me, you'd . . ."
You cherish RAGE.	■ JUSTICE	You learn that something bad happened to an enemy.	You want to know if *he's* invited too.	"Don't get mad, get even."

WHEN YOU SHOP . . .	YOUR THEME SONG	YOUR SECRET BRAG	YOUR FIRST DEFENSE	THE HARDEST THING FOR YOU TO DO
You want the smart buy.	"I should . . ."	"I'm a workaholic."	"It's nothing personal."	Give in
You want to buy the best.	"I am . . ."	"I'm too picky."	"I'm just as hard on myself."	Look foolish
You decide that you don't really need it.	"What if . . ."	"I'm too nice."	"I'm only trying to help."	Go out
You want someone else to pay.	"I feel."	"I'm too emotional."	"I can't help how I feel."	Be routine
You want the economical buy.	"How dare..." "I wish . . ."	"I'm too suspicious."	"Who needs a defense?"	Forgive or forget

strongest and most productive among us. The next chapter describes the sense of superiority, because so many of us who need to be right also feel superior, or at least we feel we must be superior in order to be loved.

From superiority we move to the fear of rejection, because that fear is usually the irritation that creates the pearl of superiority. From the fear of rejection we discuss the need to create drama. In essence, drama is simply a way to avoid rejection by creating excitement, commanding attention, and stirring up enough confusion that someone will come riding to the rescue.

From the highly emotional baggage of drama we move to a discussion of the weightiest emotional baggage, rage. Any one of us might hold on to rage. It is our universal baggage.

In this sense, each chapter is linked. If you see yourself in one, you'll get a more complete self-portrait by reading the one before it and the one that follows.

But keep this in mind: If you identify with one end of the spectrum, you will probably marry someone from the other end. (Part of what attracts us to a mate is that he or she is free of the baggage we struggle with. Later, of course, we resent them because they don't share our burdens.) Whether you lug it around yourself, marry it, or work with it, you end up coping with every variety of baggage.

You are not going to stop being who you are, personality, passions, and all. But you can lower the price you pay for being you. Stay who you are and how you are. Just don't stay *exactly* the same.

I don't want you to stay exactly the same because I don't want you to keep making your life harder than it has to be. I want you to have a good time, to feel easy about yourself, to be comfortable inside your skin. I want you to have a clearer picture of what you could achieve, and I want you to feel freer to get there, less self-consumed, less needy, less wounded. I want you to change.

Oh, but just a little change. Just a step to the right or left of your usual position. Just a slight stretch in your repertoire, a small push forward on your path. Just a small step out from behind your baggage.

Chapter Three

■

YOU NEED TO BE RIGHT

There is something so delicious about being right, so victorious, so validating. It's the A+ on the final exam, the crow of triumph when you win the argument, or the self-righteous comfort of believing that you lost unfairly.

Being right is also the sweet relief of having dodged the bullet of being wrong. Being wrong—with the accompanying feelings of shame, belittlement, and vulnerability—can be safely avoided only by being utterly, inevitably, and eternally right. Being right is smart and strong and safe and sure—and every one of us prefers it to the alternative.

But some of us do far more than prefer to be right. We *must* be right. We organize our life around this need—choosing our work, our mates, even making love—all to ensure, over and over again, that we're right.

When the need to be right is a driving force instead of just a preference, it is very heavy baggage.

■

A PORTRAIT

Remember, this, like all the other portraits that follow in *Excess Baggage*, is in essence a caricature. No one person has all these traits, so even if you do need to be right, some of what follows won't fit. Still, you'll probably be able to recognize the man or woman who needs to be right from the following descriptions:

You Are an Organized Person Who Treasures Productivity

It's Saturday morning. You are awake, you've made love, and you are ready to tear into the day. You'd like to get through the grocery shopping before noon because you thought this afternoon would be a great time to check out furniture stores. Then you two could catch an early movie and try the restaurant you read about last Sunday. Seems like an ideal Saturday.

You leap out of bed. He does not. He's reading the newspaper, flipping the remote control. You shower and dress. He's still reading and flipping, showing no signs of purposeful action. He cannot understand why you are so "hyper." You are clenching your teeth to keep from calling him "lazy." For you, the fun of down time begins when the list of Things to Do Today ends. Otherwise, your responsibilities call out to you, interrupting your relaxation, destroying your calm. At the end of a day, you want to feel as if you've accomplished something. You are perfectly capable of playing, of relaxing, of enjoying yourself. But you don't just ignore the things you have to take care of—unlike some people.

You are efficient, a person on whose competence the rest of us rely. You can run the show, and you'll do it with utter thoroughness. You find solutions to problems the rest of us never even bothered to anticipate. (When you make the travel plans, you don't just get the tickets for the best price. You remember the seat on the aisle, the special meal, and the motivational sales tape we can listen to on the way.)

You love lists—list of all the states in the Union you've visited; lists of all the things to add to your wardrobe once you get a raise; lists of long-term goals, which you update from time to time; lists of every item in your bureau drawers and what to save in case of fire (not that you'd have time to consult the list, but just writing it helps you feel better prepared).

Every day is greased along by a detailed list of chores and goals— a list that affords the twofold reward of (1) making your day more focused and under control, and (2) allowing you the small delight of *crossing something off the list,* thus creating a measurable statement of your productivity. You are attached to your list. If you lose it, you'll spend time looking for it rather than starting a new one. Some of us keep all of our lists in one perfect book—a book we keep forever. This allows us to look back at the efficient Saturdays of two years ago and reminisce.

Major lists then become schedules. You might keep a small notebook with a cleaning schedule. It reads: "bed (daily), floors (weekly), CD's (monthly), oil skis (annually)." Annual items are best scheduled for the day the clocks are pushed forward, which, by the way, is an excellent system you invented for remembering to check your smoke alarms.

Potential pleasures are listed as well, in a category called Things to Do in My Leisure Time, so that, should you find yourself with unexpected blank space, you can be productive. Each time you visit a museum, you check it off a mental list. It's a good feeling.

Your lists and schedules are tremendous assets to a productive life. Unfortunately, they may also be obstacles to a pleasant one. You are, in effect, emotionally attached to your schedule. Nothing irritates you as much as having it interfered with or interrupted. A traffic jam leaves you snarling. A friend who keeps you waiting is a candidate for justifiable homicide. You plan to bake muffins for a cousin's visit as a special treat for you both. Then your boss assigns you a project for the same weekend. Another person would just buy the muffins. You can't let go of your plan to bake them, because it was, after all, such a good idea. And by God, you do bake them, turning a special treat into a pressured chore—delivering delicious muffins through a cloud of tension. Sometimes your own plans hold you hostage and refuse to negotiate.

If you had a psychiatric label, it would be: Obsessive and Compulsive.

Your secret brag: "I'm a workaholic."

What you mean: "I am totally devoted to, fascinated by, absorbed in, and marvelous at my work. I spend much too much time doing it, and complain lavishly about its demands, and have no intention of changing either of these situations.

Your chief self-criticism: "I waste too much time."

You Are an Information Junkie

You have a passion to know everything, so you subscribe to a flood of publications. Naturally, there are not enough hours in the day to read it all and still live, but you're not about to throw a paper away unread, so you save it until there's time. Pretty soon you have stacks of book review sections, or *New York Times* Science sections, or stock market bulletins that pile up on nightstands and in bathrooms, threatening to creep onto any available chair.

And all of them are screaming out, "Read me, clip me, file me." So one Sunday you spend the day going through the pile. Interesting articles are carefully clipped and saved. Completed publications are discarded. Eliminating several piles of backed-up book review sections yields a tremendous feeling of accomplishment. On a subsequent Thursday evening, all the clippings are filed away in their proper place.

Though you've only referred to these files twice in the last five years, it's good to know they're there if you need them.

You don't simply own a personal computer, you have a love affair with it. You lavish time and attention on your computer. You buy it little trinkets—rubber mats so its mouse is more comfortable, hard disk drives to help it live longer and stay younger.

Your computer organizes massive amounts of information into tidy piles. Time spent at its keyboard is pleasant, focused. See the memos, letters, policy statements piling up beside you. Touch the graphs, charts, projections, files. Ah. Thank you for a beautiful Sunday.

In general, your memory for detail is superior, your memory for objective, factual detail, exquisite. This strength frequently translates into an astonishing capacity for absorbing and recalling factoids. You remember which dictator was recently the victim of a coup in Nicaragua and why this coup will affect soy production. You offer these facts with an authority that makes the rest of us hope you won't quiz us on soy.

You Hate to Admit It, But You Can't Stand to Be Wrong

What's so terrible about being wrong?

"It's not a reason—it's a feeling. I can feel the most horrible wince in my heart even when I make a wrong turn. It's stupid, but there it is."

"It's the bully in the schoolyard who picks on you when you show the least sign of weakness. I was little and I was slow—but I was smarter than all of them. It saved me. It still does."

"I always hear my father's voice. I hear his sarcasm, his meanness. He loved to show me up. When I make a mistake now, I am instantly back at the dinner table."

Your favorite joke: "I'm happy to admit when I'm wrong.
I'm just not wrong very often."

Not knowing an answer is, for you, just another way to be wrong. You *hate* to say "I don't know" in response to a question. Oh, you'd say it if you *really* didn't know. But it seems to you as if you must know, or you probably do know, or certainly that you *should* know.

You will tell a white lie: To make up the answer to a
factual question when you aren't absolutely sure of the
answer.

You don't think of it as a lie. You think your answer might be right.

You'll make up a statistic to win an argument. You don't think you made it up. You're sure you read it somewhere, didn't you?

You are the scientist who is tempted to cheat on his data. You would never do this casually because you know cheating is wrong. But somehow you feel that if things had been run a bit smoother technically, surely your hypothesis would have been proven correct.

You are the attorney who forgot to file on behalf of a client and then presented it as a deliberate strategy instead of an oversight. This is not merely an effort to protect yourself professionally: you argue so persuasively about your filing omission that the first person convinced of its wisdom is you.

To you, being wrong feels like an intolerable threat. And it's a threat for which there is a simple solution. Just make sure you're right.

Your Motto: "Finish What You Start."

You'll have trouble letting go of a bad business deal or a bad marriage, partly because it involves admitting you were wrong in the first place.

"When I married Matthew, everyone told me I was making the mistake of my life. I left him after three weeks, but I went back. You know

why? Because I just couldn't admit that they were right. Even now, two years after the divorce, there's a mental voice that drives me mad, tortures me, saying, 'How could you have done it! Why didn't you see?'"

"I should have admitted my first year of medical school that I wasn't right for the profession. I don't like long hours, and quite honestly, I don't much like doctors. But I'd had the plan for so long, since high school really. I'm in my second year of residency. It makes me sick to think I invested six years in the wrong future."

You Are Emotionally Reserved

"His idea of foreplay is to put down the remote control."

"My husband keeps a computer file on me. One anniversary he showed me a partial printout. It was labeled: 'Things that are good about Margaret/Things that need work with Margaret.' He had no idea why I wasn't moved."

You might feel a very deep, loving attachment to a mate, a friend, parent, child. It's just that you won't say much about it—even to yourself. You are loyal and devoted, both because you feel attached and because you believe it's the right way to act in a relationship. You expect the same commitment in return.

In general, it's hard for you to say much about how you feel, which makes you a relatively unromantic lover. If you have been made aware of this deficit by complaining partners, you may have done your determined, hardworking best to "become" more romantic. You *do* remember flowers, having been taught that these gestures are important to women. You *will* remember to put on the garter belt from time to time, having learned that your man is particularly fond of such an apparition. Male or female, if "romantic" becomes an important personal attribute, you will work to develop it, staging surprise parties or storybook marriage proposals. You'll never be one for the impulsive emotional gesture, because your feelings are too tightly reined. But when romance can be organized and produced, you can be an outstanding producer.

Sexually, you might also reflect some of your discomfort with emotional abandon. On the one hand, you might take a special pleasure in sex because it is one area where you allow yourself the freedom to feel intensely. Very often, however, your efficiency and rationality interfere with your sexual pleasure and performance. You find it difficult to relax into sensation. You might be distracted by the primitive smells and tastes of lovemaking. Sometimes, instead of an experience to savor, sex becomes something to get over with so you can get on with your day.

Premature ejaculation is a common sexual problem for men with your baggage. And male or female, often when a relationship moves beyond its first flush of passion, you might not have much sexual desire left. You are too tired, too busy to make love. Insufficient sexual desire is a common problem for both men and women who need to be right.

When you are in deep emotional waters, you can just about tolerate the discomfort. Where another person enjoys the thrill of being in love, you feel tortured by the intensity of the experience.

George exemplifies the unbearable tension of the obsessive in love. He became unexpectedly and passionately devoted to a woman seven years his senior. Their age difference and her natural reserve and polish made him utterly uncertain of her true feelings. Were they just friends? Would they be lovers? Could she take him seriously? George handled this all-too-human emotional torture in the only way he knew how. He drew up a spread sheet of the relationship, assigning numerical values to various interactions, attempting to decipher her true feelings through these analyses. I suggested that George discard his charts, go directly to the source, and ask her. After much discussion as to timing, and a fair amount of rehearsal, George took the risk we all dread: he asked her how she felt. Unfortunately, anxiety made him bury the question under an avalanche of words. Now the big scene he rehearsed is over, and he still doesn't know where he stands. What, he wonders, makes poets sing about this?

Love is not the only emotion that causes a temporary glitch in your operations. Rage can also overwhelm your normally rational self. When you are angry, you are likely to become coldly silent and withdraw. You want to pull as far away as possible from a situation that threatens you with emotional upheaval. When you do lose control, you are given to sudden explosions or abusive snarls. Your outbursts are a source of pain and tension in your family, though you feel they are quick to condemn your anger and slow to hold themselves responsible for having provoked it.

The problem is that your fury can suddenly be triggered by an ostensibly small event—a missed tennis serve in a game of doubles, a child who impishly refuses to put away her toys, a bill mislaid, a phone message forgotten. Most of the time, you absorb these evidences of human failing without an emotional ripple. (And you'd like some credit for the fact that you do.) But sometimes these events infuriate you, and it shows. Your rage is not over the tennis serve or the phone message. It's over your frustration that the job could easily have been done properly—but through laziness or carelessness an error was made. You are a fair person. You can tolerate a lost document or a tired child if effort was expended to do a job well. But lack of effort sends you over the edge.

Once offended, you may have trouble letting go of your outrage. Instead of allowing the injury to fade, you develop a vivid memory of the event. You believe you remember every detail with great accuracy. You won't be able to stop thinking about who said what to whom and why. Small differences between your recollection of a quarrel and your opponent's version of the same conflict further stoke your fury ("It was not ten-thirty when you got home. It was eleven. I know because the news was on"). Reconciliation attempts often get bogged down because you need your precise memory of the injury to be validated ("O.K., you're right. It was eleven") before you are willing to heal.

Sometimes you will structure elaborate forgiveness rituals and require the offender to apologize in just the right way ("If you really mean it, you wouldn't apologize on the phone. You would say so to my face." "It's not enough to say 'I'm sorry.' He has to admit exactly what he did wrong").

Your discomfort with strong emotion does not extend to intellectual conflict. In fact, you love to argue. In an argument (which you are apt to think of as a "discussion"), you'll aim for utter victory, using the very effective strategies you've unconsciously perfected through the years: you roll your eyes, count to yourself to avoid being swayed by your opponent, rehearse your rebuttal instead of listening. It is an article of faith with you that even when you agree with the other side on a point, you *never admit it*. You are an intellectual gladiator, forcing an opponent to fight for every inch of ground. You sidetrack and nitpick, focusing on your opponent's use of a single word. When he or she gives up in frustration, you use your favorite line: "Aha! You proved my point."

You fall into an argument without quite knowing how it happened.

Your casual comments often sound like emphatic pronouncements. (Other people frequently accuse you of being angry when you know you aren't. You're just stating an opinion.) When you make one of these comments—like, "Snow tires are not much of an improvement over chains"—it sounds as if it's meant as the final word on the subject. The rest of your family and friends go on to another topic. Maybe they agree. Maybe they are even interested to learn this and appreciate your knowledge. Maybe they disagree but they've learned long ago not to bother challenging you. Snow tires just aren't worth the battle.

But one child "won't let you get away with it." This child inevitably jumps in to dispute your statement. Pretty soon the two of you are getting testy with each other over snow tires and chains. This is the child with whom you have the running battle—or else you are that child and you have the running battle with your own know-it-all mom and dad. (The need to be right is often a torch passed from generation to generation.)

The child with whom you battle is the child most like you. You also have difficulty letting someone "get away with it" when they say or do something that's not right.

Getting and Spending

No question about it—you run the world. In our particular culture, at this particular moment in time, your drive, your mastery, your reverence for what is solid, true, real, provable, your rigor and single-minded confidence, give you a good shot at being immensely successful at work.

You are most likely to choose a profession that gives you the opportunity to be right, over and over. You will be too, because you tend to narrow the focus of your life to this one area and get very, very good at it. These likely professions include lawyer, professor, engineer, CPA, computer analyst, corporate manager, internist, chef, publisher. One reason it's difficult for you to identify the need to be right as baggage is because it's the key to your professional success. It's very hard to be critical of the part of you that has won you financial rewards, power and admiration, status and satisfaction.

You have firm strategies for handling your money. You balance your checkbook, study investments, feel the responsibility of making wise and informed choices. You consult a variety of experts for financial planning and put time into reviewing their advice and your decisions. Money is not a toy, a joke, or a status symbol. Money is a foundation, and you take the stability of your foundation very seriously.

Your bills are, of course, organized and filed for easy reference. When you applied for a mortgage, you were able to come up with all your W-2s for the last four years in less time than it takes most of us to remember our Social Security number. You forgave yourself for showing off. It is, after all, a marvelous filing system and you invented it yourself and it gets so few challenges worthy of it.

Spending requires prudence. This is not to say that you've never been impulsive, but as a rule you think and plan before you spend. You feel good about how you handle your money. It wounds you when people tease you about being cheap. But, you reason, grasshoppers have always poked fun at ants and you imagine they always will. It's a reassuring thought.

Your financial crisis comes when you make a major purchase. You must make *exactly* the right choice. *Consumer Reports* is your bible. The purchase of a car, a computer, or a sound system can leave you frozen for months because there is no one right move. You may go back and forth for days, weeks, researching, debating, discussing until the rest of us are driven to a frenzy of boredom. Your spouse screams one day, "Buy the damn CD player already. I can't stand to hear about it another minute." Eventually, in a moment of impulse after your endless deliberating, you leap forward and make a choice.

There are two possible outcomes of this financial agonizing. You either (*a*) come to believe that you made the wrong choice, in which case it bothers you forever. You are still irritated that you let a salesman talk you into the wrong camera six years ago. Now every time you go to buy a piece of equipment, you recall the camera and castigate yourself for it. Or (*b*) you feel happy with your choice, in which case you automatically become an authority on computers or cars or cameras or whatever it was you're glad you bought.

In the Social World

You are, first of all, a moral person. You're loyal and law-abiding. You're comfortable with rules that seem fair to you, and you easily understand the reasons behind them. On the plus side, you handle your obligations in a mature, ethical fashion. You have integrity, and we are all better people for having you around to set a standard.

Sometimes the problem is not that you have integrity but that you pride yourself on it. You tend toward a self-righteousness that's off-putting to the rest of us. You might develop a pattern of saint/sinner relationships: You are the saint of a twosome—the good, loyal, hard-working, mature, responsible one. Your partner, be s/he lover, friend, spouse, or colleague—is the sinner, the slob, or the lazy one, or the one prone to mistakes or to incompetence. This saint/sinner setup satisfies your self-image, but at great cost to you and to the relationship. You'll feel frustrated, overburdened, and your partner will feel insulted or hopeless.

One woman describes the all-too-common battle with a saintly husband as follows: *"If I failed to wipe out the bathtub, it wasn't just that I was sloppy, or inconsiderate. It was that I was somehow morally bad. I was made to feel unclean and unworthy. 'How could you leave the tub that way?' he'd say, with such contempt. What kind of person leaves food on a plate and calls it washed?"*

The glue in most of your relationships, whether romantic or platonic, is a common interest. Your friendships form around an interest in things rather than an intuitive feeling for people. Your friends are, therefore, in categories—golf buddies, bridge partners, professional colleagues, fellow gardeners, and so on. Your business will be a main catalyst for social interaction because it forms a solid ground of common interest ("I'm selling, you're buying—therefore, we're friends"). When you can turn a social event to a business advantage, you're delighted. You've turned what was simply passing time, however pleasurably, into something productive.

You stand on ceremony. You like formal RSVP's, thank-you notes, courteous titles. You prefer proper etiquette regardless of the intimacy of a relationship. After all, there is a right way to treat people.

▪

In any group activity, you'll take on the difficult job or the most important job, partly because you aren't sure the others are competent to do it. You don't mind the hard work yourself. In fact, it's your usual mode of operation. What infuriates you is that the other people in the group aren't working *as* hard. When you're at your desk, finishing up the printing and binding, and you hear the rest of the group laughing over coffee, it makes you crazy. Sometimes you hate the people you work with because you're the only one doing any work.

Your most likely social role: "Smarty Smarty had a party. Nobody came but Mr. Smarty."

Sometimes this children's rhyme describes you exactly. You have an enormous knowledge base that the rest of us lack. You believe in it and treasure it because it is based on *fact*. It irritates you to hear your mother-in-law express an opinion that you know she's only parroting from a morning talk show. In your experience, most people talk about things they don't know anything about. Sometimes you'll contribute and people are glad you set them straight. Sometimes you go on and on with your facts and miss the rest of us rolling our eyes. The truth is, being smart doesn't always mean people are going to like you. Quite the opposite.

Your Marriage

If you are male, you are most likely to marry a warm, pretty, charming, spontaneous woman with whom you will struggle because she's "irrational," "overly emotional," or just plain "crazy."

In the beginning of your relationship, you delight in showing her the best way to do things and she delights in being shown. You set up a stock account for her paycheck, show her a better way to talk to her boss, take over the maintenance of her car. You listen intently to her emotional ups and downs, advise her on a firmer approach to a difficult friend or a stubborn child, give her a clear analysis of her own parents. She appreciates it, and you two feel close.

Sexually, she feels things are fine. You might not be her most imaginative lover, but the actual act of making love is not the most important thing in her life. She wants a strong man who is wild about her and whom she can "respect." You more than fill the bill and she feels she is in love.

Sexually, you feel things are pretty terrific. She is responsive, willing, and affectionate. She holds your hand, strokes your neck, and seems to have an orgasm with reassuring regularity.

She is attractive, you are proud to be seen with her, and people seem to like her a lot. Having her with you makes social obligations easier, business functions less of an effort. She is able to make an astonishing amount of small talk, which relieves you of an awkward burden. She appears to be the loving woman you can cherish. You marry her.

Ultimately, the very differences that drew you together create dissension. She always had strong reactions to people, but now the person she's reacting to is *you*. You didn't get a romantic birthday gift; you didn't feel like gossiping after a party, or reporting on a business meeting; you fall asleep after sex—it's always something. Her complaints make you angry, so you withdraw. But when you try to tune her out, she escalates to a scream. She acts crazy. You back off.

You complain that she always wants more and more. She complains that you give less and less.

Depending on the rigidity of your personalities, either the marriage matures and shapes you both, nudging you toward a balanced middle, or both parties polarize and battle forever from opposite ends of the personality spectrum.

A woman who needs to be right might easily make a similar kind of match. For every woman who "doesn't wish to discuss it," there is a man who insists on knowing how she feels. It is more typical, however, that the woman who needs to be right will hook up with a different kind of man. She is most likely to marry a sweet, nurturing man, with whom she struggles because he's "passive-aggressive," "unambitious," or just plain "lazy."

This drama—the obsessive woman and passive-aggressive man—is becoming more common as women exercise their capacity for power and enjoy the delights of control. These women are more likely to connect with men who are quite happy to let a woman run the show. Eventually, both battle over the unequal distribution of work. She does most of it—which makes her mad, so she nags him to do more, which makes him mad, so he does less, which makes her angrier, so she pushes harder, which makes him angrier. And so on.

Finally, if you need to be right, there is every possibility that, male or female, you might marry someone very much like you. We recognize you two. You arrived at the party arguing over which of you made the other late. During dinner, you corrected each other twice. As you were leaving, you were overheard arguing over the best route home.

THE INNER PORTRAIT

Why? What makes you plow through life doing what is right when all around you people are merrily doing what they feel like doing? Why work harder than the rest of us when we scarcely appreciate your efforts? And what drives you to do, to be, and to know more than you yourself would reasonably expect of someone else?

The answer begins with your theme song.

Your Theme Song: "I Should . . ."

You have a psychological song—a chant, really. You move to its beat every day of your life. The song is singing, "I should . . . I should . . . I should . . ."

"I should . . . be doing my sit-ups, eating more fiber, learning Jap-

anese, saving more money, starting my taxes, calling my friends, practicing my guitar, cleaning the linen closet, repainting the laundry room,
writing a journal." You can always think of something you should be
doing—to improve yourself, to get things done, to be better, work
more, get ahead. Your idea of leisure is a sport you can practice a lot,
measure your progress in, master and eventually beat someone
else at.

You hang your sense of certainty on "I should." "I should" is *not* a
matter of your free choice. It is *not* a stance you've chosen to assume.
It is dogma.

If you felt you had the freedom to choose, you might still opt for
doing what you "should" do—because it interests you, or because you
value the result. The point is, you don't feel you have the option. Instead,
you experience the sense of "should" as dictated by outside circumstances. You stay late because the job requires it, study hard because
you'll need top marks to get into graduate school, work two jobs
because how else will your bills get paid? You turn the cup handles
facing left because the cabinet holds more cups that way. You eat at
six, though you aren't hungry, because families should eat dinner together. And on and on. These requirements are very real to you. You
cannot envision responding in another way. You did not make these
rules. They are dictated by the situation in which you find yourself.
You are only free to do the right thing or to resist and feel rotten.

"Should" is the dragon that sits on the left shoulder of every person
who needs to be right. The "should" dragon exerts a gnawing pressure,
making you feel anxious or guilty unless you are doing something
productive at all times. That doesn't necessarily mean you *are* productive. It just means you spend a lot of time feeling anxious or guilty.

The fact that other people fail to do what they "should," without
obvious punishment, is a source of shock and disapproval. You work
two jobs, and your sister quits her one because she'd rather stay home
with her baby. What happens? Your parents help her out with money
because she needs the help and you don't. It's infuriating.

You work overtime and get your work done on time. Who gets the
extra vacation days? Your lazier, louder colleague.

You both know the apartment should be cleaned. But you pay attention to "should" and your roommate doesn't. Guess who ends up cleaning the toilet?

Your ceaseless internal pressure to do what you "should," when you "should," in the precise mode and style you "should," creates your baggage every bit as much as it provides the energy for your achievements, your morality, and your self-respect. But where did this theme song come from? Why can't you turn it off—even when you are exhausted, even when you are uncertain, even when what you "should" do is trivial in the larger scheme of things?

"Should" is a hint about what makes you feel good. What makes you feel good is *control,* which is what we'd get if only we did what we "should."

Your Ruling Passion: Control

Dig a bit deeper into those of us who are productive, hardworking, reliable, responsible, and usually right, and you will unearth a full-fledged passion—the joy, the glory, the power of control.

We rarely speak about the delights of control. It seems undemocratic, un-American, to admit to a glory in oneself as ruler, dictator, czar of our own little universe. We are far more likely to talk about the burdens of responsibility than we are to acknowledge the elation of power. But it's there.

Control: "Do it *my* way. I get to say how we do it, when we do it, even if we do it. I know what's right. Therefore, I get to make the decisions. I run the show, *I* am master of the universe."

Control? Control of what? The magic of control is this: It really doesn't matter what situation provides the opportunity to experience power. Some very few of us satisfy the craving by running a country, or a corporation. But neither of these is necessary in order to taste the delights of control. Our own families, our colleagues, our day-to-day lives, will provide ample opportunity.

We decide how money should be spent—not only for ourselves but for our mates and children. We decide how the whole group should approach a project, solve a problem. We decide how other people should eat, or dress, or work—for their own good, of course, because it's obviously the right way, the best way. In our own mini-universes, we decide what goes.

But, you protest, this makes it sound like you take control just to dominate others, just to "win," just to satisfy yourself. It certainly doesn't feel that way to you. You would be infinitely happier if you could lay down the heavy burden of responsibility described here as "control." You would too, if only someone else could be trusted to do the job well, thoroughly, competently, as it "should" be done.

You would be happy to let your friends plan the weekend—if you thought they'd bother to think ahead to dinner reservations. But you know them—they won't.

You would be infinitely relieved if your husband took control of the kids' discipline. But all he is willing to do is ignore them until he's irritated, then bellow at them to get their attention. This is not exactly what you had in mind.

You would turn the committee over to anyone who could organize the group and get the job done. No one else is willing!

When you give explicit driving directions, it's not for the joys of being in charge. It's so you can get where you're going. Naturally, you were the one who bothered to call and find out.

In all of these and a thousand other examples, you might argue that you are driven more by the burdens of responsibility than by the rewards of control. Further, you might argue that control implies getting your own way and you are most definitely not someone who gets to do what you want (unlike other, lazier, less motivated, less responsible people). If your great need is control, how come *you* are picking up the clothes *they* are flinging into corners? If your driving passion is power, how come you are sitting at the computer figuring the projections and they are sitting in the lounge figuring touchdown possibilities?

In fact, the strongest obstacle to recognizing our own taste for control is the feeling that responsibility is thrust upon us, expected of us, and that we'd give it up if other people would only do a bit more of what they obviously, manifestly, should.

"I don't want, need, or enjoy control," you might argue. "But some-one needs to take responsibility."

You are absolutely right. Someone does. It's just interesting that the someone is often you. (I have long noticed that whenever I get into an elevator, whether first, last, or in the middle of a crowd, I end up being the one who pushes the buttons.)

It's not simply because other people want or expect it of you—though that's part of it; and it's not simply that you are more thoughtful or thorough than others, although that is usually true too. It's also that something inside you is *driving* you to be more thoughtful, more thorough: to train other people to expect it of you. And that part is your passion for and deep pleasure in control.

Control—because it makes you feel triumphant, and

Control—because it makes you feel safe.

Don't overreact. This is an observation, not a criticism. Control is a marvelous tool, an utterly necessary device for coping and for making progress in any important area of life. Control does entail responsibility. You, more than any of us, are willing to shoulder your share. Control does mean harder work, longer-range planning, more attention to detail, more self-discipline, less impulse gratification, a bigger bite of the chore. You are the one among us willing and able to provide all this. Control is not something you wrested from us. It's something you earned. You did the work. We meant to.

It's simply that the passion for control comes with baggage.

WHAT'S THE BAGGAGE?
YOUR NEED TO BE RIGHT

We've completed the big picture, the overview of who you are, how you probably behave, and a little bit of what moves you to act in the way that you do. Some, though not all, of it may have sounded like you. The portrait outlined strengths and suggested some of the areas where those strengths were apt to become liabilities.

The rest of the chapter takes a closer look at those liabilities. It shows you how the hunger for control, which helps to develop exceptional competence in life, also creates the need to be right. As you are reading the chapter, remember the central premise of this book: Every one of us has baggage. It's the flip side of the strengths on which we pride ourselves. But you can be ahead of the game. You can not only spot the strengths, you can identify the baggage. Once you've identified it, you can get it out of your way.

Your need to be right comes directly out of your passion for control. For one thing, a solid sense of control requires being right. (How much in control could you feel if you thought you were wrong?) And figuring out what is right in any new situation gives you new opportunities for control. An ideal relationship, right? Wrong.

The need to be right gets in your way because:

- It saps your strength.

- It turns fun into work.

- It paralyzes your judgment.

- It interferes with love.

THE STRENGTH: When Something Is Important, You'll Do the Best Job Possible.
BUT
THE BAGGAGE: Even When It Doesn't Matter, You Still Need to Do It "Right."

A sales manager calls together his support staff for an impromptu lesson on proper stapling technique. He points out the benefits of the 45-degree angle and the efficiency of holding down with the nondominant hand while pressing a staple gun with the other. Everyone nods reassuringly, then retires to the ladies' room to giggle over his lunacy.

The need to be right is, quite simply, much too much of a good thing. No situation is too minor, no choice too random to make the notion of "rightness" irrelevant. I have heard couples argue right dishwashing techniques with a vigor unmatched by neurosurgeons discussing incisions. I have seen wives in a fury over husbands who fail to reverse their jockey shorts before placing them in the hamper, husbands who snarl with frustration when a white shirt is mistakenly hung with the blue ones. And I have seen otherwise functioning families lock into a battle over broccoli, turning dinners into occasions of misery and dread, because a child "should" eat vegetables.

And this is only what we do to each other. What we do to ourselves is even harsher. We exhaust ourselves with a "should" attached to every aspect of life, to every activity. There is always some right thing you should be doing, some right way you should be doing it. You aren't able to pick situations that are top priority and *let the others go*.

I have no particular opinion as to which "right" you should keep and which ought to go. I only know that something's got to go because you are wearing yourself to an emotional frazzle over things you yourself acknowledge are not important.

If, for instance, the wife above feels that underwear turned inside out makes her work easier and she wants her husband to comply, if only to lighten her laundry load symbolically, then, she should insist on it.

If that husband takes a special joy and pleasure from a perfectly organized closet, of course he'll be frustrated when thwarted. And if those parents have made a conscious, thoughtful decision that it is important to establish boundaries for their child, then naturally they'll have to reinforce that decision every night at dinner.

But it's so rare that these decisions have been made in a conscious fashion. Even though many of us get caught up in these battles, we sense that the laundry, the closet, or the broccoli isn't really important at all. Being right is what's important. Control is what's important. Though the issue may be empty of meaning, "right" is always propelling you, sapping you, sucking you dry. The sheer volume of plans, decisions and accommodations, judgments and guidelines you generate is staggering. Because when you need to be right, nothing ever gets taken off the list.

The harm in needing to be right is that you never let up, on yourself or the rest of us. You can't. Your "should" won't shut up.

THE STRENGTH: You Are Very, Very Good at Working.
BUT
THE BAGGAGE: You'll Turn Life into Work,
Just Because That's What You're Good At.

You'd be spontaneous, only your time is already scheduled in the best possible way. You're happy to be playful, during the hours you've scheduled for play. And more and more of the play time is eaten by obligation, duty, financial pressures. Any time set aside for play you turn into a workout, a goal, or a competition.

You may make life into work by tormenting yourself on a regular basis. You worry over the possibility of making a mistake, of being humiliated or leaving something out. You can never do enough, read enough, review enough to assure yourself that you won't fail. You put too much time into a project, a case, a presentation. It's not productive time, it's worry time. You haunt yourself with the possibility of something missed, something overlooked.

Experience and success only dampen this tendency to self-torture a bit. True, the praise and respect of colleagues feels good. But you still wake up in the middle of the night worried about a new possibility of failure, or a new opportunity you don't want to miss. It's the psychic cloud over every victory. Sometimes you can only turn off the internal torture by zoning out on wine or a joint or television or a tranquilizer. None of these makes joy more likely. They just move us into the gray zone of numbness.

Your body pays a price for your intense pressure to be productive. Obstacles, lines, delays, the ignorance or incompetence of others, frustrate you powerfully. And you pay for that frustration with a vulnerability to heart disease, back spasms, ulcers, or other stress-related illnesses.

When you're good at work and it gives you a shot at being right and satisfies your sense of control, you'll turn everything into work. Then, after the exhaustion, or the divorce, or the heart attack, or the battle with your addiction, you will have to move even more slowly, master even less, be less "productive" because your wounded body and spirit will get in the way. You will chafe against these self-created obstacles.

Somehow, you have to master this lesson: Being right is not as important as *just being*.

THE STRENGTH: It's Easy for You to Be
Enormously Productive.
BUT
THE BAGGAGE: It's Difficult for You to Just Be.

"I love women. I even think I really love this woman. But I know she'll be like the rest. I have Saturday night and Sunday morning to give to a relationship. Eventually, she'll want the week."

You want love, need love, value love as much as any of us. But you are especially sensitive to the burdens and obligations of love. The burdens weigh more heavily on you, and that makes love a lot less fun.

Love, relationships, intimacy require a great deal of simple *being with*. "Being with" means being there, waking there, hanging out, spending time, being close to someone simply because your presence weaves you into the fabric of his or her life. Being there is the opposite of being productive, of having a goal. It's just the *is*, the dailiness, the availability, the presence; it's also your attention, your awareness, and ultimately, your love. Being there is the necessary condition for intimacy, though every relationship has a different Minimum Daily Requirement.

Being there is also the condition for intimacy that will chafe against your need to be right.

To be right is to be productive, to be up, to be out, to be doing what you should. Eventually, love, marriage, family, become items on the To Do list, instead of people whose presence brings you joy. Here's how it often unfolds:

When you're single, you control your own time. You may have an adult tantrum or two when you hit a frustration (are you muttering under your breath in the movie line? Crazed when your computer mysteriously crashes?). But these expressions of frustration don't interfere with your relationships, because no one is around to see them. (Your parents may notice, especially if you are living with them. But they are accustomed to your "outbursts" or "episodes." They've been tolerating them and reminding themselves it's nothing personal since you were two.)

Certainly, you see friends and have a social life while you are single. These relationships can be scheduled. You might even make a great effort to be a good friend or son or daughter. You might discipline yourself to make regular calls, send cards, do helpful chores. You can achieve a good balance.

Eventually, you become involved in a serious long-term relationship. It eats up a certain amount of time you had made available for "should." You still have a degree of freedom, but the two of you begin to fight because you feel irritable or pressured and your partner feels neglected.

As I've observed in my practice, this is where the burden of intimacy typically hits the man who needs to be right. (Therefore, the example that follows is male. Remember, though, single women can have the experience too.) You're a man with a career, a hobby and/or a deep interest. If you enjoy something like wind surfing, you are swept away with it. You want to do it, watch it, read about, vacation with it. You get a lot of pleasure from spending your free time absorbed by this activity. (Golf, football bets, your woodshop—fill in your blank and you'll see yourself here.) When you were single, you could satisfy this side of yourself completely, and still have some time left over for Saturday night. Now you find yourself in a struggle:

SHE: "I want us to spend more time together. You've been working at that computer six days a week."

HE: "O.K. What'll we do?"

SHE: "It doesn't matter what we do. We'll be together."

HE: grudgingly: "O.K." But he sighs inwardly because he would love to spend some of his weekend free time working on his stock projections. He'll be so bored doing nothing. All they'll do, he figures, is go to the movies or watch TV. The doubt begins: "If she were the right woman, maybe I wouldn't feel bored at the prospect of a night of TV with her. I don't want to marry someone who bores me. On the other hand, she's warm. She's . . ."

The man in this example does not understand that it is his own "should" dragons interfering with the demands of intimacy. Eventually, he marries her, or someone like her, and the conflict deepens. When you need to be right, it's very difficult to take something off your list of required activities. Love and marriage just make that list impossibly long. By the time you add kids to the list, you can easily be raving.

From my clinical observation, this is where women who need to be right typically feel the crunch. (Again, women most often experience the burden being described, but some men feel exactly the same pressures when they marry.) Traditionally, marriage makes more time available to men because they have someone in their life to handle day-to-day maintenance. Even if she's working, a woman today still bears most of this maintenance burden as well. If she's a woman driven by a need to do things right, she'll be in an impossible emotional situation. It's just not possible to work, parent, clean, entertain, and still remember to pick up a small gift for your in-laws' anniversary. Oh, you can do it—but you can't do it right.

She will put a good deal of energy into driving her husband to do what needs to be done. Then he either won't do it, won't do it now, or won't do it right. (See page 43 for a description of her most likely marital battle.)

He will try to point out that her list of "shoulds" is entirely too long, full of unnecessary effort: "You do not have to make the Halloween costume yourself. Buy it!" "No, I don't think the kids have to change their clothes for dinner just because your mom always had a gracious evening meal." It's hard for her to respond to this advice positively. She believes she cannot help the internal pressure she feels to be the "right" kind of wife, mother, employee, daughter, neighbor, friend, sister, and so on. All she is asking is that he relieve her of some of her chores. She doesn't want an explanation of why they don't really have to be done.

The sheer time demands of intimate relationships, and the frustration of meeting these demands along with all the others you impose on yourself, can make intimacy a heavy burden. When your need for control gets out of hand, love can become one of the things you don't have time for.

THE STRENGTH: You'll Put Thought and Effort into
Making a Wise Choice.
BUT
THE BAGGAGE: If Thought and Effort Don't Work,
You Can Be Paralyzed.

If you need to be right, you might pride yourself on your capacity
to make clear decisions—to determine the right course and proceed
accordingly. Yet decision making, like all of our greatest strengths, is
also a secret area of great weakness. It is where you are most likely to
get in your own way.

When something has to be done, but the right thing is not immediately obvious, you freeze. It's the situation where you must make a
decision, yet the pros and cons are so delicately balanced you cannot
be assured of deciding correctly.

Choosing between any two good options might momentarily give
you pause ("Brownie or cookie? Ah, cookie or brownie? Uh . . . cookie.
Wait. Uh . . ."). You grow accustomed to an internal voice that always
accompanies these small daily choices ("Should I get the gas now, or
will I be late? If I get it now, I won't have to go out after dark, but I
could be late . . . I'll see how long the line is . . . Two cars . . . I could
wait for the two cars, or I could . . ."). If you are one of those whose
internal obsessing over day-to-day moves is out of control, you know
how much it can interfere with your productivity: Lunch now or later?
Tuna or ham? Alone or with friends? Rye or white? *Aagh!* If this sounds
like you, you are probably stuck in a procrastinator's nightmare. The
impressive thing is how much you're able to accomplish despite this
moment-to-moment evaluation of right choices.

But most of us who need to be right function well in our decision
making on a day-to-day level. Our hard work, efficiency, and solid
information base give us confidence; in fact, we pride ourselves on
being the one in the group who knows how to proceed on any given
project, down to the paper clip requisitions.

In a sublime example of pride preceding falls, the pride we take in
our decision-making capacity is a good measure of the paralysis we
experience confronting the major, or the difficult, or the new. Some-

times this major life decision takes the form of a significant material purchase—be it a house, a car, or almost any technological object (car phone, fax machine—you name it). The problem is, there is no way to assure oneself of being right. There are too many choices, too many factors to consider. "Should" plus desire push us forward ("I should buy a house, I really should. These taxes are killing me. Besides, I want one. It's time. I have to. I will . . ."). Ambiguity, the risk of being wrong push us back ("I don't trust that real estate agent. I think I could get it for less. What about the plumbing, the roof, the heat, the neighborhood . . .").

There we rock, in magnificent uncertainty, on the fence, unable to give the project up ("I have to live somewhere!"), unable to push the project forward ("I just need to see a few more houses, watch interest rates a few more months, discuss this decision with a few key people").

A career fork in the road is certainly another commitment where we can be paralyzed by ambivalence. Private practice or a large firm? Corporate management or the autonomy of a small business? Leave the security of teaching for the uncertain satisfactions of the arts? These are typical of the career choices and significant life decisions that confront us as we move through adulthood. Unfortunately, the need to be right is a major obstacle to making these decisions, because neither side of the fence is clearly "right."

Also, hard as we may try (and some of us put an amazing amount of effort into it), none of us can see the future. What we need to know in order to take these forks in the road with perfect confidence is: "How will I feel in five years, in ten, in fifteen?" We feel we must be guided by what will turn out to be right far, far down the road. And that information is unavailable.

Financial commitments and career commitments are two likely areas where our need to be right often gets in the way of success and satisfaction. The third arena where we are apt to be most frozen is, unhappily, in the area of love.

In the most typical scenario, you are in your late twenties to mid-thirties. You have a life established away from your parents—friends, a home, a gym membership, and a history of relationships that have all stopped short of marriage. (Alternatively, you might have one marriage behind you—the one you made in your early twenties when you were sure that getting married was the right thing to do. So of course, you went ahead and did it. Only it turned out to be wrong and you've never forgotten it.) You feel you'd very much like to be married today but . . . only if you choose the right person.

You may be in a long-term relationship where your partner is pushing for marriage and you just can't bring yourself to feel comfortable. You're not sure. Is this potential mate sexy enough, polished enough, interesting enough, tall enough, ambitious enough to keep you in love and loving for the years to come? You two may live together, have a deep emotional attachment. You don't want to put this person out of your life, nor do you want to move forward. Here you sit, the executive capable of huge financial decisions, the administrator daily negotiating personnel decisions, the physician comfortable with life-and-death decisions, and you are frozen facing a decision about love.

As we've just discussed, if you are burdened by the need to be right, it is likely to impair your decision making, whether on a daily basis or in one of the significant arenas: love, work, or money.

Instead of making one of these decisions in an active, forthright manner, you find that your paralysis creates three negative consequences:

- perfectionism

- procrastination

- impulsiveness

"I never am happily surprised by life. I'm usually disappointed. First, I get a mental picture of exactly how something should be, like how my boyfriend will act on my birthday if he really loves me. Sometimes he acts like how I pictured it and that makes me feel good. But usually when I compare him to my ideal picture, I'm disappointed or worried about the differences."

To handle the ambiguities of adult life, those of us who need to be right are apt to construct ideal solutions to whatever problems we are facing. We fantasize a perfect house, ideally located, priced, and constructed; or a perfect mate, down to his or her age, sex, height, smile, dimples, religion, wit, occupation, income level. To some degree, these detailed descriptions of our version of perfection help us. We will scour the marketplace with a good deal more confidence because we can now be guided by a clear picture of the right choice. The problem is that real life often requires compromise—and we find this compromise agony.

Our ideas of perfection are not just guideposts. They become deep emotional investments. Realistic compromise becomes emotionally impossible. It just makes us too anxious. In other words, when you need to be right, your image of the perfect choice soon becomes the *only* right choice. Anything short of perfection looks wrong. And since so few major decisions in life offer perfect options, it's inevitable that you will find most big decisions painful, if not impossible.

(Ironically, the fact that life does occasionally present a perfect option, or at least appears to, makes the whole thing worse. When Billy Joel married Christie Brinkley, three different men in my practice mentioned it as "proof" that some men get a goddess. If your brother found an ideal house at an unbelievable price, you'll find it much harder to compromise on a nice house at a reasonable price.)

Since these realistic big decisions are so painful, what you're most likely to do, if you need to be right, is not make one. *You procrastinate,* choosing over and over the no-decision alternative.

Making no decision *is* a firm decision, a firm vote for the status quo. We'll do almost anything to keep things as they are, because we can't be sure a move would be the right move. A person less burdened by our baggage can take more risks, enjoy more adventures because he or she can forgive the inevitable failures that might ensue. Of course, along with those failures comes the exhilaration of the unexpected successes on which we miss out.

The no-decision course means we let life decide for us. It means we ask our lovers for "more time," as if time would help us to tolerate better the compromises required by relationships. We ask our real estate agents to see one more house, we decide to consult one more expert, wait one more year at the current job. Eventually, the girlfriend we're not sure of moves out, stung by rejection; or the house we're deciding on is bought by someone else; the career move dries up, the moment of opportunity passes. The world does not stand still while we're procrastinating, so we allow ourselves to be carried along by the tide of events outside our control. At the very least, this way we weren't wrong. It was just something "that happens." Ironic, isn't it, that those of us who love control will let life control us when we're afraid to decide.

Yet sometimes we can't or won't procrastinate. Much as we loathe our own decision-making disabilities, sometimes we force ourselves to act or we allow outside events to force us: Your lease is up and you've got to live somewhere. . . . Your girlfriend is pregnant. . . . Your gift certificate is good only until January 1. . . . The company closes, fires you, forces you into a career change. In these instances, you are likely to leap forward impulsively, driven by the anxiety of the moment.

The consequence of an impulsive act is often emotionally unfortunate. You are at risk of agonizing indefinitely: "Could I have gotten the house for five thousand less if I'd bid less going in?" "Would I have been happier turning down the transfer now that reorganization is a possibility?" Or worst of all, "Yes, I married you—but I never wanted to. You forced me."

To live comfortably with a decision, we need to think through its consequences and make peace with its costs. An impulsive decision does not allow for tranquil self-acceptance. Neither does perfectionism or procrastination. All three of these obstacles to self-love are generated by your very heavy baggage: the need to be right—every time.

THE STRENGTH: You Are Usually Willing to
Follow the Rules.
BUT
THE BAGGAGE: You Are the One Reading
from the Rule Book.

"We go into a restaurant and she'll say, 'Oh honey, I know you're going to order the chicken salad because you love it here.' I do love it, but she makes me want to order the pizza."

If you need to be right, you will, quite naturally, try to help other people do right too (especially the people you care about, like your family and friends, and especially the people you are responsible for, like your employees or students). They don't think of it as doing it "the right way." They call it doing things "your way." And they fight you on it, overtly or covertly.

SHE: "He won't let me use the washer without criticizing how I fill it with clothes. He has the ideal washer/dryer system, naturally. I have to do it exactly like he says or he gets furious."

HE: "Why does she make such a big deal of it? I read the manual. I know how the washer works. I tell her. She starts a fight over it. I don't get it."

HE: "She watches everything I do. When I pay the bills. How I put my underwear away, how I cook a steak. If I choose to do things differently, or later than she scheduled, she's on top of me."

SHE: "It's not a matter of differently, or later. It's not doing it at all, leaving it for me, doing it half-assed."

You do three fourths of the work—plan the party, keep the books, organize the project. Do they appreciate it? No! They complain that you're always telling them what to do, and you're not fun to be with either.

Remember, baggage is a blind spot. It really *is* difficult to understand when someone close to you complains that you are "rigid," "overbearing," or "controlling." You yourself are entirely controlled by "should." These "shoulds," these "right ways" are not reflections of your own whim or preference. In fact, quite often, you don't like them any better than anyone else. You don't feel like cleaning up in the kitchen before bedtime any more than he does. You do it because it has to be done. You don't feel like showing up at the office on Saturdays any more than your associate does. But the work needs doing. You force yourself to make the effort to do things appropriately. Why shouldn't the rest of the world make the effort? You wouldn't be so bossy if they were willing to boss themselves a little.

Here's your blind spot: You are the one who holds the rule book.

From your point of view, you didn't write the rule book. Life writes the rule book. You just got stuck being the one who reads from it.

To someone on the receiving end, these seem like *your* rules, not *the* rules. And people end up feeling it all has to be your way or no way at all. Which is, in a sense, true.

When we need to be right, we have a lot of difficulty letting others be right also, or be wrong if they so choose. Sadly, this need can force us to bully our lovers, best our children, and prove, over and over, that we're more right than our parents or friends. We win. But they don't love us more for it.

Rx: EASE UP

What is wonderful about the person who needs to be right is his or her purposefulness. We are the doers, the drivers. What hurts us so deeply is that we slow ourselves down shouldering unnecessary burdens, and we crash into the self-esteem and spirit of people we love.

If you could let go of your need for control, even a little, you could minimize both of these costs considerably. You'd see a tapering off of marital hostilities over who did (or didn't do) what. Your loved ones would put up less of a wall to protect themselves from you. Letting go of control means you'll feel less stress because you'll focus on life's important issues and respond less frequently to the trivial "shoulds" that exhaust you. Finally, when you stop trying to get other people to do what they should, they may do out of love the very things you've been trying to get them to do by nagging.

To make yourself feel better and to make your life work better, concentrate your formidable will and focus your very powerful attention to detail on this one goal—*ease up*.

"Ease up" means resist your compelling need to be right. Reduce its urgency. Relax the inner tension that pushes you to strive and pushes the people connected to you to do the same.

Naturally, you will still need *control* and you will still want to satisfy that need often. But you can become the driver instead of the driven.

Each of the following exercises gives you the opportunity to resist taking charge, being right, or doing what you should. Remember, though the task may be as simple as leaving the bed unmade or going along with someone else's plan for fun when it's your idea of stupid extravagance, you'll probably feel uncomfortable doing it. It will make you feel vulnerable, unnatural, even wrong to be other than your usual in-control self. It's worth it to withstand these inevitable discomforts of change, because the long-term payoff feels so good.

There is a specific benefit you can expect with each exercise, a benefit that is outlined for you in each assignment. Ultimately, the purpose of these exercises is to change how you handle your need to be right as it comes up over and over again in your life. It is true that even small change requires effort and makes us anxious. But the payoff is freedom, freedom from your personal baggage.

All of the exercises in this book are antidotes for the same central problem: Everyone has baggage, because everyone has some ruling passion that gets in his way as often as it helps him. When you learn to resist that passion, to gratify it consciously rather than automatically, you lose none of your strength. But you sure do make your life sweeter.

Here's how to do it:

Risk Losing Control—Part I

The simplest way to learn to redirect your passion for control is to identify situations where others could realistically take charge, and then force yourself to sit back and allow them to do so. In other words, take control of your need to be right. (Yes, this is a bit like "Be spontaneous," but bear with me.)

Part I of this exercise suggests you begin with small, day-to-day events. You'll need to identify areas where you typically run the show. Then pick one or two and turn them over to someone else.

For example:

▪ Let someone else drive.

▪ This time, have no opinion on which movie to see, which restaurant to go to, which video to rent. Let your companion pick.

▪ Let the other people with whom you eat plan dinners this week. While you're at it, let them cook and/or clean up afterward.

▪ Hand over the checkbook this month. Aren't you tired of managing the money anyway?

▪ Don't be the one who takes the time to find out how to get there. You are usually the one who calls for directions or plans the route. This time, sit back and watch the scenery.

▪ If everyone usually comes to your house, make a point of going to theirs for a change.

▪ Give up your role of scheduler and timekeeper. Don't remind others it's getting late. Don't plan someone else's day unless you are being paid to do it. Don't decide the best time to leave. Don't worry about when everyone should wake up or if they might oversleep. Just get yourself together and be prepared to wait while your companions slowly learn to move under self-generated power.

▪ Give your mate the money and/or credit card when you go out together. Don't pay, don't look at the bill, don't take the receipt (even if you are sure he'll lose it).

One important note: When you hand over responsibility, you lose your criticism privileges. Be prepared. Most of the time, the people who have assumed your customary tasks will do them differently than you would have. That's to say, there is a great probability that they will do them wrong, poorly, late, or not at all. Don't take this bait! They are just luring you into continuing to do most of the work while they sit back, enjoy the ride, and complain about your bossiness along the way. So when someone else says he or she will do something, don't end up doing it yourself just because it wasn't done when or how you'd like it done. Let the dishes sit. Let the wet wash mold in the washer. Just *back off*. Your focus is on lightening your load of baggage. That has to have priority over your laundry load.

Now, let's assume that you decide to take on (or rather, let go of) one of the assignments listed above. What can you expect to get out of it (other than dull restaurants, boring videos, seven pizza dinners, three bounced checks, and a load of underwear accidentally turned pink because he washed it with the red sweatshirt)?

Well, aside from getting anxious over all of these possible negative outcomes, here is what could happen for you:

Let's say that you and two friends are going to dinner and a movie this Friday night. Ordinarily, you would automatically be the one to suggest the movie and the restaurant, coordinating movie preferences, dietary needs, schedules, and transportation time with the ease of an air traffic controller. This time, however, because you are giving this exercise the benefit of the doubt, you stun your friends by saying, "You plan the evening. Just let me know where to go." (They will certainly try to urge you into expressing at least an opinion or a preference. They know how picky you are. Besides, people always want you to be who you always were, even if they didn't like you that way. It's just more comfortable. Still, you have this private baggage-reduction project in mind, so you resist.)

What do you gain?

Well, it's possible that you'll be delightfully surprised and they will pick a wonderful restaurant, with your meal scheduled to end in time for a leisurely stroll to just the movie you were dying to see, just at the moment it begins. You will have learned that the people close to you are stronger, more resourceful, and more thoughtful than you previously knew them to be. You don't have to exhaust yourself being in charge of absolutely everything, because other people can take on part of the burden.

While this outcome is possible, it's not especially likely. For one thing, you have a far more detailed definition of "right" than others do. Besides, your friends and family are probably used to your deciding and they are bound to make the mistakes of inexperience.

So most likely, if you let someone else take charge of dinner and a movie, you will end up at the boring rock movie that they like, but you knew would be awful. You may feel you wasted not only the $7.50 for the ticket plus the parking but your time as well.

How, you might wonder, is that going to make you feel better in the end?

Here's how:

1. You made a trade. You didn't put in the tension and effort of planning a great evening. You did not add to your already crowded to do list the work of checking the newspapers, calling your friends, making a reservation, and plotting travel time. Yes, you do these things well. But they are work, and they cost you energy.

They cost emotion, too. The reward of the "right" movie costs you the unpleasant, if ever present feeling of being responsible for everyone else. When you pick the movie, you are the one who gets to worry about whether they'll like it. Why not give yourself the opportunity to let someone else worry over whether you like it? All that this opportunity could cost you is a boring movie.

2. You gained because you surprised people. You gave them room to see you differently, not just in this way but in a lot of ways. You gave them the opportunity to show a different side of themselves, too. And if by chance, your need to be right has made them feel personally controlled or pushed around, well, you may hav reduced an obstacle between you. The chance to be different and interesting to the people in your life and the rare opportunity to be intrigued by a new side of them are huge gains. All it costs to be interested in these people is the potential of a boring movie.

3. The ultimate gain of this exercise is that it proves to you that you *can* liberate yourself from a "should," from your own need to be right.

You see, your goal is to learn to set priorities. "Should" resounds in every corner of your life, but you can be in charge of when you'll respond. In order to quiet this ceaseless internal voice, you have to discover that you can ignore it and you'll be O.K. Even better than O.K.—actually, you'll be free.

You start with the movie. You don't pick it, and it ends up being a bore. But it's not such a big deal. Remember, a boring movie never gave you colitis. Your need to be right gave you that.

Once you learn it's possible for the movie to be wrong, the restaurant to be wrong, the evening to be wrong without your doing a lot of unnecessary agonizing, you'll find that this freedom from pressure will generalize. You are being liberated from "should." You still hear it, but you decide when to respond. You use your skills where they matter, and let the rest of life flow around you as it will. But first, you have to force yourself to stop taking charge where it doesn't count. So change begins with a small step like not picking the movie.

Risk Losing Control—Part II

When you feel you've had sufficient success resisting your impulse to make the small things go right, take on something more meaningful. Reflect on the major arenas of responsibility in your life: money, your sex life, household maintenance, your social life, parenting. Focus on your job, too, and review all the areas of responsibility that could potentially be on someone else's plate. Then identify at least three ongoing situations that could become someone else's show to run.

Here's a sample list taken from Anna. Anna is a twenty-eight-year-old caterer whose stress level became intolerable after the birth of her son. She was in a constant rage with her husband, who she felt contributed little to the increased burdens of their life. Her husband felt unjustly accused, explaining that he'd be happy to help more but "everything I do is wrong," and "a lot of what she insists on doing is just unnecessary." This marital conflict is classic and complicated, but one necessary component of its resolution was to ask Anna to identify situations where she automatically took charge. Her list looked like this:

1. I control our son's care—what he wears, when he eats, when he naps, if he goes out, whether he gets a bath—everything.

2. I plan our social life—will we see friends, who—where—are they coming over, if so, what will be served—everything.

3. My in-laws are coming next month and I've been planning the whole visit. I make sure the house is clean, I plan the activities, I make the phone calls to the rest of the family, make the cookies my mother-in-law likes. I even arrange for basketball tickets so my husband and his dad can have some decent time together.

This sample list is typical of a woman who takes control and therefore totes the baggage of needing to be right.

Make your own list. It could include a major task you are always in charge of ("We both work, but I do the taxes"). You could include a special event ("I have to call everybody or there'll be no birthday dinner"). It could be an area where you're in charge and you hate it ("Night after night I have to decide on dinner. Somewhere after my meals-around-the-world phase, I ran out of steam"). Or it might be something where you feel your control is deeply important ("This money came from my parents' estate and I want a say in what happens to every penny").

Step two of this exercise is simple. Pick an item on your list and practice letting someone else be in charge. Anna (with much protest and anxiety) selected her in-laws' visit as a place to start. She told her husband that she would be happy to help him with any assignment he might give her—but she wasn't going to be in charge of the visit.

Truly, only extreme stress and much prompting could have gotten Anna to try this exercise. Her in-laws are important to her, and since in her view, it's a wife's responsibility to run a house and a social life, she feared that she'd bear the criticism if her husband forgot anything crucial. She dealt with these fears as you will have to deal with yours, by confronting them as directly as possible.

Anna made a "what-if" list, which included every minor and/or catastrophic consequence of her not taking control of this particular event. Although her list (probably like yours) began with a tendency to fantasize about every possible negative outcome ("What if it rains? What if he forgets to pick them up? What if the sheets aren't changed? What about the towels?"), the *what-if* list usually settles into several familiar themes.

The first of these is: What if . . . it doesn't get done? followed by that torturous thought: What if . . . it's done wrong, poorly, late, partially? There's also: What if . . . someone important is angry, is hurt, sad, disappointed? Not to mention those two great mental bogeymen that make those of us who need to be right loath to put another person in charge: What if he wastes money! What if he wastes time!

Then Anna had to look at her list and ask herself, "Can I live with these consequences?"

This is not to say that the worst will occur. Actually, it's unlikely to. Note that the defining limit is "Can I live with" the consequence? The question is *not* whether Anna will enjoy these consequences. It's just —can she tolerate them?

Anna had to face the fact that there really were no catastrophic consequences to her not running the weekend. Her in-laws would arrive, and eventually leave. In between, they would all be together. True, they might not eat as well as if she had planned the meals. They might not even have as much fun, see as many sights, cover as much ground as when she structures the time. She's good at it. But the worst that could happen is that he could forget to defrost the chicken and they'd order pizza and her mother-in-law would wonder why she hadn't remembered the chicken, and Anna would either explain the new system or let it remain a mystery, as she saw fit.

Anna's gains from this difficult exercise were substantial. The very struggle she had with herself to let go of being in charge showed how deeply she was emotionally invested in doing even small things right. Once she stepped out of the pattern of deciding what should be done and then telling her husband which of them to do, he stopped resisting her in small ways. When he was in charge of what needed to be done, he was much more apt to do it. And the more he did, the less angry she was with him—a crucial gain for this or any couple.

It was not an easy process or an easy weekend for either of them. Anna and her husband have very different ideas about what "should" be done for an in-laws' visit. (Or actually, Anna has about twice as many ideas as he has on the subject.) He was not thrilled to take on responsibility for something that had previously run well without the least effort from him. He left several glaring omissions in his preparations (not cleaning the apartment, for example, even though he knew his dad was sure to make a critical remark). The omissions were positive lures for Anna to step in and nag, so they could go back to their old dance where she complained and he said, "Well, if you're going to criticize everything, do it yourself!"

But they did get through the weekend, and it had a profound impact on them as a couple. He found there was a lot involved in planning a weekend and he was more closely connected to his parents because he'd had to think about them. Anna found that an apartment does not have to be that clean or meals that planned, in order to be *good enough*.

But her main lesson would be an invaluable one for you: Just because you "should" do something, doesn't mean you have to.

When you've made your choice of an important arena of responsibility you are willing to turn over, draw up your own what-if list.

Then when you've examined your what-if list and found that you can tolerate the risk, resist your impulse to take control and improve things. Let your husband (Mr. Spontaneous) plan the two-week vacation. Let your colleague (Ms. Late) handle the newsletter. Allow your child (Miss Irresponsible) to remember her own homework, lunch money, and permission slip.

Tolerate the consequences for the sake of learning one lesson that can be achieved only through this experience: When something is not done as it "should" be done, it doesn't very often matter.

Break a Rule!

This exercise is for those of us whose need to be right translates itself into an endless list of rules for living. Those rules make life work. One way out of your prison of "should" is to break a rule and await the catastrophic results. Who knows? You might break so many rules that you accidentally break free.

Below is a list of challenges. Identify the ones you feel would disturb you the most. Of those, pick three and force them into your life.

Eventually, if you make enough effort, they'll come easily.

- Make a list of the things you are not going to do today, even though you "should." Then don't do them.

- Balance half your checkbook.

- Leave the dishes until tomorrow.

- Walk out of a movie that bores you.

- Leave your bed unmade.

- Declare one day a week a nutrition-free zone. Eat what you feel like and let your kids do the same.

- Take a cab.

- Wear the shirt with the spot and don't pretend it just happened five minutes ago.

- Put your underwear in your sweater drawer.

- Waste money.

- Use the same dishrag for the dishes as you do to wipe the table.

- Cut classes/play hooky/take a mental health day.

- Use a pot or pan again—without washing it in between.

- Turn down an opportunity. It could be an opportunity to make money, make an important business contact, meet a potentially helpful friend. Waste the time instead.

- Ignore your mail.

- Erase your telephone messages without playing them. If it's important, they will call you back.

- Give a party and invite only the people you want. Resist including the people you "should" invite.

Force Yourself to Falter

"I'm sorry."

"I'm wrong."

These two sentences are the wonder drug for the baggage of needing to be right. You will probably find it very difficult to swallow.

"I'm sorry" and "I'm wrong" force you to confront your baggage head-on. You usually feel the urge to explain why you were not wrong, why you are therefore not sorry. You always automatically argue your own point of view, recounting to yourself your reasons, your motivation, your understanding of a situation. In other words, you automatically prove to yourself you are right. Then it's just a short step to explaining to someone else why you are.

For this exercise, for the purpose of stretching yourself psychologically, you will need to oppose that line of thinking. You'll need to do a mental backbend, to give the other fellow more than a fair shake. You will have to say what you *don't* believe, in order to leave room to change. In other words, you'll need to say "I'm wrong" when you cannot quite convince yourself you are.

("What! Isn't that a lie? How can I sincerely acknowledge wrongdoing when I don't believe it? Besides, it would never work. S/he'd see right through me.")

Maybe. Or maybe the person who receives your acknowledgment will see it differently. Maybe he or she will appreciate your effort to be flexible, your willingness to let go of your own version of "the truth" to make room for someone else's.

If you are a person who needs to be right, you are breaking through a powerful barrier when you apologize. Naturally, that feels insincere. It's very different for you. You'll find it easier to break through this barrier if you understand the enormous payoff that comes with relinquishing your version of "the truth."

The first payoff is that you can come to understand that there are many versions of truth. This increased understanding represents growth in both sensitivity and flexibility for you. The truth might be that you said you'd call by eight. But it might also be true that he *heard* you say seven-thirty. You could both be right.

Obviously, there are situations where there is only room for one version of truth, namely yours. Statements of your personal feelings, tastes, and preferences are an example of this. If you don't like pasta, no one else can say you do. But you might be able to say "I'm sorry" or "I'm wrong" if you commented at dinner, "This pasta is overcooked!" After all, that "truth" is just your version of al dente.

When you are able to leave room for someone else's version of the truth, there's a second payoff: They feel good—about themselves, and about you.

Truth is, as they say, cold comfort, especially when you compare it to a warm body whose embrace you invited with an apology. The truth might be that you really *do* know an answer, but you might say, "I don't know," anyway, in the interest of serving someone else's self-esteem or autonomy. Besides, when you are open to someone else's version of the truth, you might learn something.

This exercise will help you to reach these goals. Your assignment is to count the number of times you say either "I'm sorry" or "I'm wrong."

Count means exactly that: give yourself one point for every time you say one of these sentences. Try the exercise every day for a week, to establish a baseline. Then set a goal of doubling your production.

You will need to seek out opportunities to apologize, and being you, you may have to search hard to find occasions when you are wrong.

Here are the ground rules:

1. One point every time you say "I'm sorry" or "I'm wrong."

2. Zero points if you use the word "but," as in, "I'm sorry, but you really shouldn't have . . ." If you defend yourself or explain yourself or blame someone else, it doesn't count.

3. Two points every time you say one of these sentences *even though* in your heart, you don't completely mean it. You get double the points here because this is the hardest place to get you to budge. It will be a struggle to avoid defensiveness. It will feel odd and insincere to acknowledge the possibility of error, when you feel it's unlikely. Take the risk.

This exercise is an attempt to assault a core psychological obstacle. It's a way of saying: If you need to be right, give yourself permission to be wrong. Yes, it will be awkward. Yes, it will make you anxious. But it will also stretch you and free you.

The Quiet Mind

"I hate to meditate. All I do is get anxious about everything I should be doing."

If you are a person who needs to control life, the endless stress of stemming the tide of chaos saps you mentally and physically. The need to be right has, as its greatest cost, the exhaustion that comes from constant striving.

There are a variety of psychological techniques that are highly effective at counterbalancing these costs. Unfortunately, with the exception of physical exercise, few of the techniques have been incorporated into mainstream Western life. We're suspicious of goals we can't quantify, or ones that require stillness and belief as compared to action and profit. So many of these techniques are relegated to the mystical, the ethereal, the "New Age." Well, we're missing out.

Three simple mind-quieting techniques appear to be especially successful for beginners on the path of inner exercise. They are:

- deep muscle relaxation

- visualization

- meditation

The three can be used individually, in combination, or as mental adjuncts to physical programs like yoga and long-distance running. You can learn these techniques through a night class, a private teacher, or a trip to the library. Each technique has many variations, much written about it, and its own cadre of disciples (if not fanatics). To get you started, I've included references in the bibliography to some basic texts that have proven helpful to my patients.

All of these techniques are easy to start. They need to be used on a regular, preferably a daily, basis. It will require both discipline and commitment to incorporate them into your everyday life. It will also require something of a leap of faith on your part, because when you need to be right, you are accustomed to measuring yourself according to outer results. Inner development has no external measure. You'll have trouble believing it's worthwhile. It is.

The previous exercises, like all the ones in the following chapters, are deceptively simple. Taming the passion for control, like your hunger for self-esteem, for security, for attachment or justice, requires conscious, focused, even strenuous effort. But your rewards for these psychological efforts will be great. You will make your work more fun, your goals more accessible, your sleep deeper, your waking moments more content. Best of all, because your efforts make you more lovable, more love will come your way.

If you are fortunate enough to be a person with a gift or a tradition of assuming control, you have a great advantage. It is very likely that your life runs smoothly, and that its path is clear before you. When you stretch to free yourself of your baggage, when you can be wrong (even though it mattered) or indifferent (even though you could have made it better), and when you can let the rest of us be wrong and love us anyway, your ride down that path will be a delight instead of a duty.

You may have recognized some part of yourself or someone you know—your boss, your spouse, your too-smart-for-her-own-good sister—in this chapter. You are all very different people, but you have a common coping style. You try to soothe the normal anxieties of daily life by insisting that you stay on top of things. That driving need to stay on top of it all is part of what weighs you down.

Some of us take the need to be right one step farther. We not only need to control the game, we need to be seen as the best in the game. We add to whatever piece of us wants to be right—no matter what the cost—a piece that insists on being superior—no matter what the contest. In the next chapter, you'll read about your superior baggage, which often forms a matched set with your need to be right.

Chapter Four

■

AIN'T I AWFUL?
AIN'T I SWELL?

"In high school, I was voted cutest couple."
—THE TRACY ULLMAN SHOW

We know who we are. We have a secret, held very dear to our hearts. And here it is: We're just a little bit better than the rest. We are just that cut above, just that extra special. What we are, in fact, though rarely are we so graceless as to mention it, is *superior*.

How could anything ostensibly so positive cost people so much joy?

In some ways, the sense of superiority is the most subtle yet the most costly of all our baggage. Because it is easily mistaken for self-esteem, superiority may be the baggage to which we cling most tightly. People usually suffer over their phobic boundaries, rue their penchant for drama or control, and long to be released from the poison of their rage. But it's rare that someone walks into my office and states, "I wish I didn't feel so superior. It's really getting in my way."

But it does get in the way—enormously. Superiority sours every intimate relationship with scorn, disappointment, or fatal uncertainty. It builds grandiose visions of achievement without supplying the necessary building blocks of accomplishment. At its heart, the sense of superiority forces us to live in a world of fantasy because real life is so pale by comparison.

A PORTRAIT

You Feel Special

Something about you makes you outstanding.

You are beautiful, smart, or exceptionally athletic. Or your family is prominent—or your nose is not. You are unusually good at math, gifted in music, or clever about selling. The exact nature of your gift is not important, nor does it matter how realistic or distorted you might be in your perception. Maybe you are brilliant and maybe you are merely glib. Either way, you feel special.

It's a feeling that can pay off for you throughout your life. It might help you to be a risk taker, an entrepreneur, a leader. You can take that great leap forward into the unknown, because your inner sense of destiny gives you confidence. You dream big dreams, and sometimes these dreams carry you to material and social success. You might not simply feel like a star, you might actually become one.

"Only the best" is your personal mantra. "Best" can mean any number of different things, but however you define it, you have to have it. You deserve it too. After all, you're special.

Your secret brag: "I'm too picky."

What you mean: "I have extremely high standards, which reflect me, my taste, my values, my sensitivities. People tell me I'm hard to please, but that's not true. It's just that I know what's good, I know what I like, and I know what is possible. I don't settle for less."

▪

Because you are special, you unconsciously assume you are entitled to special treatment, special rules. This belief betrays itself in small ways. You don't put money in parking meters, or you park in a disabled spot though you have no physical handicap. You'll go through a red light and feel perfectly comfortable with the explanation "The lights are too long." When only passengers are permitted to board the plane, you will try to walk on for a moment anyway. You understand that there are laws and rules. You're just not one hundred percent sure they apply to you.

When seeking help, it's typical for you to do something that establishes you as a special client or customer. You routinely turn professional relationships into quasi-personal ones. You'll ask to use your physician's personal phone, feel comfortable calling your lawyer on Sunday afternoon. You're the one who brings in the theater tickets or the bottle of good wine for your cardiologist. We are all slightly "one down" when we consult these professionals. But you are only down on the power ladder temporarily. Your behaviors are automatically geared to reestablishing that balance suitable to your self-image.

You might have a deeply cherished feeling that someone or something watches over you. That someone might be a deceased parent or grandparent. It might be a treasured part of nature or it might be God. Either way, it proves that you are unique and makes you stronger.

If you had a psychiatric label, it would probably be: Narcissistic personality.

Your Motto: "I can do anything I want if I put my mind to it."

This can be an extremely positive and motivating personal vision. When it's packaged with a balanced sense of self-esteem and a realistic assessment of strengths and frailties, it can be the motivational juice needed to make a championship push. But when you burden yourself with the sense of superiority, this positive statement also carries a psychological curse.

The curse is twofold: First, when you believe you can accomplish anything you put your mind to, you can set your mind to a lot of inappropriate things. You try to be an artist, but you fail to take a realistic measure of your talent. You want to be a manager, but you don't want to get the graduate degree you'd need to be a good one. You can create failure after failure because your belief in yourself makes it difficult to assess accurately the possibilities of success.

On the other hand, you may end up trying nothing at all. It feels so good to believe you *could* do anything you set your mind to that you don't want to risk losing the feeling by failing. How to avoid failure? It's easy—don't try. You might be so fearful of challenging your beliefs that you try almost nothing, content with a job and a life significantly below your capacities, because you are safe from the devastating disruption of failure.

So, paradoxically, your motto might make you an extreme risk taker or no risk taker at all. Or you might be both at different times, speeding your powerboat through a storm, but unable to leave the corporation to start the business you've envisioned for years.

In your fantasies, however, you are a hugely successful risk taker. You invest a lot of your time in these daydreams and you enjoy that time enormously. You'll be driving or exercising or listening to music—all the while lost in a fantasy of creating the board game to replace Trivial Pursuit, or winning the Olympics, or being chairman of the board. You may or may not have real-life plans to reach these goals. Your fantasies are rich and rewarding either way.

There are no paths to success in these visions, no how-to elements. You simply see yourself having arrived. And in your vision, the crowds are roaring their approval and acknowledging you as the person you knew you were all along—someone superior.

Your best fantasy: Rehearsing an acceptance speech.

At the end of the Vietnam War, I received this thank-you note from a friend: "I'd like to thank you for anything you may have said or done to end the war." All the charms and liabilities of superiority were expressed in this gesture. It had the marvelous grandiosity of a man who saw himself as one entitled to send the note, as if peace, like everything else on the planet, were there for his personal satisfaction. On the other hand, there was my great delight in receiving the note, smiling over it, over the sentiment, over the sender. This was a man who grew impatient or simply tuned out if you were sharing an experience in which he was not directly involved. ("Don't worry," I'd say. "This conversation is really about you. I'm just taking a long time to get to your part." "Well, hurry up," he'd respond.) But he was also someone who once sneaked into the home of his three best friends on Easter eve, leaving secret Easter baskets for us to discover in the morning. After all, special people do special things.

You Feel Acutely Self-Conscious

"What makes you think she's self-absorbed?"
"Well, her license plate reads 'Mindy-1.'"

Self-consciousness is not the same as self-awareness. Self-awareness means I know what's going on inside me. Self-consciousness means I wonder about what you are thinking of me. You are exquisitely conscious of yourself and of the impression you are making. It's a burden that is difficult to shake.

You loom so large in your psychological space that it can be very hard to have the energy to attend to the rest of the world. Often you find it difficult to listen, because you are framing your next remark or evaluating the impact of your last one. Even when you are able to lose yourself in a conversation or an interaction, you'll burden yourself later with endless self-critical replay. Did they understand you were joking? Were you too abrupt? Why didn't you try to turn the drinks into dinner? Did they think you were rude? Or did they like you? These analyses exhaust you, but you can't seem to stop yourself. They seem so natural to you that you assume they are "just human nature."

You care very much about how you present yourself. Your clothes and appearance tend to be immaculate. You'll have more difficulty than others coping with a physical change. A broken limb that heals peculiarly, a visible scar, or hair loss are an adjustment ordeal for you because you feel they violate the image you've cultivated so carefully.

That image is very, very important to you. It is part of what you might refer to as "the whole package." Whether your image is an accurate reflection of you or an inflated one, you are devoted to its creation and maintenance.

You wouldn't find the concept of an "image consultant" the least bit ironic: the impression one makes on others is obviously a key element to success. You understand completely why a politician needs to hire someone who will plan the impression he ought to make on people. You would certainly do the same.

You are always aware of the image you project, not just by what you own but in what you do—where you vacation, what you eat, what games you play, where you play them. Everything from your house to your underwear has the potential to project your sense of self.

"Image-conscious" is not synonymous with "materialistic," though the two occur together so often they are easily confused. It is true that you usually prefer "the best" in a material sense. In fact, even when you protest the importance of labels and logos (and you do hate them, you do, you do), there are some obvious signs of status to which you are drawn—a certain golf course, a certain handbag, shoe, hotel. It's not the label that lures you. It's the sense of quality. Everything is not equal, nor is everyone. You have a strong inner sense that you belong at the top of the heap.

Your heap, however, is not necessarily made of money. You do have a detailed wish list, but it may not read: "BMW/Three-bedroom Tudor/Rolex." It might as easily read: "Jeep/Log cabin/Timex." This scaling down of financial ambition does not necessarily reflect a scaling down of your self-image. In fact, in terms of baggage, it might be quite the contrary. Some of us seek a simpler life materially because it satisfies our spirit. Others choose the Timex as an expression of moral superiority over those shallow Rolex wearers.

Superiority can burden the man or woman whose only goal in life is owning more and more. But it can also be the stumbling block of the person who wouldn't deign to own anything of material value at all. It is possible to feel superior in a simple log cabin, and possible to feel nonjudgmental and self-aware while living in a palace (difficult, but possible).

The hardest thing for you to do: Look foolish.

"I think David would have put it in our wedding vows: Don't Do Anything to Embarrass Me."

You would *never* be part of the horse costume, just to be a sport. You are not goofy or a joker, or undignified. You cannot lose yourself in the moment because your eternal consciousness of the impression you make won't let you. Sometimes drugs or alcohol can get you to be silly—a fact that lures you to them as powerfully as it makes you shun them. You are mannered, decorous, and shocked by the emotional abandon or careless lapses others allow themselves. Or, as a woman noted, conscious of her every gesture, "I don't want to laugh too loud."

You absolutely detest being teased. It's not that you don't have a sense of humor. In fact, you may be a marvelous wit with a keen appreciation for life's absurdities. It's just that you don't enjoy seeing yourself as one of those absurdities. You are not easily able to laugh at yourself, but you are even less able to tolerate being laughed at. When someone apologizes by saying, "I was only teasing," they may as well have said, "I'm sorry. I only slapped you."

Sexually: If you have any problem at all, it's that you try too hard.

The self-conscious voice in your head reviews your sexual performance, plotting moves ("I'd better stop at the other breast before I move down. She likes that." "I'll moan faster now—he needs to hear passion") and calculating audience reaction ("Did you come?"). You care about your partner's sexual response, in great part because you see it as a review of yourself as a lover. This might mean you put extra effort into being a good lover, or it might mean that you put extra pressure on your sexual partner to respond positively ("Sure I fake it. He isn't convinced by my real orgasms"). Because it's hard for you to lose yourself, you may miss out on some of the intense emotional moments possible in a sexual experience. Your concern with performance interferes with pleasure.

You Hate to Admit It, But You're Critical to an Extreme

You don't think of yourself as being critical, of course. You feel you simply care about excellence.

As noted earlier, you are the first target for your own critical review, assailing yourself with what psychiatrist Otto Kernberg describes as a "crushing self-judgment." You can't seem to turn off the mean-spirited inner voice, the one that finds you lacking, the one that reminds you that other people—important people—might see through you too.

In a paradoxical way, you take pride in this ruthless inner voice. You will deliberately turn up its volume and rely on its criticisms as a motivator. If you want to go on a diet, you'll tell yourself over and over again, "I'm too fat, and fat is disgusting." Chanting this helps you to resist desserts, sometimes forever. To inspire yourself to greater professional heights, you make a mental note of every place you've fallen short ("The last report should have been researched more." "I could have been more aggressive in my summation").

In your mind, these are realistic self-criticisms that give you something to aim for. And sometimes they are. But sometimes they are a ruthless distortion, a reflection of your inner fear that if you are average or ordinary, you won't be loved or valued. Partly you fear that if you are ordinary, other people won't think you are worth the bother. But mainly you drive yourself because when you see yourself as average, *you* don't value you much.

Whether accurate or harsh, your self-criticism works. That is, quite often, the critical voice in your head will lash you onward. Your sense of never being satisfied might push you to great success where a more complacent person relaxes halfway there. Undeniably, some of us respond to criticism by trying much, much harder.

You'll use the same critical technique to motivate those close to you, though with mixed results. When they complain that you are too tough on them, you will fall back on your favorite defense: "I'm just as hard on myself." (You are, but so what?)

Because criticism is your motivational tool, praising people you care about makes you nervous. You are afraid there is hidden permission in a positive statement, as if you're saying, "*Stop trying.*" So your positive statements are always mixed with critiques, just to make sure you are still pointing the way to superior performance.

"After an evening's entertainment, Doug always reviews us—or actually, me. I never hear, 'I'm so proud,' or God forbid, 'That was great.' I hear, 'The fish was wonderful—let's work on the hors d'oeuvres.'"

Doug responds, "I am proud of her and she knows it. I just think everything both of us do can always be improved. We're not perfect. What's wrong with that?"

You don't have the same problem accepting praise as you do bestowing it. You're very comfortable being flattered. (You've watched other people squirm when they were being appreciated or admired, but you wondered if they were faking.) But you see, there is no risk that you will *stop trying* just because you received a compliment. You always have your disapproving inner voice driving you on to a higher standard of performance.

There is one grand exception to your reluctance to praise people:

*You will tell a white lie: Very often—because if people
really knew how critical you were, they'd hate you.*

You sense that and protect yourself by giving lots of casual compliments.
You are the person most likely to greet someone with a charming
"Sally, you look great." "Love your dress, your hair, your . . ." You do
it warmly, if sometimes insincerely. These social compliments are easy
for you because you don't care much about the people receiving them.
If your colleague John makes a speech, you'll be the first to tell him
he looked great and sounded even better. But if you are married to
John, or if John is your son, you'll tell him he should have worn a
different tie and he might have polished his opening statement. After
all, you love John and you want him to be the best he can be.

In fact, the people you criticize most are those closest to you. In
part, this is an expression of your own self-interest because family is
a "reflection" on you. When you see something shabby in that reflection, it makes you wince ("If I were really as wonderful as I know
myself to be—how could I be married to a bald man who wears fish
ties and belches?").

But in part, your free-flowing criticism of those closest to you is a
sincere if somewhat unsuccessful expression of your love. You really
do want them to be the best, do the best, have the best—for their own
sake, not just for yours. (Actually, you censor more critical thoughts
about them than you express, a gesture of restraint for which you feel
you get very little credit.)

You are less openly critical of your parents because, as their child,
you are not responsible for improving them. Still, they sense your
disapproval. Sometimes they embarrass you by their tastelessness or
their lack of polish. Your father's poorly fitting false teeth, your mother's
fondness for blue eyeshadow annoy you no end. You aren't necessarily
proud of these feelings, but they are difficult to shake.

If you have elevated your own social status by virtue of education,
income, or a socially fortunate marriage, you may be especially uncomfortable with the signs of your parents' inferior social class—be it
Mom's fake French furniture (when you have graduated to the real

thing) or Dad's pinkie ring (worn years after you learned the virtues of quiet good taste).

The ethnic traditions of your youth might also embarrass you. You worry that your relatives will insist on foisting a dozen tasteless rituals onto your wedding: "Mom, I will not have a wedding cake surrounded by bridesmaid dolls." "Mom, I will not have ice sculptures on the buffet table." "No, Mom. I don't care whose heart is broken. I am not dancing publicly to 'Daddy's Little Girl.'"

You don't particularly like the part of yourself that is embarrassed by your origins, but the feelings won't go away. You may have difficulty acknowledging them consciously, so they go underground. You end up with a lot of reasons why your family could not or should not be a big part of your life.

"Only the best" extends far beyond your intimate circle. It is the standard by which you form friendships, choose lovers, and in general, sort through all the people in the world.

If you are single, you might be very eager to marry if you met the right person. But you are likely to go to a party with scores of single men and women, come home, and say, "There was no one there." What you mean is that there was no one whom you found worth meeting—no one well dressed enough, attractive enough, polished enough, or just generally superior enough to interest you. It leaves you feeling sad and discouraged.

Friendships and relationships with colleagues suffer from the same critical reserve. In new situations, you are far more likely to reject than to approve. You feel comfortable accounting for your distance by explaining, "Not my type," about a lot of other people. When confronted about your behavior and its resultant professional or social isolation, you explain defensively: "You can't expect me to like everybody, can you?"

Paradoxically, you are extremely sensitive to criticism when it comes your way. Criticism threatens rejection, and you dread rejection, because it means you were rated "not good enough" or "second best." (In the next chapter, you'll get a full picture of how your fear of rejection might be getting in your way. It's baggage that is very common to superior people.)

First, you'll automatically review yourself and ward off someone else's critical comment with your own instant self-criticism. When you have a visitor, you are quick to point out the couch you intend to re-cover or the picture arrangement you intend to improve upon. When you hand in a piece of work, you mention the flaws before your boss can.

When you are criticized, you are easily wounded. You might not show it, but an offhand remark stays with you for days. "What did you do to your hair?" becomes, "I hate that haircut. You look weird," as it resounds over and over in your mind.

You often construe lack of appreciation as criticism. In a group project, you're upset when one of your ideas is ignored. "These people wouldn't know wonderful if it were under their noses," you mutter to yourself. You feel a strong urge to withdraw verbally or physically. After all, if they don't appreciate you, who needs them?

You overreact to criticism, even in the form of affectionate teasing, precisely because the sense of superiority puffs up your ego like a big balloon. When an ego is stretched that thin, the pinprick of even a very small criticism can burst the bubble. Your overreaction is the screaming ouch of deflation.

Your Financial Statement

Your professional performance could be outstanding, underachieving, or anywhere in between. You might be a Pulitzer Prize winner with a lifetime track record of standing above the competition, or you might be chronically unemployed with a strong inner sense of all the things you could do if you wanted to. Your profession might be the "proof" of your superiority, the linchpin on which you hang a huge sense of entitlement. ("As a person, he's a helluva baseball player," goes the saying about Pete Rose.) On the other hand, your sense of superiority could be the reason why you don't need a profession. You are already special.

Your personality, with its combination of risk-taking, power, capacity for fantasy, and the sense of boundless possibility, does, however, tend to draw you into certain professions more than others. These include real estate developer, entrepreneur, public relations specialist, film producer, politician, designer, writer/creator.

The family business is another strong possibility for you professionally. In fact, if there is a family business, you will probably end up in it, though you may wander away and attempt to establish yourself elsewhere for several years. It pays better, you're more secure, and besides, in that business you are automatically special, in a way that you could never be if it were just a job. No matter what your job title, you are in effect heir to the boss. Regular corporate rules don't apply in a family business. Where most jobs require that you submerge your personality, the family business tends to indulge it. The family business is apt to challenge your self-image less because, after all, these are the folks who helped you build it in the first place.

Therapist to passionate shopper/aspiring architect: "But do you really think you'll feel better about yourself when you are able to buy all the things you're missing now?"

"I wonder that myself. But I think I'm going to have to get them first, just so I know they're as meaningless and shallow as we suspect."

No matter how you pursue earning money—from a lifetime dedicated to aggressive accumulation to a lifetime spent playing the lottery—the money itself is of supreme importance.

Money is worth, is self-worth, a measure of power and status and personal value. True, most people in our society use money as a measure of success. But you *need* this success more than most. You crave visible proof of your worth, and since money is a socially recognized signal, you focus a tremendous amount of attention on it.

Money—how much you have, how you'll get more, what you'll do with it when you get it, who else has it, how much they have, what they do with it—is an endless source of interest to you. (For the superior antimaterialists we spoke of earlier, money is still the object of deep emotional investment. It's just that they care intensely about not having it and feel a cut above the people who do.)

Spending is a serious business for you. You could take weeks to research a significant status purchase. Your research is not focused on "value." In fact, "value" is sometimes synonymous with "cheap" in your mind. You are trying to determine "best." What is the best fountain pen, ski boot, handbag, lamp, in your price range? (Yes, you do consider your price range. You might inflate it a bit, but you aren't delusional.) You will be far less interested in consulting *Consumer Reports* than *W*. Then, having ascertained the "best," you'll stretch yourself financially to spend a bit more than your ceiling, and get the very best you can.

If you can't afford anything you could remotely describe as the "best," you'll do without. "I'd rather live with blank walls than reproductions," one woman reasons. "I'll buy a car when I can afford a car I want to buy."

At Heart, Superiority Is a Social Statement

All of your specialness, criticalness, self-consciousness, has one focus: to measure yourself against every other person whose path crosses yours, in order to determine your relative standing. For you, life is an ever shifting social contest. One of the great costs of your baggage is the time and energy devoted to keeping score.

Usually, the answer to who is on top is you. (If that weren't the case, it wouldn't be much of a sense of superiority, would it?) This dominance gets established quickly in your own mind, by virtue of some quality that allows you to dismiss the other person.

You might rule people out because of their lesser professional status or income, their unimpressive physical appearance, their marriage to someone who does not interest you, or some other criterion important to you. (Gary does not care to bother with homosexuals, no matter how talented or interesting other people may find them. They are automatic losers in the social contest because he simply does not value them. Cynthia feels precisely the same way about Jews. Neither Gary nor Cynthia would ever admit this aloud.)

When you do come in contact with one of the many who are not in the running for your attention, you are not necessarily rude about it. You might be practicing a kind of noble condescension, priding yourself on having rapport with your cleaning woman or the bus driver. The difference is that while you are not really rude, you're not really interested either.

Basically, you do not extend diplomatic recognition to people who are not, in your opinion, worth knowing. "She's not my kind of person," you'll say, as if this explains everything, or, "What would I talk about to a person like that?"

You trust your first impressions, believing you have a knack for assessing people. "I make snap judgments," you'll admit. "But I'm usually right." Whether or not you're right is something you only rarely get to test out, because your most frequent first impression is negative: one look and it's "Not my type"—again.

Ah, but with the few who do merit your interest, you are quite a different person. You can be warm, engaging, even entertaining if you have the talent for it. You have great charm. You just don't use it with everyone.

Along with your charm, you have the capacity to be a leader—energetic and charismatic. You are a big-picture person, one who can put together a team of worker bees, outline the general goals, and then leave them to accomplish the task. Think of Ronald Reagan when you think of your kind of leadership. Apparently, his presidential style involved stressing a few major themes and letting his staff use them to run the country.

Reagan appeared to handle his sense of superiority cleverly: He married a woman with the same superior baggage, and then she saw to satisfying that less-than-politically-attractive need. This left him free to assume the bluff geniality and popular touch that won him enormous support. (Many of us delegate our wish for superiority to our spouse. That way, we are always assured of the best table in the nicest restaurant but we didn't have to expend the psychic energy necessary to make the reservation.)

So you might be a star, a standout, a leader of the pack. But some people look at your leadership qualities and see you as a user. They feel you exploit others, taking advantage of their strengths and talents to further your own ends. Since this is, in effect, a necessary quality of any leader, the judgment as to whether this trait is positive or negative rests in the eyes and interests of those led.

In any event, it's very like you to be open about your goals, publicly proud of your triumphs. You love to talk about yourself, especially about your accomplishments and your possessions. (The truth is, you brag—though bragging has become socially acceptable now that we call it "marketing.") You are a salesman of *you*, of your ideas, your plans. You believe that what's good for you is right for the rest of us. Your confidence usually convinces us that you're right.

Your Most Likely Social Role: Critic/Connoisseur.

You are not necessarily famous, but in your social group, you are the one who *knows*. You are an environmental guru, a movie buff, or an art appreciator. Your sensitivity to image and to externals makes you the arbiter of taste, design, style, and etiquette. We call you to tell us where to shop and what to buy, where to eat and what table to sit at. You have established some area of expertise and tuned your critical bent into a resource for those around you. You set high standards and contribute more than your share to maintaining them.

You are not just a critic when it comes to improving something. You are a participant as well. You contribute your highly developed visual and aesthetic sense, your deep appreciation for quality as well as your energy, money, time, and talent to a project that intrigues you. Of course, the standards you follow must be your own, and any compromise with someone else's version of "best" will grate on you. (Unless that someone else is an acknowledged master in the field. Then you'll back off, possibly humbled, probably exhilarated because now you are learning from "the best.")

You often have a wicked sense of humor, with a devastating ability to poke fun at the mediocre. But you increase the quality level in many areas, simply because you insist that things get better.

You are intensely competitive.

Since superiority is, in effect, a social contest, it only stands to reason that you would be.

You can turn anything into competition. An afternoon jog becomes an imaginary race if another runner happens to be at the track. A younger sister's engagement feels like a personal indictment (how can you still be the pretty one? the favored one?). A doubles tennis match comes to symbolize which team has the better marriage.

You may feel anxious about losing when other people don't even know there's a contest. You hate to introduce one friend to another (what if they like each other better than either of them likes you?). You aren't comfortable hiring someone superbright, supercompetent (how do you maintain status with that kind of competition?). You feel most relaxed with friends who are just a rung "lower" than you on some important "ladder"—less educated, or less wealthy, or less professionally successful, less something.

These inhibitions may be unconscious. That is, you might not acknowledge or even be aware of your reluctance to hire a star, or to bring people together. You usually have other, more acceptable reasons for not making these uncomfortable choices: "He was very competent, but I think he was overqualified for the job." "I like seeing people one-to-one best. That way we get to talk."

Still, when people do come together in a way that threatens the dominance of your position, you are sure to notice: "I introduced my best friend to my boss at a holiday party. Now they're a couple, and I just can't stand it. I know my friend didn't do this deliberately to bug me, but I feel betrayed. He's *my* boss."

Variation on the theme: You love to put one over on us.

Some of us lie, cheat, or steal (albeit on a small, possibly even insignificant scale) in order to enjoy a secret sense of winning. We make a great show of loyalty, but take a sales kickback the boss doesn't know about. We are the waiter padding a check, the clerk deliberately giving the wrong change. We cheat on our taxes, partly because we believe cool guys do. We lie to customers, not just to increase business but because it's a subtle way of putting the customer down.

Each of these examples describes the same process: In our ongoing social contest, putting one over is one way to "win," to be secretly more powerful, to reassert our superiority, especially where we feel dependent, as with a boss or customer.

There is a catch to your competitive spirit. As we discussed earlier, your need to maintain a fantasy of special powers might also make you avoid a contest. That way, you can maintain your victory fantasies without having them marred by the experience of real-life failure ("I could do anything I really *wanted* to do. This contest isn't one I care to enter, that's all").

In general, we resolve the conflict between our intense desire to compete and our passionate dread of failure in a few different ways. Some of us are so overwhelmingly confident and competitive that we deny even the possibility of failure the instant we spy the prize. At the other end of the continuum, some people find any competition a sickening threat. But most of us resolve the conflict issue by issue. We confine ourselves to areas of confidence. We'll compete intellectually, physically, or sexually, if we happen to feel superior in one of these areas. But we might dodge an area of weakness for fear of losing.

Your Marriage

"I was talking to a couple at a gallery, when a friend of theirs came up to say hello. The friend was adorable—pretty and happy and excited

because she'd just gotten engaged. This couple was fussing over her—kissing her, congratulating her—when over came the fiancé. He turned out to be a short, kind of fat guy, with brown teeth. Everyone was warm and wonderful and friendly to the happy twosome. When they walked away, the husband of the couple turned to me and said, 'Wouldn't you put your head in an oven first?' His wife started laughing. 'How about just a gun to the temple?'"

Marriage too is first a measure of your worth. Only when you're sure your potential mate measures up do you give yourself over to the pleasure of love. (No, everyone else does *not* attribute this meaning to his or her choice of mate, or at least not nearly to the degree you do.) Your choice of mate (*a*) confirms the fact that you're special, and (*b*) announces that fact in a very public way. You need people to look at your partner and say essentially, "Wow. Carole must be something. Look who married her."

The first effect of the marriage-as-a-measure-of-self-worth stance is that it's hard to get yourself married at all. You have a serious struggle with commitment. What if someone even better came into your life twenty minutes after you got engaged? Up close to the person you are thinking of marrying, you are acutely aware of flaws. Off in the distance looms the rosy, ego-enhancing possibility of perfection. You find it a very difficult vision to surrender. If you marry someone with visible flaws, you face more than the problem of how to cope with these flaws through the eternity of a marriage. You also face this wounding worry: "What does it mean about me? Why did I settle?"

No matter whom you find as a likely prospect, commitment to marriage itself may be a struggle for you because the very fact of being married makes you feel like everybody else. As long as you are single, you have the daily possibility of a transformed existence. Who knows whom you might meet and the life they might open to you? Marriage is the end of the "possibilities," the start of adulthood, the drudgery of a mortgage. How will you be special then?

Of course, the opposite might be true too. You might be a single woman whose sense of superiority makes you especially vulnerable to the inferior status of unmarried women in our society. In this case, your baggage will contribute to a desperation for marriage, all the while making it more difficult for you to love a flawed man.

Eventually, however, through some combination of love, timing, luck, and suitability, you probably will marry. In the course of building this marriage, you may struggle with several issues that are a direct outgrowth of your passionate need to establish your worth—and your baggage of superiority.

First, your critical nature plays a big role in your marriage. You are aware of it, you try to control it. But it's very difficult for you to tolerate a wife who gains five pounds, or a husband passed over for promotion. These are true injuries to your self-image.

The marital misery created by your tendency to criticize is compounded if you, like so many people with your baggage, married a person who is also highly critical. You can see how this would happen. You're special, so you need to marry someone special, right? And how do you know if someone is special? Well, you can tell because he or she has high standards. And how can you tell someone has high standards? Well, you know he has high standards if he doesn't think you are good enough.

This all-too-familiar Groucho Marx's "I wouldn't belong to any club that would have me as a member" is played out frequently in the marriages of "superior" people. The net effect is that you, who look down on most of the world, may marry someone willing to look down on *you*. Or you are both equals, and equally critical of each other, setting an emotional tone where snide remarks pass for foreplay. (In *Love Story* by Erich Segal, the hero was gorgeous, rich, athletic, and brilliant. The heroine took one look at him, yawned, and called him a stupid preppy. Naturally, he fell wildly in love.)

Finally, you could marry "beneath" you, identifying some quality in your mate that makes him or her less important than you are—forever. Your payoff is the satisfaction of superiority, but the price is perennial disappointment. You married an admirer but you've stuck yourself in the role of critic.

Worst of all, that admirer you chose can become a critic over time (see the discussion of catcher-flier marriages in Chapter 5). Eventually, if your mate feels neglected or resentful, he or she becomes critical. You cannot bear the pain of criticism, however justifiable. You have to push the attack away. When we push away the criticism, we push away the critic. This stretches the bonds of love very thin. Sometimes they snap.

It can be a huge shock to you when a love you counted on turns critical. Your baggage can make you blind to your partner as an individual. It's hard for you to believe that the people close to you really don't feel the way you do. You operate on this principle: If I'm happy, we're happy. You are genuinely shocked when you discover that your mate is, in fact, not happy at all. You are likely to be the partner who comes into a couple's first therapy session saying, "My wife (husband) is being ridiculous. She's moved out. She took the kids; she won't give me a chance to talk about it. How dare she!" The wife's (husband's) version is different: "I've been talking about it for years. You never bothered to listen."

It's not just that you didn't bother to listen, it's that you would have felt trapped if you had paid attention. Marriage requires an accommodation to a mate that you find it difficult to honor. Why should you have to spend an evening with her friends who aren't very bright? Why should you have to put in a night at a baseball game when you couldn't care less and you are so busy as it is?

If your "specialness" has been confirmed by outward success, you will find it particularly difficult to sacrifice for the sake of a mate's happiness. Monogamy might be especially tough for you—not that any of us always find it easy. Part of your increased likelihood of infidelity is your increased opportunity because your success sexually excites the rest of us. But part of the push toward infidelity will be your sense of entitlement. Success has validated your suspicions. You are a unique person, entitled to exemptions from the rules.

When your mate responds bitterly to this violation of trust, you won't be enormously sympathetic. In a way, you blame him or her for your transgressions in the first place. If she had kept up with you more, if he had carried his half of the load, you wouldn't have been driven to sexual adventuring, you argue. This viewpoint feeds into your tendency to be harshly critical of a mate in the first place. Eventually, your mate may be too hurt, too humiliated, or too angry to tolerate the relationship further. He or she leaves.

It's very hard for most of us to forgive a mate who leaves us, however justified his or her unhappiness. Even if we were repeatedly unfaithful, even if we were critical, impatient, or driven to moments of physical rage—we still don't forgive this abandonment. In couples a decade or more postdivorce, the supersuccessful man may still not be able to hear the name of his first wife without boiling inside. True, he had ceased to love her. True, he had little respect for her. But how dare she force him out of his home, destroy his family, and use his money to finance the rest of her life! For these assaults on his superiority, she can never be forgiven.

Superiority does not doom you to a bitter divorce. But your unique combination of self-critical drive and great expectations does make you more likely to achieve professional success. And professional success can make the compromises required by marriage less palatable.

THE INNER PORTRAIT

How come so many, many of us are walking around feeling superior to the people who are feeling superior to us? Why do you *need* all the trappings of materialism, all the outer signs of status—even when you don't approve of your own aspirations?

Well, first of all, the values of our consumer culture give all of us a push in the direction of superiority/inferiority. In other times and other cultures, great value was placed on the development of inner resources: self-discipline, integrity, commitment, the capacity for sacrifice and service. In our highly materialistic society, we receive love and approval based on our outer shell, on what we look like and what we own. So we spend a lot of energy polishing up the package instead of building up the inner base.

That cultural bent provides the first push. A heaping share of one of our image-conscious society's highly valued commodities—physical beauty, intellectual capacity, athletic prowess, or wealth—gives you a powerful shove in the direction of a sense of superiority. That's why those of us who feel superior often *are* better-looking, smarter, stronger, or richer than average.

But not everyone who is bright or beautiful is burdened with superiority. (See the notes on this chapter for family dynamics that make you especially prone to developing this personality pattern.) If you are something like the person in the portrait you just read, then you are particularly vulnerable. Your intense self-scrutiny, your competition to be the best, your deep appreciation of quality—all these traits work together to reassure you, over and over, that you will win the great emotional prize you seek so passionately.

That prize is a feeling of self-worth, and you spend a lifetime trying to prove yours. The most conscious inner evidence of this drive to prove yourself is in your theme song.

Your Theme Song: "I am . . ."

Your inner voice sings a constant reprise of "I am . . ." That is, "I am" as in "I am special. I am successful, pretty, rich, young, a doctor from France, a great skier, my father's son, and so on." Your voice focuses your attention vigilantly on your identity, reminding you of what makes you important, valuable, and especially what makes you lovable.

Quite literally, you cannot get your mind off yourself. Where the person who needs to be right is preoccupied with doing what he should do, you add to that concern an ongoing assessment of how important you are while you're doing it. With each new person, you are chanting unconsciously, "I am smart," or, "I am tasteful," or, "I am a good sailor"—anything to remind you of why you win the competition for "best" in the face of this rival. At the same time, you are automatically criticizing this person, mentally downgrading him for flaws, so that he is less of a threat, more likely to be an admirer. Actually, the most complete description of your theme song would be: "I am . . . and you're not."

You see, your theme song is not primarily a love song. It's also a song of scorn for yourself, of self-derision and self-denigration, that repeats over and over in your mind. That is, "I am" as in "I am stupid.

I am dull, loud, short, boring, a poor kid from a family of ignorant immigrants, a little girl who picks her nose, a boy who secretly masturbates and fantasizes about his teacher." You include in this song whatever is your private catalogue of weaknesses, failings, or secret sins. Then you remind yourself of these over and over.

Sometimes "I am . . ." is a thought you project into the minds of people around you. "I am . . ." turns into an agonizing question, an unanswerable self-torture, as in "Do they think I am pushy? Does he think I am sexy enough? Does she think I'm interesting?"

Then, caught in the inexorable cycle from the pain of inferior uncertainty to the soothing balloon of superiority, you will refute this constant stream of inner self-criticism by focusing on all the ways you are special, outstanding, superior to those around you.

"I am" has both a dark and a light motif, but it always focuses your attention on one dominant theme: it requires a moment-to-moment reading of your worth.

Your Ruling Passion: Self-Esteem

"I feel like I put all my energy into building a huge shell around me and I'm this little guy hiding inside. It takes all my strength just to drive this huge shell around . . . But I love my shell—it's my house, my career, my title, my car. I would not want to be without them . . . I worked for it all. What's wrong with that?"

Inside each of us with a sense of superiority is an insecure little guy. This little guy worries about being good enough. The sense of superiority is the psychological attempt to make this little guy inside feel bigger and stronger and braver.

You may go about it in an elliptical fashion, but the drive that gives rise to the sense of superiority is the drive to feel good about yourself. Essentially, you try to feel good about yourself by winning the love and admiration of others. Ah, but not loved by just anyone, not admired just anywhere. You are on a constant quest to win love, approval, and admiration from only the most worthy sources. And if that person— that rich or famous or popular or powerful or smart person—values you . . . you must be valuable. And if that object—that expensive, important, rare, or beautiful object—is yours . . . you must be valuable.

And you know what? It works! When we do wear beautiful clothes, or finally buy the Porsche, or get invited to the classy party, we *do* feel better about ourselves. When we're with people who did not get the invitation, or the car, or the clothes, that makes some of us feel better too. All in all, outward signs of status and outranking others socially are definite sources of a very good feeling for you. Get a taste of that feeling and it's not surprising you want more.

Mentally criticizing others feels good too. Your self-conscious scrutiny of your own shortcomings has left your self-esteem shaky. Criticism of others soothes those self-inflicted wounds. It reassures you that other people really are flawed, even more flawed than you. The net result: a reassuring, invigorating, ego-inflating sense of superiority.

Because superiority is so intoxicating a sensation, it doesn't feel like baggage. It feels like secret power. It feels that way because, as noted at the very beginning of this chapter, we confuse it with self-esteem.

Self-esteem and superiority are superficially similar. Both appear to describe a good feeling you have about yourself. Without doubt, feeling good about yourself *is* a secret power—in some ways, it's the most powerful psychological weapon available. Naturally, every one of us wants some.

But the good feeling we get from being superior to someone or some group is very different from the good feeling associated with a solid sense of self-regard:

▪ High self-esteem is an absolute, meaning that it's a feeling I have about myself that does not depend on reference to anyone else. Superiority is a relative feeling. I am only superior in regard to someone else. I automatically measure my status and rate yours. My feeling good about me depends on my feeling not so good about you.

▪ Self-esteem is a solid core. Superiority is a brittle surface. I do everything I can to decorate that surface beautifully, but it is still vulnerable. And it hurts when it breaks.

■ Self-esteem absorbs criticism, tests reality, makes changes. The sense of superiority is shattered by criticism. It takes a long time to reinflate.

■ Self-esteem is an inner issue. It refers to one's deep feelings about one's self. Superiority is an outer issue. It refers to one's standing in the world.

■ High self-esteem tends to make us feel positive toward other people. We're not so threatened, not so anxious. We can afford to tolerate more, disapprove less. A strong sense of superiority tends to make us negative toward others. After all, it's our negative evaluation of them that "proves" our superiority.

In the end, superiority is self-esteem with a leak in its tire. You need a constant flow of compliments, flattery, praise to keep it pumped up. You need endless love and approval to keep the good feeling going.

And that good feeling becomes harder and harder to get. When you need a lot of hot air to pump up your balloon, you need frequent reinforcement from other people—the *right* other people—and that's not always possible to come by. If you don't get that reinforcement for whatever reason, you do not adjust. You deflate.

WHAT'S THE BAGGAGE?
YOUR SENSE OF SUPERIORITY

Somehow, of all the kinds of baggage, the idea of superior baggage seems to be the one with which we're most uncomfortable. Maybe it's that when we spot the superiority, we come face-to-face with the little guy behind it and he frightens us. If parts of the portrait you just read do describe you, keep in mind that the fountain of your strength is the inevitable wellspring of your weakness. And the strengths that bring with them superior baggage can be truly outstanding.

Your pursuit of self-esteem fuels your achievements, and the love and approval this pursuit can generate are great sources of joy for you.

Your insistence on excellence before you bestow love and approval keeps the rest of us reaching just a bit beyond our grasp too. You hold us to a standard for quality, and quality often enriches life.

It's just that you've assured yourself that you are high quality by pointing out all the ways we are not. Your sense of superiority makes you feel good about yourself, but it also:

- Makes you vulnerable to those who are "superior" to you.

- Makes it tough to be a grown-up.

- Makes life a disappointment.

> **THE STRENGTH:** Superiority Is a Magic High, a Giant Enjoyable Ego Inflation.
> BUT
> **THE BAGGAGE:** It Leaves You Vulnerable to the Crash of Jealousy, Envy, and Inferiority.

Remember the little guy inside? Superiority is your medicine for his uncertainty. But that superiority is easily punctured, leaving you vulnerable to the three great psychological poisons:

1. Envy: The passionately unhappy feeling that you have something I don't have. And I want it!

2. Jealousy: The sick and anxious hatred that floods my spirit when I fear that you want someone (or something) that I have. And you might get it!

3. Inferiority: The secret dread one layer beneath my belief that I'm special. I'm not outstanding, I'm worthless.

These three emotional blights are the unavoidable companions of superiority. Superiority is "proven" by the ongoing contest you mentally stage between yourself and everyone else. Even if you win nearly all the time (which makes most people a disappointment to you), some of the time you will lose.

How secure can I be about being loved, if there exists someone more beautiful, smarter, more successful? Naturally, I'm jealous. How confident can I be that I'm superior if you own something, create something, do something of value to which I don't have access? Naturally, I'm envious. How solid can my superiority be if I'm constantly seeking out those superior to me? Naturally, I feel inferior.

The pain and bitterness of these three emotions are difficult to overstate. In the grip of envy, we turn petty and negative, willing to diminish someone else, to disregard a relationship because we envy her job, his car, their engagement. Years of friendship can be soured by our uncontrollable material lust. Envy makes us mean-spirited, and we turn that mean spirit out to the world and in on ourselves.

The great destructiveness of envy is that it makes us devalue ourselves. It is a direct blow to the self-worth we are so hungry to establish. Envy is a form of self-criticism. It says, "What I have, what I am, is not good enough. I need what you have in order to feel good."

Jealousy is even harder. It is one of the most tormenting inner experiences you can have. It destroys concentration, focusing all your attention on sickening thoughts of betrayal and horrifying visions of loss. Once jealousy seeps into a romance, it is difficult if not impossible to erase. Jealousy is the absolute enemy of love, but those of us with superior baggage often find that it is almost a side effect of our falling in love. We feel we can't help it. As we love deeply, we fear that a more superior person will win away our beloved. This is a paralyzing, poisonous anxiety that can ultimately destroy the very relationship we were seeking to preserve.

And inferiority is a pervasive disease of the spirit. It shakes your will at every step on the path, whispers uncertainty under your mask of confidence. It pushes you away from risk and from achievement because inferiority feels certain of failure. Inferiority is your reason for why you have not, are not, and will not. It feels hopeless. Inferiority plagues you because your inner sense of self-esteem is shaky. Instead of building it up from the inside, you tried to hide the damage with a superior shell.

You can best protect yourself from jealousy, envy, and inferiority by having a strong, realistic core of self-esteem. But you can't feel good about yourself in a solid sense without letting go of the overwhelmingly good feeling you get from being inflated.

> **THE STRENGTH:** You Have a Deep and Powerfully
> Motivating Conviction That You Are Meant
> for Great Things Someday.
> BUT
> **THE BAGGAGE:** You Don't Want to Grow Up and Find
> Out What Happens.

"Every morning, I fight with myself to get out of bed. I play a game of 'five minutes more, five minutes more.' And every morning, I'm late. I can't convince myself that I have to get up just because everyone has to be at work at a certain time."

It's hard for many of us to feel superior and be regular old grown-ups at the same time. So much of what grown-ups have to do is deflating. Your solution is to resist being an adult in a thousand different ways. The message you communicate is: "I don't have to . . . I'm special."

Superiority makes it difficult for us to move from one status to another—from single to married, from student to employee, from child to adult. We do very well with the rewards associated with these changes of status, but we fight like hell against any loss of prerogative such a transition involves. We like the freedom and respect of adulthood, but we resist the responsibility. We like the companionship and security of marriage, but we object to the obligation and loss of autonomy. We like the paycheck but balk at doing the job.

One man who made the transition to adulthood for the sake of his marriage had this to say: "Marriage is not so difficult if you can give up trying to be who you were when you were single. I had to stop fighting for my right to come home at night and say or do whatever I felt like—to have my drink or read my paper and just generally feel entitled because I'm a terrific guy who earns a decent living and therefore my family shouldn't make me do things I don't feel like doing."

He is describing the inevitable loss that comes with moving on in life. Yes, he has all the rewards of a marriage and family, but he also loses power and independence. Your discomfort with being just "one of the family," instead of the star with star privileges, creates conflict and misery for both you and your mate.

Work too can deflate your sense of importance. It usually requires that you be part of a team, or under someone else's supervision. You put a lot of fantasy time into envisioning yourself on top. But you didn't picture the real-life sacrifices you'd have to make to get there. When you are required to make such sacrifices—whether they are sharing credit, doing paperwork, being in the background—it's a struggle for you.

Some of us are extreme in this resistance to adulthood, unable to leave home, unwilling to have a checking account, uncomfortable committing to a career. Most of us are not quite as extreme and express our superiority in pockets of resistance, like refusing to be on time for work, or living in a mess because we are above having to clean.

Superiority interferes with success on the humdrum, day-to-day doing-what-needs-to-get-done level. Unfortunately, that's the level where success starts.

> **THE STRENGTH:** Your Insistence on "the Best" Makes
> You Far More Likely to Be "the Best" and to Receive
> "the Best" from Others.
> BUT
> **THE BAGGAGE:** In Order to Maintain Your High
> Standards, You'll Find Most of Life
> a Disappointment.

"My older sister has the family completely at her disposal. It drives me nuts because we all play the how-to-make-Fran-happy game. I'll take her out to dinner and she'll study the menu and look sad and say, "Nooo . . . There's nothing here I really want to eat.' 'How about the lamb chops?' I'll start asking. (I can't help myself.) 'Uh, no. I don't think so,' she'll say, shaking her head slowly. 'Too fatty.'

" 'The veal, maybe?' (I'm still in there pitching.) 'Well, maybe a little,' she'll acquiesce. 'But plain!'

"We stop by my parents' house. Everyone starts dancing around her. 'Maybe some tomato soup?' my mom will start, having heard immediately that dinner did not entirely please her. Fran makes a little negative shake of her head, looking disappointed or disapproving. This starts my dad off. 'She's not hungry, Helen! Maybe she's tired. Why don't you go lie down, honey?' No response. Finally, my brother George pops his head in. 'I'm watching a Fred Astaire movie. Why don't you come sit down with me?' 'Oh, O.K.,' she says. George can't help himself. He starts to smile. He won! He won! He made Fran happy."

As you would be the first to admit, you are difficult to please. Naturally, it's one of the ways you are special. The people who love you may make grand and persistent gestures to gratify you, all of which satisfies your ruling passion by making you feel more worthy. And when you feel more important, you make your standards even higher, which makes you more difficult to please. Neat system, huh?

In this way, high standards nicely satisfy your ruling passion for self-esteem. But as a reward for maintaining these lofty and uncompromising standards of quality, you reap the following harvest: you get the chance to feel disappointed, disapproving, or disgusted as often as possible. Superiority maximizes your opportunity for unhappiness.

It stands to reason that when you are burdened with the sense of superiority, most of life's experience will disappoint you. Most of the people you meet won't interest you. Most of the parties you go to will be "not really that much fun." Even your own moments of glory will privately be assessed as falling short: "It wasn't what I imagined." "It wasn't what it might have been."

You know who has the very best time? Those of us who are too dumb to be picky and too unsophisticated to have high standards. Our standards are so low we like nearly everyone we meet. Without the benefit of superiority's discriminating eye, we're happy with most everything, including ourselves.

To be superior, to be picky, to have high standards, is to maximize your chance to feel bad. (How high could your standards be unless pretty much everything didn't live up to them?)

To have low standards, or worse, no standards at all, is to take every experience as it comes along, to appreciate what it has to offer, without judgment, without comment, without measuring yourself or your worth against it. This attitude will never give you the opportunity to feel superior. It will, however, maximize your chance to feel happy.

Rx: MOVE FROM FANTASY TO REALITY

What you need—to diminish jealousy, envy, inferiority, to be comfortable with the deflation of adulthood, to eliminate the fatal negativity of pickiness—is to trade superiority for self-esteem.

At the heart of genuine self-esteem is a realistic picture of your own strengths and weaknesses. This can be a bitter pill initially, because our real self is never as grandiose as the person we are in our dreams.

The shift from superiority to self-esteem involves one of the most difficult losses of all—the loss of a fantasy.

"The illusions which exalt us are dearer than a thousand sober truths," said Goethe. And no illusion is as exalting as the illusion that we are superior. You may fear that without this illusion, you are stripped of any worth at all. That fear is your sense of inferiority speaking, the inferiority you have not had the courage to face, to wrestle with, and ultimately, to heal from.

The loss comes first. It's what makes this change so uncomfortable and so anxiety-provoking. But if you can stick it out, the gains that come from solid self-confidence are so significant they more than compensate for the loss of feeling superior.

You'll have more friends, for one thing, or you'll get more pleasure from the friends you have. Right now your superiority is an invisible barrier between you and the rest of the world. It leaves you lonely.

Without superiority reminding you of all that's missing, you'll find it easier to fall in love. More important, you'll find it possible to stay in love. That's a reality worth trading any fantasy for.

And you'll be frightened less frequently. You know how scared you get whenever you're going to meet a big shot, or date one of the truly gorgeous people, or make the presentation in front of the boss? (That's also partly your fear-of-rejection baggage, which you'll get a clearer picture of in the next chapter.) When you feel better about yourself, you won't torture yourself over how these important people might be judging you. If you like yourself, the verdict's in. You pass.

As with the exercises suggested for every other kind of baggage in this book, the exercises that follow are based on the principle that you have to frustrate the automatic ways you have been satisfying your ruling passion, because your automatic reactions have a way of becoming self-destructive. Specifically, your need for self-esteem is necessary and normal, but the superiority you rely on to establish that self-esteem gets in your way. First you have to take the difficult step of deflating that superiority, of resisting its quick fix. That's tough to take, but it will leave room for growth.

Four exercises follow. They focus on techniques to help you make a genuine self-evaluation and presentation. They may seem absurdly small and concrete in the face of something as grand as superiority. But it takes only a pin to puncture a balloon, if you are willing to poke it.

"It's Not a Problem"

This is an exercise to correct your tendency to negative thinking and pickiness. "Picky" proves your superior standards. "It's not a problem" forces you to let go of your critical pout and develop flexibility, tolerance, and the sense of humor you keep mentioning as such an important quality in others.

The exercise is simple. Use the phrase "It's not a problem" seven times in a week. Use it every time you would ordinarily explode with frustration over someone else's negligence or stupidity. Use it as you see a solution to what might have been a problem.

You may find this exercise difficult because you'll have to resist the temptation to criticize or complain. It's tough for us, because how will people know we're special if we don't remind them when things aren't good enough for us?

Nonetheless, give the exercise a try.

Your secretary ruined the letter. . . . It's not a problem. You'll just ask her to redo it.

Your girlfriend broke your plans at the last minute. . . . It's not a problem. You'll use the unexpected time to clean closets.

Your brother left the directions at home and now you have no idea where you are. . . . It's not a problem—you'll ask someone.

The saleswoman can't work the cash register and you've been standing here for ten minutes watching her puzzle over it. . . . It's not a problem—she'll figure it out eventually.

You get the idea. Compile your own list of opportunities to be angry at, frustrated by, or disappointed with other people's lapses. Give yourself a point every time you resist these opportunities to feel superior. When you hit 10,000 points, buy yourself a Patek Philippe.

"It's not a problem" is silly and fun, and it works. In a way, negative thinking and critical disappointment are habits; you learned to complain, to review, to disapprove. "It's not a problem" is a mental tool you can use to reverse your training in defeat and increase your opportunity for delight. Furthermore, "It's not a problem" makes you infinitely nicer to be around. What you lose in opportunity to prove your high standards, you will gain in your increased opportunities to be loved.

Realistic Self-Appraisal

This exercise is about seeing yourself accurately. It is the single most effective medicine for your baggage. The questions are very simple. Most people, and especially most people who feel superior, find the answers very difficult.

I. List five reasons why someone would want you for his/her mate.

Now list three reasons why they would *not*. That's right—three reasons why someone would have to settle (if you're single) or already did settle (if you're married) for you. List three reasons why you are less than perfect, three aspects of your personality that might make you difficult to live with, three ways you are less than the prince or goddess of your partner's dreams.

2. List five reasons why someone would want you as an employee. List three reasons why your boss would have difficulty with you.

3. List five reasons why someone would want to work for you. List three things about you that could make an employee want to quit.

You could try this same exercise analyzing your strengths and weaknesses as a friend, a parent, a sibling, or any other role important to your life.

Now take a look at your responses.

I know, you didn't do it. You'll do it later. You don't believe in these things. You don't have a pen handy. You knew all this already. You don't know and couldn't care less.

You did do it, sort of. You could think of a few reasons why someone would be or definitely is lucky to have you. (Actually, if given the proper amount of time, some of us could think of more than a few, as long as we were sure that no one else would see our lists.)

The problem for most of us is with the negative list. Take a look at yours. Were you able to identify three facets of your style, your personality, your behavior, which might be less than ideal to another person? It's tougher to do, isn't it?

When you review your negative list, check to see if your overtly negative statements are, on closer scrutiny, secret brags. This is the most common self-image distortion. A secret brag, as we've discussed, is a way of saying something ostensibly negative about yourself that is really a disguised pat on the back. For example, here is one woman's list of why someone might not want her as a mate:

1. I'm extravagant.

2. I like nothing but the best.

3. I'm picky.

Secret brag translation: I am very special. My standards are exquisite. A more aware description of the same traits might read:

1. I sometimes spend money irresponsibly.

2. I am very concerned with "best." I have a hard time enjoying what I have if there is something better out there.

3. My "pickiness" can make me negative and cranky. People find me unappreciative, and often I am.

In this list, the same traits—i.e., extravagance, a concern for quality, and pickiness—are presented with a realistic appraisal of their downside. There is no brag, nor is there utter self-contempt. There is just a realistic statement of the part of your personality that might be a problem for others.

Review your own responses, checking for secret brags. To the extent that you are unable to complete the negative list or unable to distinguish a brag from a real limitation, you are probably still caught up in the shroud of superiority's fantasy.

In one way, the even-handed self-appraisal of this exercise is a major psychological task of adolescence and early adulthood. That's the time when we are focused on: "Who am I? What do I care about? What am I good at? What am I struggling with?" Out of the years we take to refine our answers to these questions comes the solid, balanced sense of self on which to base self-esteem. But if your passion for proving your worth created a feeling of superiority, it probably interfered with this developing identity.

In another way, the entire course of a psychotherapy can be about completing the questions in this exercise. Whether a person seeks help because he or she can't set realistic goals, can't make a commitment to a marriage, or can't seem to feel positive, confident, or relaxed, to reduce superiority and replace it with realism is a big step toward solution. Together we might work for a year or more helping this person to develop an accurate sense of self and to tolerate the pangs of loss along the way.

But whether you devote a developmental decade to this task, or go and work with a psychotherapist to help you accomplish it, the questions you must answer are no different from the ones in this simple paper-and-pencil exercise. The more refined your answer, the more likely you are to be developing a clear and affectionate picture of yourself. If your answers are too self-critical, you are reflecting your underlying feelings of inferiority. If your answers are too self-serving, you are reflecting the inflation we've spoken of.

This exercise builds a sense of self not simply by getting the right answer. The process of asking these questions, of struggling to answer them in an even, balanced manner, is the path to self-acceptance. When you can see yourself and live with what you see, you don't need to feel superior in order to feel good.

Exercises to Ignore Yourself

It's painful and difficult to overcome the chronic feeling of self-consciousness that usually accompanies the sense of superiority. You need to drown out your theme song "I am . . ." because the more you focus on you, the more your self-critical assaults devastate you. Then you need to rip apart everyone around you in order to feel O.K. about yourself again. To move beyond this cycle of inferiority/superiority, you have to focus on something other than you.

The best way to reduce consciousness of self is to become emotionally invested in something greater than yourself. This usually requires that you extend yourself beyond the world of family and friends, because they are seen as extensions of ourselves. Most people find that the emotional investment needs to be in something that dwarfs the self. For some of us, it's a charity where we are exposed to overwhelming need in a way that helps us put our own neediness in perspective. For some, a cause, a social issue, an injustice, becomes a positive focus of attention. These larger issues affect so many people that it helps us to see our psychological place as one among many, instead of one above many.

Some of us find this release from self in the presence of God. Religion, spirituality, concern for the earth, sensitivity to the forces beyond the known, are all aids to quieting the self so we can tune in to what is out there.

Sit and talk with someone who is a part of your life, but about whom you know little. This might be your garage mechanic, your baby-sitter, your dry cleaner, the person who sits next to you in class. It could also be a social acquaintance, an office colleague, or the spouse of a good friend. Focus on inquiring about that person's solutions to problems you might have in common: beating rush hour traffic, or losing seven pounds, or keeping your kid from being a TV junkie, or meeting a man. Put a face and a personality to as many stereotypes in your life as possible. It's good medicine for superiority.

Finally, with every person who crosses your path, ask yourself this question: "What hurts this person?" And: "How can I help?" What "hurts" is meant broadly, as in what makes his or her life more difficult, painful, or troubling. "How can I help" is straightforward. What could you say or do that would make it better for someone else?

This antidote to your theme song is obvious. If you are thinking of them, puzzling over them, you are not simultaneously consumed with the question of how they are judging you. And when you help, if you can help, you will discover you don't always need to be Lady Bountiful, stooping to help the poor. You give yourself a shot at being one human being who lends a hand to another and accepts one too, when your own turn comes.

Tell the Truth

The truth is wonderful medicine for the sense of superiority and its underlying self-doubt. This exercise requires that you tell the absolute truth about all events, large and small, for a specific length of time. Period. Just don't let yourself lie. If you'd like to do something, but you feel you'd have to lie about it—don't do it. If you do it—don't lie about it.

You aren't allowed an iota of exaggeration for the sake of self-enhancement. (You aren't allowed to say that you were fifteen minutes late when the truth is half an hour. You aren't allowed to say you read the book when you actually read the book review.)

You aren't allowed a single lie for the sake of making money ("I have two other people interested in this apartment, lady. You'd better decide"), for the sake of avoiding someone's anger ("That project will absolutely be done Tuesday." "I did call you back, but your line was busy"), or for the sake of making someone like you.

Try this exercise for a week at a time, then review your experience. Maybe you routinely tell the truth, except in those instances where it would inflict gratuitous pain. But you may notice how superiority tempts you to twist the truth, to pump up your accomplishments or your attributes, to avoid conflict through pretense.

You'll be inclined to rationalize. You'll argue that everyone lies, or all business people lie, or that you are only lying to spare someone's feelings. Actually, these rationalizations are also examples of dangerous lies—namely, the ones you tell to yourself.

Self-esteem is built on seeing yourself clearly and then presenting that authentic self to the world. The truth will clear up an astonishing amount of the confusion you feel about who you are, what you want, what your goals are, whom you love, who loves you, and what you are worth.

Once you see that accurate view of you, the next step is to be it. Present yourself to the world honestly. Consider the truth as your first option, and reject it only because you can make a strong and thoughtful case that the truth will do more harm than good. So often when we have to consider how to deal with an issue, we ponder the "right" thing to say, or the "smart" thing to say. The "honest" thing to say is considered last, if at all. Just move the honest option to the top of your list.

You might be concerned about how this honesty will affect your relationships. After all, many of your lies are mask for your private, plentiful criticisms. "Honesty" here does not mean sharing an unsolicited barrage of your nitpicking dissatisfactions. You can still keep those to yourself. (Besides, as you grow more self-accepting, you'll be letting go of this pickiness more and more.) Honesty means making sincere statements about how you think and feel. It means being open about your own motives instead of blandly denying them. It means letting people know if you are disappointed, angry, or unusually touched or pleased by them. It means being a real friend instead of a secret competitor. Close friendship and a deeper marital bond are potential benefits of this exercise.

There's another benefit too. When it's easier to be honest with other people, it's easier to be honest with yourself. When we tell other people only what they want to hear, we get in the habit of telling ourselves only the good news too. You can't make constructive changes if you can't tell yourself what needs to be changed. And you can't move toward a deep self-acceptance until you can present this self to the outside world, flaws and all. As you get more and more comfortable with the truth, you can accept that some part of you will elicit criticism and disapproval. You don't enjoy the criticism, but you can learn to live with it. You proved that when you did the second exercise.

When you don't disguise yourself in order to sell yourself, you feel good about yourself in a way you never could when you needed to be superior to feel adequate.

Remember, superiority is disposable. Once you see how feeling special might keep you from feeling happy, you can let it go, bit by bit.

As you do, that self-conscious, self-critical voice that so preoccupies you will gradually quiet, freeing you to take more pleasure in the world around you. The exercises described here are techniques for focusing your effort. The aim of that effort is straightforward: Come down and join the rest of us. It only hurts for a minute, and actually, we're having a very good time.

You'll discover a great blessing, a windfall really, if you tolerate this step down. When you release the balloon of superiority, you begin to set aside the fear that acts as its helium. Fear is your secret fuel: fear that you are not the best, fear that you are not lovable, fear of failure, fear of being found out. Along with your sense of superiority, you carry one other very heavy load. You dread rejection, and that fear is the dead weight that you use your superiority to counterbalance. The next chapter tells you where it came from and what you can do to cut yourself free.

Chapter Five

■

YOU DREAD REJECTION

The twenty-pound weight loss should not have made such a cataclysmic difference. But in our body-conscious, beauty-worshiping culture, it made all the difference in the world. Men are looking at Meryl, smiling at Meryl, considering Meryl.

This is exactly the reaction Meryl hoped for—indeed, dreamed about obsessively—during the eight weeks of self-imposed isolation required to shed the twenty pounds in the first place. Now Meryl, minus her fat, is back out in the world attracting attention.

Her reaction? Joy. Panic. Excitement. Humiliation. Paralysis. After all, Meryl reasons, she's still not as thin as she plans to be. Her thighs still rub together in a way that would surely repulse a man who saw her naked. And even if her looks passed muster, she believes her conversation will eventually disappoint anyone clever enough to be of interest to her in the first place.

Every man who looks at Meryl with interest stirs a sickening anxiety. To meet the eye of a man who is frankly appreciating her newly designed body is to take the first step on the road to an eventually devastating rejection. Whatever it is they expect, she believes she will fail to deliver. Meryl has only one remedy for this intolerable anxiety. She goes home, turns on the television, and gives herself over to eating.

Glen dreamed of fast, sexy, sophisticated women—women who were educated, funny, and polished, women who dressed just to get you hard and expected you to know what to do once you were. He dated a dozen such women once he moved from his small hometown into Manhattan. He dated and dated and dated, but he rarely risked a sexual encounter with such a discriminating audience.

Eventually, Glen married a sweet girl from a small town. He doesn't love her. He's not even particularly interested in her. But she takes good care of him and she's never going to judge him.

Linda is single. She has always been single, though it still surprises her sometimes, so clear were her expectations of marriage and a family. For a while, she was depressed, even distraught about her single status. Somehow she got less upset as the years passed. She has a group of kind, funny friends who enjoy seeing themselves as a family. She has an attractive apartment now that she has finally allowed herself to furnish. (It took her years because she could not buy a good couch. The man she met might already own one.)

Linda didn't date a lot, because men who interested her seldom asked her out. She didn't travel much, because it wasn't fun to go places alone. She didn't try very many new things, because she was busy doing the old ones.

Over time, friends' lives moved on. The single ones married, the married ones had children. The ambitious ones left the office, the restless ones got themselves into trouble. But nothing much happened to Linda. And she believed nothing was going to happen, barring the miracle of love (a miracle that seemed ever less likely, though she hadn't totally abandoned hope).

Her life stood still. And slowly, imperceptibly, Linda started to lose interest, first in her activities, then in herself, finally in life itself. The spark was going out, her emotional energy ebbing away. Linda had virtually eliminated risk, and with it, she had eliminated hope. This is the point at which we met.

People come to my office speaking with great pain of the things that are missing from their lives—love, excitement, financial stability, challenge, a sense of deep satisfaction. All these joys are available in the world, floating just out of the grasp of the person who, like Linda, is suffering. She knows they are out there. She sees other people enjoying what she can't seem to achieve. Why can't she reach out, move forward, create the life that was promised to all of us?

She can't because she is trapped in a prison of fear. She can't see it. She might be utterly unaware of it. But the fear is as real as a prison bar, and she is living a life tucked safely behind these bars, mourning all the wonderful things that exist in the world on the other side.

The fear from which we build this emotional prison is the fear of rejection.

Fear of rejection is a cultural cliché, a concept so familiar that it fails to convey the anguish it is meant to describe. Fear of rejection is not simply the clutch of dread most of us feel when we're about to ask for a date or a raise or a favor. The possibility of rejection in any of these circumstances makes all of us hesitate while we gather our courage. But most of us will eventually face up to that possibility, plunging ahead, however awkwardly, asking for the date, hinting about the favor, until finally we either get what we want or get turned down and live to try again another day.

Some of us just can't complete this cycle. For these people, the fear of rejection is not a tolerable pang of discomfort that will pass. Instead, it is a sickening anxiety that goes on and on.

Fear of rejection keeps a bachelor who has many friends but no lovers from making a sexual overture, because he can't convince himself that he won't be laughed at. And fear of rejection keeps the woman who is crazy about him from helping him out by letting him know how she feels.

Fear of rejection keeps the bright man, the talented woman in a deadly job for a decade. Both of them could do more and be more but for the ongoing spasms of dread they experience when they face the possibility of risk and failure.

Fear of rejection makes a frenzied manager unable to lighten her load by delegating; it makes an artist hide his work and deny himself the possibility of success. It makes you settle for less than you deserve, simply because the *possibility* that you might try for more and fail is intolerable.

You cannot avoid the possibility of rejection unless you avoid life. This is precisely what the person who dreads rejection tries to do: He tries to hide in a small, safe, familiar world where the possibility of rejection is almost erased because he has already been accepted there. If the possibility of rejection does not exist, he doesn't have to fear it, or suffer all the dreadful side effects of that fear. This eliminates a highly unpleasant internal state, but it can cost you a life worth living.

The following portrait may help you recognize how much time you spend in your own safe prison.

A PORTRAIT

You Stick Close to Home

Home is the center of your universe, and you are the center of your home.

We need you—you're our mother. We come home to you and you're always there to greet us. You worry over us, care about the smallest details of our well-being, nurture us when we're sick. You make home safe and, since you never change it, familiar and secure. You work at it, and that frees the rest of us. You manage life's maintenance—clean clothes, hot meals, tidy rooms. You maintain our family's emotional core, and that gives us the strength and courage to explore the edges.

You are our surrogate mom as well. You make the office into a home, the friendship circle into a family. You perform this magic the way moms always have—by listening to our problems, by telling us what to do, by feeding us, organizing us, gathering us together to celebrate the great moments. You are the friend we can trust, the colleague we rely on. You are loyal, committed, responsible.

You are the support to our spirit; you root us on, keep us focused because our goals are important to you. You do this as a friend, teacher, parent, mentor, nurse. And of course, you never reject us. You are a necessary, if unacknowledged, condition to our happiness.

"Home" is more than a symbol of your security. It is also a physical place of great importance to you. Home is not just a refueling spot, as it might be for someone who needs to be right. And you don't care about its being on the best block of the best neighborhood you can afford, which is important to the person burdened by superiority. (In fact, if it were on the best block, you'd be uncomfortable unless you were born and raised there, because you'd rather be familiar than fancy.)

For you, "home" is your main stage.

You tend it endlessly, acutely aware of all that is yet to be done. Grass always needs mowing, closets always need straightening, ovens always need cleaning. You feel most at ease when you are there to keep an eye on things. You decorated it yourself and you don't change it very often. It probably looks like a modern version of the home you grew up in. It's not new, fashionable, or meant to be strikingly beautiful. But it is well maintained.

You believe you sleep best in your own bed. You are interested in the rest of the world and think about the Grand Canyon, or a world cruise, or European food with great delight. You've traveled away from home some, and while you had a good time, it wasn't an entirely comfortable experience for you. You find new foods, new places, new roads a strain. Besides, in the back of your mind is the nagging feeling that it's not really safe to leave a house empty.

Of course, "home" refers to a great deal more than the building. In fact, "homeandfamily" are one word for you, an inseparable unit, familiar, central, emotionally crucial to your well-being. (Which is one of the reasons why leaving your parents, or your children leaving you, or anyone leaving anyone is so upsetting to you. More about that later.)

You might have a large, intact, extended family who still live within astonishing proximity of one another. ("My sister moved twenty minutes away to Hoboken. Ma still talks about 'why she did it.'") You live down the street from your mother or your sister or both. You see them on a daily basis and fight with them at least weekly. But that's O.K. You can afford to get mad at your family. They can't reject you, because there is an unwritten but irrevocable rule in your family against it.

You've spent very few nights away from your spouse since the wedding. If you were forced to go somewhere alone (your brother was sick in Florida—naturally, you had to go), you felt a bit uneasy. Would they be O.K.? You left home with all the family meals precooked and labeled in the refrigerator. It infuriated you to discover on your return that they ignored your casseroles and ordered pizza. See? When you aren't home, things fall apart.

(If the "home" you are leaving is an office, and the "spouse" you are leaving is your boss, you will be equally concerned about his or her well-being while you are away. You will pay special attention to appointment books, files, completed projects, trying to anticipate your boss's needs. You might even phone in once or twice from vacation, just to make sure things are O.K.)

"Home" refers not just to your place, or your people, but also to your routine. When you go out to dinner, you go the same restaurants over and over. This seems eminently sensible to you ("It's easy. We know it will be good and we like it. Why change?"). You visit the same seashore or mountain over and over for the same reasons.

On major occasions, you venerate tradition. Change is suspect. No one new ever gets invited to Christmas dinner. Nothing new ever gets cooked either. The holidays are a nightmare of frenzied preparation, though you are quick to say you "love Christmas." You do, too. It's just that you're driven to a thousand chores by that internal voice nagging, "But we always . . ."

If you always make eleven dozen homemade cookies, you'll make them this year, that's for sure. And if a daughter who always helped isn't interested now, you'll feel betrayed. If you always bake the family birthday cakes from scratch, you'll do it this time, even if you have the flu. The absence of a beloved ritual signals change and loss.

Television is probably very important to you. It's true, its impact is enormous for all of us. But its importance to those of us who fear rejection goes very deep. Television makes it possible to extend the unit of homeandfamily without having to risk leaving the house. You form emotional attachments to the characters in your favorite shows. You visit with them on a regular basis. You care about them, and they have the great advantage of being people who can never judge you.

Television entertains you and distracts you from noticing the limits you've set on your life. It fills the dead air in marriage and makes it more tolerable than it might otherwise be. It brings the family into the same room at the same time (without any of the conflict that usually comes up when a family talks about the same topic).

Television helps you to tolerate your prison. The more you tolerate it, the less likely you are to leave it.

If you had a psychiatric label, it would be: Avoidant personality, or in more casual psychiatric conversation, Phobic personality. Generally, we associated "phobias" with isolated, irrational fears—a fear of bridges, for example, or of heights. But it's also a general style of being in the world: it's a need to make your world cozy and secure and utterly without risk.

In the Social World

It's not that you don't enjoy meeting new people. You do. It's just that you couldn't go to the party because you don't like to go out during the week or to run around on a Sunday when you have to work the next day, or to be on the road on a Saturday when all the loonies are driving, or to have to get dressed up on a Friday night when you're tired from the week.

When you do go beyond the world of homeandfamily, you are a very different person. In the safe, familiar environment of home, or the homelike comfort of close friends, you are able to be open, spontaneous, even silly. But out in the social world, anxiety forces you to clam up. If you do a good job of covering over that anxiety, people will see you as cool, aloof, detached. They read your polite protective shield as lack of concern. If they themselves are insecure, or if you happen to be very attractive, relatively wealthy, or notably intelligent, people are apt to interpret your reserve as snobbery. Actually, you are just a person whose fear of rejection stands between him or her and a stranger.

Much of your social life exists in your fantasies—especially, but not exclusively, if you are single. Your fantasy life might be as active as that of the person who needs to feel superior, but the content is very different. The superior person daydreams about magnificent moments of achievement when his or her preeminence is established unequivocally.

Your daydreams are a bit different. You create fantasy relationships that keep you company in your isolation. For example, you might create a fantasy romance. You'll pick someone in your real life whose path crosses yours regularly, but with whom you have no real romantic connection. The association could be distant—a tall blonde who sits in the front row of your night class, a professor, an attractive neighbor who smiles in the elevator. The fantasy might also fix on someone closer to you—a friend or a member of your marketing team.

Once the fantasy is stirred, your feelings are very intense. You'll spend hours visiting it, dreaming of how the two of you might actually connect. You might rehearse what you'll say the next time you meet, or practice asking for a date. It's rare that you'll risk taking one of these steps, however. The fantasy is very satisfying, whereas a move to make the fantasy a reality risks rejection.

Sexually: You inhibit your pleasure because it takes a long time for you to feel secure.

"I could never feel comfortable in a sexy nightgown. I feel like a fool, like I might look like I think I look good, when I know I don't."

It's very easy for you to feel foolish in bed and you can be relaxed only with a lover who is both aggressive *and* reassuring. Under those circumstances, you can enjoy sex a great deal, though it takes a unique situation for you to make the first sexual move.

You will tell a white lie: To agree with someone who seems to hold a strong opinion.

You will state that you are going to vote for someone, or you'll concur that a mutual friend was wrong, or that your boss was unfair to your co-worker, when in fact you don't agree. You don't call it lying. You call it "going along."

You would by far rather *be* the angry one than have someone angry with you. In a long-term relationship (whether a marriage, a friendship, as a parent, or as an employee), you'll unconsciously ease yourself into the security of the *done to,* the angry one. It's simple enough to do this. You just keep a running list of disappointments and inequities: "He won't let me see my friends." "I hate how my boss talks to me." "On my birthday, she didn't even bother to call."

Your resentment over these injuries naturally builds. *When you do express your anger, you:*

▪ *Complain*. Your resentment leaks in small jabbing remarks. It dribbles out in sighs, or burdened airs. You won't say, "I'm angry that you kept me waiting." You'll look sullen, upset, and mention how hot it was sitting there. You'll go quiet, distracted, make a negative remark on another subject, hoping someone will notice and ask what's wrong. Even if you are asked directly, however, it's hard for you to be forthcoming. You might just change the subject.

▪ *Cut the other person off*. You'll stop calling a friend who hurt your feelings, decide you never really liked your officemate anyway. Then you'll reason that you shouldn't talk things over with the offender because:

    a. it will only make things worse.

    b. s/he isn't worth it.

    c. s/he is impossible to talk to. You tried it once, or you "know how he is."

▪ *Get depressed*. When you can't cut someone off who has hurt, insulted, or offended you, you tend to turn the anger in toward yourself. Rather than blast a parent, or child, or friend who was thoughtless or cruel, you will mope for days, focused on the sadness or hopelessness of your life.

Sometimes depression—its intensity, frequency, duration—is a measure of the depth of your rage. When you are depressed, anger is a poisoned arrow aimed at your own heart. It's too scary for you to unleash it on the world. That might threaten your security. So you direct this anger inward, where it festers.

"My dad had chest pains for three hours, *but they just sat there because they didn't want to bother the doctor in the middle of the night."*

When you dread rejection, you tend to live by a single rule: "I'll live my life as I please, as long as I don't get anyone mad."

Your Motto: "If I have to ask for what I want, it's not worth having."

This is a peculiar piece of logic, used predominantly though not exclusively by women. It is sister to the belief: "If you loved me, you'd know what I want," which we will discuss in the next chapter. (You have a lot in common with the person in the next chapter. You may discover when you read it that you have more dramatic baggage than you'd realized.) Your beliefs are similar, though your motive is different. As we'll see, the drama lover sees gifts and deeds as testimonials to her worthiness, expressions of the love and passion she inspires. They should come, therefore, out of someone else's feelings, rather than at her direction. (After all, you can't throw a surprise party for yourself.)

The woman or man who fears rejection has a far more straightforward reason for believing it's bad to ask for what she wants: If you don't ask, you can't get turned down.

On the other hand, you rarely turn someone else down. You hate to say "no," despite the fact that "yes" means you may be exhausted, exploited, frustrated, or unappreciated. This inability allows you to be pushed around by your friends, hopping in service of your in-laws, and volunteering for an endless round of committees, community boards, fund-raisers, and newsletters.

You hate to rock the boat, think very little is worth making an issue of. It's certainly not worth the unpleasantness that will follow if you confront a salesclerk who was rude or return a mediocre steak. And when it might be worth it—such as in a relationship that's not moving to marriage, or in a marriage that is bordering on abuse—your fear of rejection by these key people silences you.

Assertion is incredibly difficult when we fear rejection. In the end, we settle for crumbs—partly faithful lovers, sometimes-kindhearted mates, friendships that take far more than they give. We rationalize away our dissatisfactions, reasoning, "It's better than nothing."

The Hardest Thing for You to Do: Be Judged

Any situation where you will be judged overwhelms you with the feeling, "I'm not good enough." (This is particularly true if you have a sense of superiority cloaking your fear of rejection. Judgment threatens to strip the superiority from you and leave you naked in your fear.)

Naturally, you will be inhibited in all the obvious ways. Interviewing for a better job, meeting an interesting person, asking for a raise—all of these potential sources of pleasure are, for you, only sources of paralyzing anxiety.

But more subtle interactions can also make you feel you are risking judgment: *"I hate it when my husband asks me to call another couple to make weekend plans. I never say 'How about a movie Saturday?' I always say something general like 'So, what are you guys doing this weekend?' That way, they'll make the plan and I won't have to worry about them saying 'no' to mine."*

You sense the potential for being judged everywhere. A rude saleswoman must have decided you weren't worth the bother. Any opportunity to be the center of attention—to give a speech, to host a party, to chair a committee—is an opportunity to be judged inadequate.

You might cross the street to avoid an acquaintance, or pretend you don't know someone to whom you've been introduced. You fear that you aren't important enough for them to remember.

Rather than be judged, you opt out of the contests of life. You remove yourself from competition by fixing on an ironclad explanation for your inevitable loss. The three that I have heard most frequently are:

1. There's no point in going; I'm not attractive enough. (I'll try to go someday, next month, next year, when I lose twenty pounds, when I've worked out, when I get something to wear, but until then, why bother.)

2. There's no point in trying; I'm not smart enough. (I don't test well—I never did. I won't be able to think of anything to say to those people.)

3. I don't know what it is, but it never works out for me. (I'm not unattractive. I'm not stupid. But I know in the end I'll get left. I always do. Maybe it's terminal bad luck, maybe it's a fatal flaw.)

These "reasons" for rejection seem so predictable, so clichéd. Intellectually, even you doubt the accuracy of your own explanation. But this intellectual doubt can't hold a candle to your feelings. You feel too fat, too dull, too stupid. You feel your inadequacy to the depth of your being, even when you "know" that you are exaggerating. And, though you try to confront your illogic about luck and fatal flaws with a strong dose of reason, a piece of you remains forever wedded to your conviction that, if you try, you'll be rejected.

You Are Flooded with Guilt and Worry

"If two people next to me are arguing, I wonder what I did to cause it."

"If I wake up in the morning with nothing to feel guilty about, I'll stop and think until I find something."

"I told my father I bought a Saab and he went berserk. 'Never buy a good car! Someone will only wreck it or steal it.'"

Your best fantasy: The weather outside is bad and everyone you love is tucked safe and warm inside the house.

With luck, you'll all be snowed in together tomorrow.

You worry about what the neighbors think, though not in the superior sense of wondering if they think you're terrific. Instead, you're on constant guard against their disapproval. Everything you do, from mowing the lawn to mannering your children, is motivated largely by the need to ward off criticism. Because you are so extraordinarily sensitive to the criticisms of others, it is impossible for you to be relaxed or open with most people. "Don't get too personal" or "Don't tell other people your business" could be inscribed on your family crest.

"I'm sorry" is your automatic response when something bad actually does happen. Pretty much everything is your fault—at least everything that happens in the kingdom of homeandfamily. If your mate is rude or your child clumsy, you are the one who is apt to apologize.

You may suffer from a chronic self-doubt that, at its worst moments, can escalate into pure self-torture. You *know* that if you make a decision, if you extend yourself, something bad could happen. And when it does, it's hard to forgive yourself.

Where mistakes are concerned, nothing exists only in the past. Mistakes you made last month or last year can still make you squirm with self-loathing today. You are still rethinking and regretting the college you chose, or the time you made a fool of yourself in junior high. Paradoxically, the *fear* of rejection and failure can make us hold tight to actual life experiences of rejection and failure. It's as if you are saying, "See, I'm inadequate. I can't trust myself, and holding on to the past helps remind me not to."

The Sanctity of Money

Your likely profession: wife and mother, nurse, bureaucrat, administrative assistant, military professional, teacher, civil service personnel, social worker. Your job, in whatever field, is valuable, relatively secure, and underpaid. You are hardworking, but not the boss. You may have had a chance to be, but the prospect was overwhelming. Most likely you turned it down.

Sometimes, with enough outside encouragement, you do move up the ranks professionally. Unfortunately, you are likely to take doubt and worry with you along the way. As your responsibilities increase, so does your self-torture.

If your money is earned in a daily plod of professional routine, it is spent conservatively, thoughtfully, or not at all. You pride yourself on thrifty habits, especially at home. You save tinfoil, or wash your coffee filters, or choose only the less expensive dented cans. These small rituals concretize your desire to monitor your resources carefully.

You nurse other people's resources too. You are uncomfortable with lavish gifts and can't really enjoy the VCR your son gave you last Christmas. First of all, you worry about his money. (What if he got sick? What if he lost his job?)

But there is a second reason for your discomfort. You are the one who is supposed to be the giver. Family and friends are supposed to rely on you, to be in your debt. You always feel most at ease when the relationship scales tip away from you, when you give a little bit more than you get. That way, at least on an unconscious level, there's something coming to you.

You Hate to Admit It, But You're a Martyr

"Don't bother. I'll take a bus from the airport."

"You don't have to fuss over our anniversary, dear. The only gift you could give me is to be happy."

"I'll meet you at the beach later. Someone has to wash these towels."

The part of us that fears rejection turns us into martyrs, sacrificing ourselves in order to secure love. Then we give gifts that weren't solicited, and feel hurt because the gift was not adequately appreciated. Sacrifice itself is a necessary component of love, but you have taken it to an unreasonable extreme. In your case, what is sacrificed is the self, in the form of:

- *Self-interest:* "I wanted to go to my cousin's engagement party, but my husband wanted to see a Lakers game and he's not crazy about family stuff, so . . ."

- *Self-respect:* "You know, I had sex with him but I really didn't want to. It just seemed like it would insult him or hurt his feelings if I said no."

- *Self-awareness:* "I was only trying to help."

It's hard for us to see that the sacrifices made on behalf of our loved ones are partly motivated by our need to keep them close to us and dependent on us so they will never, never leave us. If they left, or even moved far enough away to leave a big space, we'd have to fill that space with new people, new work, new purpose. And all of that opens the possibility of new and dreadful opportunity for rejection and failure.

Your secret brag: "I'm too nice."

What you really mean: "I am essential to the people who are important to me. See? How could they make it without me?"

Your Marriage

"I say 'I love you' all the time, even when I'm really furious with him. I think it's because 'I love you' for me is really a way of saying 'I'm scared.' I'm scared of a lot of things. But especially, I'm scared of what I'd have to face if I admitted, 'I don't love you.'"

When fear of rejection is painfully acute, people tend to dive into marriage as a safety zone, a perfect and perfectly acceptable place to hide out. In an effort to build an utterly secure nest, you might form one of three kinds of marriages: catchers and fliers; nurses and stray puppies; symbiotic couples.

Before we examine these relationships in detail, it's important to note one fact: Any of these three marital patterns has the potential to become abusive. As a group, people who fear rejection run a greater risk of tolerating abuse than people with other kinds of baggage.

For one thing, since you crave security, you are attracted to powerful people whose strength makes you more likely to feel taken care of. Unfortunately, it is easy to confuse abusive people with powerful ones. Also, fear of rejection makes you reluctant to set limits, uncomfortable with confrontation, and likely to blame yourself when trouble erupts.

These traits make you vulnerable to mistreatment. Be aware. And if you are in a physically or emotionally abusive relationship, *get help to get out*. Nothing you do to lighten your inner load can be effective while you are living in the psychological poison of abuse. (See the notes on this chapter for target signs of abusive relationships and additional sources for support.)

The Catcher and the Flier

The success of every trapeze act is built around two elements: A flier who does the breathtaking triple flips and wins all the applause, and a catcher, the person on the other trapeze, swinging back and forth, waiting with exquisite timing to clasp the flier and haul him in to safety. Those of us who dread rejection tend to be catchers in search of a flier to conquer the world for us.

In our society, the flier is traditionally male, though these sex roles are more and more frequently being reversed today. A full-fledged flier is powerful, successful, attractive, and probably financially established. He or she is not famous necessarily but, in some circle or other, is well known, looked up to, or sought after. S/He is prominent in the community—as a judge, a business success, a sports figure, a noted writer. People everywhere try to attract the attention of a flier. As a catcher, you begin the relationship inflated with pride that you have been chosen.

The catcher-flier couple is the extreme version of the traditional husband-as-breadwinner, wife-as-keeper-of-the-domestic-flame roles (or, in the contemporary version, wife as successful career woman, man as househusband). The flier is usually an exceptional breadwinner, which makes the catcher necessarily a bit more accommodating and eager to please.

The flier is, in reality, as dependent on the catcher as she is on him. He needs a steady and secure base from which to launch himself. He needs to fuel himself with the faith and support of someone who knows him well and loves him anyway. He needs his attention free to grab center stage and perform his magic. Fliers often have difficulty, however, acknowledging the mutuality of the relationship. Fliers like to see themselves as independent. How could he really need someone? Love her, maybe. Marry her, possibly. But need her to catch him? That's a hard one for him. He tends to feel that he has carried her along on his coattails. Eventually, he may come to feel that he could fly higher if she weren't dragging him down. At this point, he may opt to leave, usually for love of a younger, sexier catcher.

The female flier also has difficulty acknowledging the contributions of a male catcher. It's hard for her to feel taken care of by a man she supports financially, even if she "knows he's contributing in a lot of different ways."

So your first problem as a catcher is that your flier tends to diminish your importance. But even if the flier does acknowledge your value, the rest of the world doesn't pay attention to your contribution. You go to a party and people elbow you aside to get to your partner. Your opinions are less interesting *and* your presence is less desirable.

One woman described a dinner party she attended with her fiancé, a heart surgeon. She was angry with him because, once again, he had promised to arrive early at her house and discuss wedding plans. Once again, he was too busy to make time. She was approached at the party by a grateful patient who asked, "What's it like to be engaged to a god?"

A catcher gets resentful. Your own natural needs for recognition may eventually begin to assert themselves. You might mature and lose some of your fearful baggage along the way. Maybe you want to fly a little. Often you don't quite know how to do it, so you start to criticize your flier. You want to be appreciated. You want to connect with someone who is catering to you for a change. A flier does not take kindly to what he perceives as the grossest ingratitude. This significant shift in the power balance of your marriage produces a relationship crisis. Like every crisis, this one is a mixture of danger and opportunity.

The Nurse and the Stray Puppy

This is the relationship on which the codependency movement focuses. When we fear rejection, we often marry someone so wounded, so troubled that he or she:

- Can never leave us. "How could he leave? He needs me to function."

- Can never challenge us. In this relationship, *we* are the good, the brave, the smart ones. He or she is the one with the problem.

Although most of the codependency literature focuses on relationships with drug or alcohol abusers, there is actually a range of troubled partners available from which to choose. The pattern in the relationships stays the same.

The "nurse" is the man or woman who is described in this chapter. You are the friend who is perfectly willing to be awakened at four a.m. if someone has a problem. You've been divorced for four years and you still remember your ex-in-laws' birthdays. You are bright, cheerful, energetic, capable, competent. Often you are disappointed in people because they are not as good to you as you are to them. You are an all-time giver whose biggest sadness in life is not finding someone who can give back equally.

The person you do find is the "stray puppy," the man with the problem, the woman who is falling apart, the person who needs help.

You'll give your stray puppy a stream of help, an absolute flood of therapist recommendations, job possibilities, second chances. You'll take over for your puppy where he or she can't or won't function—visiting his mother because he is "too depressed" to do it himself, calling her children on their birthdays because she is going through a bad time and can't call herself.

Nurses are not saints. They get angry at their puppies over and over. As a nurse, you probably keep a running tally of the puppy's omissions: "Can you believe I was sick and he never bothered to cook a meal?" "Can you believe not even a card on my birthday?" "Can you believe she didn't even show up at the airport, and I waited for an hour?" After each disappointment, you confront your mate with pure rage. He or she either defends him- or herself ("Well, I didn't like your tone of voice this morning"), or pleads mental illness ("I felt so awful. I just couldn't seem to think clearly"), or promises to do better ("Honey, you're right. I'm going to start that program tomorrow"). As the nurse, you criticize, you rant, you encourage, you sob. And you never give up.

However frustrating or infuriating you find this marriage, it has one enormous advantage: You two are bound by the steel bands of security. The stray puppy may disappoint but he will never go away. He can't —he's wounded. He needs you.

There is a second subtle payoff. In this relationship, the nurse is the good one, the strong one, the "healthy" one. The marriage focuses on the weaknesses and inadequacies of the stray puppy. You never have to fear that your mate will push you to take more risks, get a better job, meet more people. The world of the puppy is so small that yours looks large by comparison.

Sometimes this marriage falls apart when the stray puppy begins to heal. To get stronger, he has to be independent of his caretaker. As the wounded spouse heals, the nurse spouse can feel abandoned.

More commonly, the nurse–stray puppy marriage has a crisis when the nurse begins to demand some nurturing in return. She's ready to examine her own baggage and she wants support and encouragement. If he is rigidly locked into his wounded role, and he probably is, he won't be able to meet her needs. She gets angry at the injustice. He gets angry with the demand.

They lock into battle.

The Symbiotic Couple

Symbiosis is the likely outcome when people who fear rejection marry someone with baggage exactly like their own. Carole and Mike are an example.

Carole and Mike met in a college class as sophomores and glued onto each other like shipwreck victims. Both described it as falling in love.

Carole always seems to have a part of herself draped on Mike. And he's always monitoring her out of the corner of his eye, checking himself out. One friend observed, "When Mike looks at her, he sort of straightens his tie. It's like he's looking in a mirror."

Carole and Mike are together as often as possible. They take classes together, now that Carole has switched her major to his. As a result, her grades have improved. Mike takes school seriously, so Carole studies along with him. She's dropped her little-theater interests. She used to love amateur acting, but it's not fun now because Mike isn't involved.

Mike has made fewer changes to accommodate Carole, but that's because he felt he had fewer changes to make. He was always a serious student with just a few friends and no real hobbies. He opened the magic circle around him once, to include Carole. The gates slammed behind her.

Carole and Mike have submerged their individual personalities in the interests of fusing into one. They are symbiotic. "Symbiotic" is the biological term describing two organisms who are necessary to each other's survival. When psychologists use the term, they mean a relationship where two individual identities merge into one, for the sake of the psychological survival of each.

In a way, most couples who fall in love go through a stage of symbiosis. Then they move past it, identifying their individual differences and struggling to find a decent way to accommodate them. The symbiotic couple, like Carole and Mike, never moves to the stage of establishing and fighting over the individual needs of each partner. Instead, they bond together to handle life as one.

Symbiosis provides more than a buffer against the world, it also reduces Carole and Mike's need for the world. They do not seek friends, acquaintances, or colleagues. They risk no rejection. It is utterly safe and entirely stifling.

It's stifling because in order to maintain the safety of symbiosis, you must never change. You must move in lockstep with your partner, want what he or she wants, believe what he or she believes. You don't develop new interests. You don't connect with new people. You are frozen in time.

When one of you starts to change, to move out and explore the world, the symbiosis is threatened. The struggle for one or both of you to break symbiotic bonds is wrenching. It feels life-threatening.

As different as these three marital patterns are, they have one common feature: each undergoes an upheaval when you face and push past your fear of rejection. The upheaval comes when:

- Catchers are willing to risk a flight (or fliers pull too far away).

- Nurses are willing to examine their own wounds (or puppies begin to heal).

- Symbiotic couples pull apart so they have room to stretch.

Upheaval is inevitable, but the result of that upheaval does not have to be the catastrophe you fear. In fact, it can be the magical realignment of power that reawakens love.

THE INNER PORTRAIT

Your relationships tend to be stable, your surroundings familiar, and your aspirations modest. Naturally, under these circumstances, you experience rejection infrequently. How is it that you fear it so enormously?

Your theme song hints at the answer.

Your Theme Song: "What if . . ."

That's "What if . . ." as in, "What if I make a mistake? What if it snows? What if they have cats? What if I'm dressed wrong? What if the road is icy? What if I can't think of anything to say? What if . . . I think I'd just better stay home."

"What if . . ." plays over and over in your mind, freezing you in your tracks. Most of the time, it plays in a preconscious whisper, just loud enough to create an inner state of vague concern. Should anything mildly alarming occur—say, a relative who is half an hour late from the office—it amplifies; then you tease yourself with disastrous fantasies ("What if he was mugged in the parking lot? Does he have ID?"). When you face an actual situation where you will be judged, like a first date or a job interview ("They'll ask why I didn't work for six months— what if they don't believe me?"), the volume on the "What if . . ." theme song is turned so high you literally can't pay attention to anything else.

If you face the prospect of serious risk, "What if . . ." can become a complete preoccupation. One mother came to see me after reports of prowlers in her neighborhood disrupted her sleep for weeks. "I'd lie awake at night thinking, 'What if someone broke in, what would I do? Would I run to the kids first, or would they hear me and find the children? I could lock their bedroom door, but then what if there were a fire? I could call the police first, but then what if that gave burglars time to get the children?' No matter what I do, there is always the risk of something bad happening."

Of course, there *is* always the possibility of something bad happening in life. The problem is that your attention is focused on that possibility most of the time. We are all automatically, if unconsciously, analyzing any situation. Where one person focuses on what he *should* do in that situation, and the next uses the situation to take a reading of his own *self-worth,* you are the person who reviews the situation to figure out *what could go wrong.* And once you identify what could go wrong, you worry about it.

Worry is the fuel for your fear of rejection.

As psychologist Thomas Borkovec points out, when you are a chronic worrier, you play constant fear images over and over in your mind. Catastrophe does not have to occur in the real world in order for you to maintain a constant fear of rejection, because it is occurring internally all the time, through the mental pictures you create when you worry. Your theme song, "What if . . ." is the process by which you conjure these pictures.

The irony is that your goal is to avoid rejection in real life, so you conjure it up and experience it over and over in your imagination. "What if . . ." creates mental pictures of failure and loss, but it helps us protect again real-life disaster. In this sense, "What if . . ." is the voice of your ruling passion: a quest for security.

Your Ruling Passion: Security

"My girlfriend once slept with a guy who never called again. In fact, he hadn't even asked for her phone number. She wanted to see him again, so the next time she ran into him, she walked over and gave him her business card. He looked at it—and gave it back! I would have been so devastated. I would have taken to my bed for a week with a carton of chocolate Ding-Dongs. She just shrugged it off. HOW DID SHE DO THAT?"

Fear of rejection has, at its core, a frantic need for a safe harbor. Rejection reminds us, in a powerful and unmistakable way, that the world is never safe, that bad things can happen, and that they will happen—to us. When your need for security runs very deep, you will naturally do anything to avoid such a reminder.

Every one of us needs security. We need a solid base, a sense of rootedness and support, in order to be happy. But some of us need this above all else and find it only in the most fixed and unchallenging of circumstances. Some of us are extremely vulnerable to the slights and abrasions of day-to-day life. We seem to suffer more deeply, diving into a secure nest in order to protect ourselves.

Why? What makes you so fragile, your fear so profound, your security requirements so enormous? Several factors might contribute. You might be temperamentally slower to respond, have a more hesitant approach to exploring the world, which means you would take a long time to adjust to change, to new people and new situations. And, if you are female, you have to some degree been socialized to be passive and fearful—you know, "feminine."

Whether or not your biological makeup or the influences of society have created your passion for security, your early environment clearly has an impact. As one woman put it: *"My mother taught me that for every silver lining, there's sure to be a cloud."*

A parent who avoids rejection at all costs, who can't have people over because the house isn't clean enough, who won't drive, travel, work, or take an obvious risk of any kind sends us a clear message: Watch out! Danger out there! Some of us (probably because of sex, or temperament, or birth order, or a lucky intervention) notice this lesson and reject it out of hand. But some of us take it to heart as the Truth.

Oddly enough, risk-taking, achieving parents can also make us sensitive to rejection in an attempt to help us develop excellence. These parents might be critics, flaw finders, people whose need to be right extends to their need for us as their children to be and do right as well. In the end, we develop the feeling that we're profoundly inadequate (or else why would everything about us require improvement?) or that we are lovable, but only when we're perfect. Since it is the sad truth that we tend to anticipate from the world what we got from our parents, critical parents train us to expect criticism; perfectionist parents train us to expect love only when we're perfect or damned close to it. In either case, it makes us afraid.

So we stay where it's safe, where we are protected, where we can avoid even the possibility of repeating the pain from which we were unable to escape as children. We crave security not necessarily because it makes us happy but because inside those familiar boundaries we know how to defend ourselves.

It is not this desire for the familiar or your deep attachment to family that ultimately weighs you down. Your capacity to create a secure niche is a great asset, and if you make it safer by an ongoing internal litany of "What if . . ." well, at least it helps you protect against pain. What gets in your way is your belief that if you expand beyond your safe borders, you'll be a failure.

WHAT'S THE BAGGAGE?
YOU DREAD REJECTION

Parts of the portrait you just read might fit you. Perhaps you are not at all the social martyr we described, but you realize that professionally you've been hiding out. Or you might be happy with your job, but you realize that you press your grown children to stay close to home more for your own sake than for theirs. Taking a look at your own passion for security might be uncomfortable, especially as we begin to outline the baggage that comes with it.

It's easier if you keep in mind that out of your passion for security come your greatest strengths—your loyalty, your capacity for love and sacrifice, the depth of your relationships. You don't need us to be fascinating, stimulating, or even especially worthy. You just need us to be *there,* and if we are, you'll be there too, doing your best to make us feel safe and secure. You are steadfast and easily satisfied, patient and forgiving. You don't need to prove anything and we don't either —as long as we all sit around the table together one more time.

But there is a cost to your capacity to build a safe nest:

▪ You might stay in that nest long past the point of satisfaction.

▪ You insist that the rest of us stay in there with you.

▪ One of the risks you avoid is the risk of feeling great about yourself.

THE STRENGTH: You Avoid the Pain of Rejection.

BUT

THE BAGGAGE: This Avoidance Makes You Feel Bad
about Yourself.

"Avoid" is your operative word, your main mode of coping, your strategy for living. Avoid risk and you can't fail. Avoid opinion and you can't offend. Avoid pursuit and you can't be rejected. Avoid all of this, and you can't feel very good about yourself either.

If you are loaded down with a fear of rejection, you really feel good about yourself only when you are being accepted. Your self-image is formed as you see it reflected back in someone else's eyes. Naturally, you'll develop a lot of people-pleasing techniques. You'll do a lot of lovely things for other people, and you'll get pleasure and satisfaction out of doing them.

A great deal of good comes out of this, but something is missing. You will tend to measure yourself and your self-worth against other people's appreciation of what you do. Then you have a problem, because other people rarely appreciate what is given to the degree to which you appreciate having given it. The difference between these two can create an enormous wound to your self-esteem.

You give and give, and not all that much appreciation comes back your way. You make everything at home as wonderful as you know how to—but still, your children leave, or your mate leaves, or your friends move on. You squelch the anger you feel, because you hate to rock the boat, and because when you vent anger, other people seem to retaliate tenfold. Your fears keep you safe—but they also keep you unstimulated and underdeveloped.

All of this might be a formula for chronic or acute depression.

You might have trouble dragging yourself out of bed in the morning, feeling hopeless and helpless. You might be prone to overeating, stuffing the emptiness and soothing your boredom. You might be drinking too much in an attempt to block out your anxieties. Either the eating or the drinking can give rise to feelings of shame and self-recrimination, which make the burden of your fear of rejection even heavier. You can grow so accustomed to the chronic state of depression that you no longer recognize it as baggage. It simply feels like life.

Even if you are not depressed, your avoidance chips away at your self-esteem. You tend to bury your identity because some aspect of you might not meet with approval. You tend to give in, go along, find very little worth fighting for. You are always trying to please others more than they are trying to please you. So how important could you be? If you let go of all the parts of you that might offend, how can you have a strong sense of the whole?

In place of a strong sense of identity, you are left with something we have come to call "low self-esteem." Chip by chip, day by day, relationship by relationship, your avoidance creates a bad feeling about yourself. And *you never even have to get rejected to feel it.* All you have to do is worry about being not good enough, bury the uncertainty under a bland mask of sacrifice. Of course, you know how much uncertainty you have stashed away. That fear of rejection alone makes you feel bad about yourself, in and of itself. And if you feel bad about yourself, you are more likely to assume that other people will feel negatively about you, and therefore reject you. Quite naturally, you pull back into the prison.

THE STRENGTH: You Are Enormously Giving.
BUT
THE BAGGAGE: You Charge a High Price for It.

"My mother-in-law sent us a sterling silver service for twelve as an anniversary present. Which was very nice except I hated the pattern and I was stuck with it for life. What was worse, I had to admire it aloud at every holiday dinner and remind everyone how wonderful and generous she'd been."

What is there about the passion to please that often drives others away from you? Why does the woman who devotes her life to her kids frequently lose her children in adulthood? Why are the husbands who were less responsible still married, while the husband who made sure there was gas in the car and life insurance gets left?

First of all, you are blind to the criticism implicit in your generosity and support. There is an edge, an implication of judgment in your unselfishness. It is probably an unconscious edge, but other people sense it.

You help a colleague by redoing the files. She thanks you, and you comment with a laugh, "Well, it would never have gotten done if it were up to you." The unspoken message? "You're lazy."

You are still doing your adult child's laundry. You joke, "At least I know your clothes are clean." Your message? "You can't do anything right. I need to do it for you."

Even without these subtle or not-so-subtle put-downs, other people are sensitive to your critical edge. You send a silent but clear message: "I'm the good one in this relationship, and you aren't nearly as good." The proof of this imbalance is in your own experience. People are always disappointing you, yet you pride yourself on the fact that you'd never let them down in the same way. You focus on your own feeling of neglect. But if you look at it from the other person's point of view, you can see how upsetting it is always to be seen as a disappointment.

Some of your criticism takes a more direct form, though this is usually limited to mates and children. We project our fears of rejection onto family because we see them as extensions of ourselves, leaving the house and going out into the world to be judged. We imagine others judging our family as they judge us. It makes us especially nuts because our family refuses to do things the way we feel would be most likely to avoid rejection. The frustration and threat provoked by their careless behavior can be enormous. We vent our frustration and concern by criticizing them: "Don't leave this house dressed like that." "Remember, what you do is a reflection of me." "Get a haircut."

The advice may be good but the tone is hard to take, so it's not surprising that the people closest to us fail to appreciate this guidance. In fact, they don't call it help. They call it "nagging."

There is an even higher price people we love have to pay for our generosity. We refuse to allow them to leave us. We experience their wish for a larger world as a rejection of our own small, comfortable one.

A daughter longs to quit a job and travel. We raise a hundred practical considerations, but the hidden knife is a passing mention of our own loneliness when she's gone. A lover wants to hold Friday nights open to party with her friends. We base our objections on rules and expectations we have for lovers, which only partly mask our motivation: What will I do on Friday nights without her? Why have a lover if you have no companion on the weekend? And worst of all, the basic gnawing uncertainty of our baggage drives us on: *"If you really cared about me, you'd want to be with me on Friday night."* If we separate, even for a few key hours, I feel rejected.

So we try to keep the people we love close to us, close physically, close to us in social class ("Now that you've made a lot of fancy friends,

I guess you won't want your sister's opinion anymore"), and close to us in terms of sharing our values, our tastes, or style of living. The closeness makes us feel secure, but it doesn't leave them much room to change or develop or grow.

> **THE STRENGTH:** You Can Burrow into a Cozy Niche, and
> Experience Deep Joy from Its Daily Rhythms.
> BUT
> **THE BAGGAGE:** You'll Cling to This Niche, Even When It
> Ceases to Satisfy.

You aren't prepared for change. Life's transitions come hard to you. You'll stay in a mediocre job five years too long. You'll stay in a painful marriage forever or, worse, until your braver mate leaves you. Then you'll be both totally unprepared for the change and devastated by it.

In general, people can prepare for change by causing it to happen in small, manageable doses. They go on practice job interviews a year before their company merges. They expand activities into the community as their children gradually need them less, or begin to date others when a romance shows signs of fizzling. These are all small steps that people may take because they get an early signal that change is imminent.

But it's very difficult for you to prepare in advance. Generally, your life is reactive. Events force a response from you, but you rarely act to shape events.

Instead of stepping out of your niche yourself, because you've changed or because you sense that it is about to change, you might shut down even further. Preparing for change, making decisions, and taking steps to manage change all make a person stronger when change is required. But your fears make you avoid opportunities to become braver. If you date someone who asks you to stop calling, it could be months before you'll risk trying to develop a new romance. If your idea isn't greeted warmly by your boss, you may never risk presenting another one. You are frightened to ask questions for fear of looking stupid, so it's hard to learn enough to feel smart.

Your reluctance to push, to challenge, and to risk makes you cling to anything familiar whether it makes you happy or not. You can learn to let it go.

Rx: EXPAND YOUR WORLD

When you have a passion for security, you get very, very good at being safe. Along the way, you can lose your ability to take a risk.

"Take a risk" means that you will deliberately have to frustrate your need for security in order to push past your emotional prison. It means that you may have to sacrifice feeling comfortable, content, and toasty to do something that feels awkward or even unpleasant—just to prove to yourself that you can. Now why would you want to do that?

You want to do it because it pays off triple, which is something you can say for very few investments.

The first payoff is obviously whatever you stand to gain by the specific risk you took. If you risk looking stupid by going back to school—you might find out you're bright and get a degree along with it. If you risk your boss's refusal and ask for the longer vacation—you might get what you ask for. Every risk that you are currently avoiding has a payoff you are missing out on. After all, you can't win the game if you don't play it.

The second payoff is indirect, but maybe even more important. The small risks you take can improve your relationships with other people. Each tiny step you take to expand your world means that slightly less of your emotional weight is being carried by your family, your friends, your old standby supporters. As you lean on them less, they enjoy you more. As you move slightly away, you have more to say to them, more to share. They seek you out more, drawn by affection now rather than by sheer obligation.

Yes, it's true that as you move a bit apart, you are less automatically available to bear the weight of their dependency. A child, a mate, a friend, might resent your new interests, your newly strengthened self. But with that temporary resentment will come a new appreciation of your worth. That's a big payoff for a small risk.

The third benefit you'll receive for having disrupted the contentment of your familiar routine is the best of all. You'll impress yourself. You can do what you thought was beyond you, succeed where you had been living only with mental images of failure. With each new risk, you'll discover that you are unlikely to experience rejection as often as you anticipate, and that you will be rejected sometimes, fail sometimes, do or say something incredibly foolish sometimes, and nothing very awful happens.

As you take risk after risk and discover you can survive the consequences, your "What if . . ." fears diminish. You replace fear of rejection with confidence. Yes, bad things happen, but you can handle them. THE GREATEST PAYOFF TO RISK TAKING IS THAT YOU END UP FEELING MORE SECURE.

To reap these benefits, to lessen your fear of rejection, you need to force yourself to take risky action. It's worth it. More than any other form of baggage, fear of rejection poisons your spirit and strips the vitality from your life. If other baggage gets in your way, fear of rejection stops you dead in your tracks. That makes the exercises here of special importance. It takes only small steps to widen a life, as long as the steps are in the right direction.

Worry Management Strategy

To break free of the prison of fear you've built, you'll need to get your tendency to worry under greater and greater control. All those worry visions have helped to create your fear and they are a large part of what sustains it. Control the problem behavior of worrying and you will probably reduce the fear.

There are several techniques for controlling worry behavior, depending upon whether you are a chronic worrier, or you are paralyzed by one specific worry.

If you are worrying about a specific event where rejection is a possibility (for example, you might be reluctant to go to a party of strangers, unable to ask for a raise, or anxious about a performance review), the following strategies will help you reduce the frequency or intensity of that worry:

1. *Write down your worry.* ("I'm afraid no one will talk to me all night." "I'm afraid if I ask for a raise, my boss will turn me down flat *and* hold a grudge.")

Sometimes just this clear focus on your worry helps to reduce it. A specific fear can live in the back of your mind, creating a vague but pervasive sense of dis-ease. Bringing that fear to the forefront of your attention gives you a sense of its true scope. It reminds you that it's not your whole well-being that is threatened. It's just a raise, just a party.

2. *Evaluate your worry, in writing.* How likely is it to occur? (Reality testing.) Is there anything more I can do to minimize the risk? (Planning.) If the worst happens, can I handle it? (Affirming.)

For example, Shelly agonized over the possibility that her lover's teenage daughters wouldn't like her. Since she hoped to be their stepmom someday, it seemed crucial that the relationships get off to a good start. In Shelly's mind, however, that was an unlikely outcome, as she'd had no experience with teenagers, not to mention with potentially possessive daughters who would probably see her as a rival. Shelly found one excuse after another to delay the introductions.

It was easy for Shelly to write down her worry ("They'll hate me, I'll hate them, and that'll be the end of Bruce"). The next three steps required more effort.

■ How likely is it that the girls will hate me?

Shelly rated this possibility fifty-fifty. Daughters might reasonably be expected to have mixed feelings about a divorced dad's new girlfriend, and teenagers are not noted for their grace under pressure. Oddly enough, acknowledging in writing the strong possibility that her worry was realistic eased some of Shelly's dread. She could see that there was a good possibility of rejection for reasons largely out of her control. A difficult beginning might just be a sad fact of life for Shelly and the girls. She could detach herself to a degree and see the problem less personally.

▪ Is there anything more I can do to minimize the risk?

This required consideration. Shelly read a book on stepparenting, but it wasn't very helpful about the first meeting. Then she put a little research into the girls themselves. She discovered that one was a history buff, the other took art classes at a local college. Shelly planned the initial meetings around this information. She invited one to a World Affairs Council meeting, took the other to lunch at the museum. At least the setting was positive and her efforts communicated caring, both to Bruce and to his daughters.

▪ If the worst happens, can I handle it?

Finally, before the meetings, Shelly accepted the fact that these young women had issues of their own that might make Shelly a target for their angry feelings, no matter what she said or did. She dropped the idea that it all had to go well from day one, and accepted that even if her worst fear came true and they *hated* her, they might change over time. She would endure, and she'd do her best to help Bruce through it too.

The process of writing the answers to these questions moved Shelly closer to taking the risk. She faced the fear instead of blurring it inside a pervasive sense of worry. And in accurately assessing its size and actively taking steps to minimize a poor outcome, she was shaking herself out of paralysis and inching toward action. Finally, by facing the worst in her imagination, she was reassuring herself and giving herself permission to take the risk. This last step is especially important. If you could not live with the worst possible outcome of a risk, you probably shouldn't take that risk. The thing is, the worst possible outcome of most of our risks is usually not that bad, after all.

3. *Visualize success.* Having put your worry into writing and realistically analyzed its size, scope, and likelihood, put your writing aside. Now close your eyes, relax your body, and practice visualization.

Magically, the single greatest tool for overcoming fear of rejection is to visualize yourself as brave. Create a powerful enough mental image of yourself and it will help you to face down fear. See yourself as overcoming resistance, as facing up to your bogeyman, and—if you see it clearly enough and often enough and successfully enough in your mind's eye—that is exactly how you will act in the real world.

In Shelly's visualization, she pictured the initial meetings. She saw herself smiling and talking with each daughter. More important, she saw, in her mind's eye, the daughters smiling back, pictured the whole group laughing together. These positive mental images relaxed Shelly and helped her to behave as she most wanted to during the actual events.

Visualization works on the simple principle that we never really do what we can't see ourselves doing. When you fear rejection, flirting with a stranger or asserting yourself in the office feels like "not me." If it's not you, chances are you won't do it or that you won't do it well. Visualization works on your inner picture, restructuring your own vision of your capabilities.

As we said in Chapter 3, visualization can be self-taught, though again it requires commitment to add anything new to your repertoire. Several books are included in the bibliography to help start you out.

Fear of rejection stirred by chronic, generalized worry raises a different set of problems. Realistic appraisal, planning, and positive visualization reduce fear around specific risks. But chronic, intrusive worried thoughts don't necessarily revolve around a specific problem. Instead, they create an overall atmosphere of concern, negativity, and paralysis.

The most successful intervention here is to treat worry as a behavior problem that responds to self-control strategies. The goal is to contain your tendency to worry, limiting it in time and circumstances. Thomas Borkovec has designed such a program, which involves six steps:

I. Listen carefully to yourself and identify the very start of your worried thoughts. Catching your worry behavior early is crucial, because the longer you let a worry episode go on, the more you strengthen your habit of worrying. Borkovec recommends that you count your worry thoughts—actually count them on a notepad or with a wrist counter. This helps you to focus your attention, to identify worries earlier, and to track your progress later.

2. Pick a "worry period"—Borkovec recommends a half hour every day. It must be the same half hour, and your worrying must take place in the same location every day. The idea here is that if you are an out-of-control worrier, you behave much like an out-of-control eater. You have allowed worry to become associated with a whole variety of places and activities. Then, when you enter one of these many locations, or engage in one of these activities, it automatically triggers a worried thought. Borkovec's idea is to disconnect these associations by scheduling your worrying behavior, limiting its locale, and sticking rigorously to your schedule.

3. As soon as you catch yourself worrying, postpone it until your worry period. Write the topic down if you are afraid you'll forget to worry about it later.

4. Shift your attention away from your unscheduled worry thoughts by focusing on something else immediately present in your environment. Worry has to do with thinking about things from the past or especially about the future. Focus on what is happening now. Read, count, write, something. Focus on the present.

5. When you get to your worry period, worry intensely. Here's where you can use the techniques suggested earlier for reducing a specific worry. The worry period is for problem solving. Write down each worry. Review it logically. Estimate its probability. Confront the worst possible outcome. Shape and repeat affirming thoughts.

6. Finally, deliberately relax. Use a technique of deep muscle relaxation, meditation, or self-hypnosis and slow yourself down. You are about to confront a risk. Do it from a position of calm and strength.

Like any change technique, this one requires effort, self-discipline, and a fierce commitment on your part to stop spreading the poison of worry through your life. If you are willing to commit the energy and attention to the problem, you may find this technique of scheduling worry amazingly effective.

Risk-Taking Strategies

Ultimately, to reduce the fear of rejection, you have to risk rejection. Period. Risking rejection will extinguish the fear when it is unrealistic, because you'll learn that the feared event, rejection, does not always occur. You'll never have the rewards of that learning experience without taking the risk. It will also reduce the fear even when it is realistic. When you are rejected, as you inevitably will be, the pain is not nearly as devastating, nor the humiliation as overpowering, as you envision. Unfortunately, you can't learn to tolerate the sting of rejection without actually experiencing it.

Yes, yes, sure, sure. You know. It all makes perfect sense and you know you should and you have to and just as soon as whatever it is that you are waiting for happens, you'll go right ahead and risk it. Right?

Wrong. Risk it today. Now. Stop waiting for someday. It won't come. Or worse, when it does come, and you do take the risk, you'll be filled with pain when you realize how much of your life you spent sitting on the sidelines because of an exaggerated fear. Therefore:

▪ Stop waiting until you are thin enough or fit enough! It's partly your fear of rejection that is urging you to be fat and flabby in the first place. It gives you a "reason" to avoid taking a social risk. Take your body out into the world and let it get to feel comfortable while you are perfecting it. The one doing the fiercest rejection of you and your body is *you*.

▪ Stop waiting until you are successful enough! Stop looking at the women who interest you the most and saying, "I wouldn't ask one of them today, but in a few years, when my practice is established, when I'm more financially secure, when I get the promotion, *then* I could attract one of the ones I really want." You are already good enough. Risk it.

▪ Stop waiting until you have "time," until you aren't as busy at the office, or until the kids don't need you as much, or until your aging parents are better situated, or until whatever obligations you have are met. Yes, they are responsibilities. Yes, they are a top priority and they do take time. But very often we fill up our lives with obligations so that we don't have to take risks.

▪ Stop zoning out! Give up whatever techniques you ordinarily use to quiet your longings and/or soothe your anxieties. Take one identifiable chunk of time, preferably a three-month period, and stop indulging your addictions. Unplug your television. Don't drink. Don't use any drugs. Eat moderately with an eye toward nutrition. Bring yourself back to the surface. Then you'll get a fair idea of the fears and aspirations you've been pushing out of your consciousness.

Fear of rejection is baggage that can be unloaded if you're willing to take active, risky steps—now.

Identify Your Fear

We tend to think of ourselves globally as "good" risk takers or poor ones. Actually, you are probably strong in some areas and need to work on others. The same man who can make a breathtaking professional leap might never challenge himself to ski the expert slope. But the daring skier could be bartending by day, afraid to challenge himself professionally. The competent physician might be too shy to smile at a strange man who excites her.

Consider a person sexually, socially, emotionally, professionally, and romantically. Here is an example of specific risk objectives she might have:

Socially—I'd like to be able to walk into a party alone.

Emotionally—I'd like to have the courage to tell my mother-in-law that we want to spend Christmas morning without her.

Sexually—I would like to put on a garter belt and lingerie without feeling silly.

Professionally—I'd like to ask my boss what she has in mind for my future.

Romantically—I'd like to be brave enough to talk to someone gorgeous first, instead of just responding to the ones who want me.

Now consider yourself socially, emotionally, sexually, professionally, and romantically. Write down a specific risk objective for as many of these areas as you can. Begin each statement, "I would like to be able to . . ." and then complete it with a goal or a behavior that would give you great delight, if only you weren't too scared to try for it.

Can you do it? Can you think of at least one risk you feel motivated to move toward, one challenge you'd like to set yourself?

If you're having difficulty, that could be an indication of just how deeply you've burrowed into your secure niche. When you're in bed with the covers pulled over your head, it's easy to forget there are challenges in the outside world that hold any allure for you. Give yourself a few days to look around; then come back to this exercise. Our whole goal here is to get you to take more risks. Only you can determine what reward might be worth risking something for.

Make Your Plan and Act on It

Pick one of the objectives you completed above. Set it as your goal. Pick a date by which you will take the action. Circle the date in your calendar.

Next, break that goal into as many small steps as possible. For example, Arthur's emotional goal was to tell his boss "no" when he was asked to do something inappropriate. Arthur couldn't set a date because he couldn't tell when his boss would next send him out, for example, to pick up the dry cleaning. So he decided that if such an offense happened three more times, he would have to act. The effect of committing to the third time helped Arthur rev his adrenaline and strengthen his resolve. Counting forced him to pay attention to the actual frequency of the problem so he couldn't just ignore the problem. Finally, choosing the third time allowed Arthur the reassuring fantasy that maybe he'd never have to take this risk. The fantasy made his other preparatory steps easy. ("I'll get ready just in case. But maybe 'just in case' will never come," went his thinking.)

He broke down his specific objective into smaller risks by:

1. Saying no to other people who were less intimidating than his boss and paying careful attention to the outcome.

2. Creating an easier climate to say no, by scheduling a meeting with the boss to discuss his job duties. That way, when he was asked to do something outside those responsibilities, he would have that discussion to refer to.

3. Identifying in writing every likely opportunity to say no to his boss, so he would be more prepared for a confrontation when the third time came.

4. Rehearsing exactly what he'd say. Arthur wrote a script: "Frank, I'm not comfortable doing those personal errands for you. It's not part of my job as you described it to me last Thursday. You know, I owe you an apology. I should have told you this from the beginning so I wouldn't have to put you in this awkward spot."

Arthur practiced variations of this speech until his boss committed the third offense. In fact, Arthur froze initially and found himself driving the boss's car to the auto body shop. But he was so clear that he was breaking a commitment to himself, and so rehearsed, that when he got back to the office, he found an opportunity to deliver his speech. His boss was neither wonderful nor horrible. He got a bit defensive, changed the subject, and stopped asking for favors. Arthur worried on and off for a week about whether his boss would hold a grudge, and the boss himself was a bit distant for a few days. Finally, the incident receded into the past, Arthur was more comfortable at work, and they both got on with the job.

Kim used the same strategy to take a social risk—namely, the risk of initiating a friendship instead of waiting to be chosen. Kim's closest friends had recently married and moved away, leaving her with no playmates for a Tuesday night movie or a Saturday afternoon shopping adventure. Kim was so embarrassed to find herself friendless that she hid out for a while and pretended to be busy. Finally, bored and lonely, she steeled herself to take action.

First, she gave herself a target date and a specific written goal: "I will invite at least two different women to do something with me before next Sunday."

Next, she made a list of every interesting person who could be a potentially pleasant companion. These included a friendly stranger she sometimes ran into at the health club, a neighbor in her apartment building, a colleague at work.

Kim did two further things to make the risk easier. She wrote down phrases she could use to extend an invitation. She notes, "I felt sort of stupid writing down lines on a three-by-five card like, 'Got time for a drink after work?' or, 'Want to stop in for pizza tonight?' But when I'd see one of these women, I'd kind of freeze up. Writing down a sort of script helped me get past it."

The other thing Kim did that pushed her past the barrier of her fear of rejection was to visualize success. Twice a day, for just a few minutes, she'd close her eyes and picture herself extending an invitation, and then she'd see the other person happily accepting.

All in all, Kim's strategy to extend herself socially worked well. That is not to say that she never got rejected. Some people said no, some accepted her invitations gratefully, and two of those eventually became real friends. Kim's greatest payoff was an overall reduction of her social fears. The more she extended herself, the more comfortable, the more natural it became. "When I think that I used to be too shy to ask another woman to go grab lunch—it doesn't even seem like me. Now I wouldn't think twice about it. I've met a lot of interesting people that way."

Make your own plan, including a commitment in writing as to your target date. Identify in writing the specific steps you could take toward your goal and schedule them.

Get Support

The risk-taking program you've just mapped out occurs first in your mind. The paralyzing difficulty usually comes when action is required and the risk of pain and rejection is real.

You may have excellent intentions with respect to the risks you need to take in order to be happier in your life. But good intentions can be very weak motivators when they come up against the intensity of your dread. You might need an outside agent to help push you.

A therapist can absolutely fill that role. Very often someone will tell me that he or she only made the phone call, raised the touchy question, faced the fear, because he knew we had an appointment the next day and he'd have to talk about it if he didn't act. By this, some people mean they don't want to face the possibility of my rejecting them for failure to carry out a plan. (I wouldn't, of course, but people fearful of rejection always worry.) Some people mean they don't want to waste any more money talking about something they are going to do. It's too expensive—they'd rather do it. And some people use therapy as their calendar, and a therapist as a quick and appreciative audience for a fear they've overcome.

A mentor, a parent, or a respected friend could fulfill the same function (although these people sometimes have an investment in our keeping our baggage). We don't want to diminish ourselves in the eyes of people we admire. If you make an agreement with one of these people that you'll act, it's an extra incentive.

Support comes from a therapist, a friend, a public statement of your intentions, a written commitment, and a plan for rewards. Take all the support you can get, in every form available. Take the support, then *take the risk.*

One final thought: The suffering engendered by our fear of rejection is very real. But the desire to get what we want without risking rejection is pure fantasy.

We suffer from our fear because it confines us to such very small lives. We grow stifled and unsatisfied, living in the same place, clinging to the same long-since-mastered job, holding on desperately to people we no longer care for or who no longer need to hold on to us. So we anesthetize that dissatisfaction with fantasy: "Someday . . . when I meet the right person, when the kids are grown, when I win the lottery, when I graduate . . . then I'll have the life I know is possible, without having to risk the pain, the humiliation, the panic of failure."

It's just not so. Achievement, toward whatever goal, is a mountain we climb. So many people spend their lifetimes tucked safely into a valley at the base of that mountain, dreaming of life on top. The people who live at the top did not get there because they failed less on the way. They got there because they were willing to endure more failure.

The goal is not to avoid rejection or even to reduce its frequency. The goal is to reduce your fear of it. The *fear* is the baggage. Rejection itself is just part of the path up the mountain.

Every one of us is slowed on our path because we are carrying heavy baggage, and because the people we love, work with, depend upon are carrying baggage too. If you fear rejection, it's probably not the only thing slowing you down. You might feel you can only avoid rejection by running every show. If so, your need to be right is probably also a stumbling block. You might avoid rejection by clinging to the idea that you are above the fray, in which case, a sense of superiority is probably getting in your way.

Whatever your other baggage might be, if you fear rejection you are probably a person who needs other people too much. You need their approval and acceptance, of course. If you didn't overvalue these, rejection wouldn't be such a threat. But you need more than someone else's stamp of approval. You need his love, her attention, his admiration, her support. You need attachment, and sometimes you'll go to great lengths to get it.

You might become helpless so the people you love have to stay around. You might get in trouble so the people you love have to rescue you. In other words, if you are a person who dreads rejection, sometimes you might also create drama, just to ward it off. You'll find that piece of your baggage in the next chapter.

Chapter Six

■

YOU CREATE DRAMA

There was a little girl
Who had a little curl
Right in the middle of her forehead;
And when she was good
She was very, very good,
And when she was bad she was horrid.

—HENRY WADSWORTH LONGFELLOW

At the opening of her book *Some Men Are More Perfect Than Others*, Merle Shain describes a man who abandoned everything he had built in his lifetime—family, financial stability, respected career—for the sake of a wrenching, heartfelt love. The love affair ended badly. Shain then describes a friend observing this broken man, a man who has lost his wife, his children, his job, his assets, his love, and his hope for happiness. The friend's comment? "I envy him."

Passion, that elusive, exhilarating state of transport, is the prize of prizes for some of us. Passion, and its near cousins—anticipation, excitement, enthusiasm, longing, sexual arousal—are our very lifeblood. These fuel our energy and fire our imagination. Even their intense opposites—hatred, dread, fear, rage—are preferable to the alternative, a daily trudge through the emotional desert of homework, housework, paperwork. We crave the one sweep of emotion that will convert this black-and-white life into a colorful, engaging, lively play. In other words, we crave drama.

The woman or man who craves drama, creates drama, or feeds on drama is the person who adds color to all of our lives. Here is a general description to help you recognize yourselves.

A PORTRAIT

It's Not Simply That You Enjoy Drama—You Are Drama

"What a disaster. Oh my God!"
"Ma. Earthquake is a disaster. You burnt a chicken."

"I can never say exactly what makes her different. She just gets us to do things we'd never do otherwise. She'll call and say, 'I'm picking you up in fifteen minutes. We're all wearing red.'"

"No one has his sense of the moment. Once we were on a long, hot, miserable drive through India. At the lowest ebb, he pulled five Tootsie Roll Pops out of his backpack."

It's automatic, it's unconscious. With no particular effort, you create theater of the everyday. You are the entertainer—center stage, and worthy of the spotlight.

Things are always happening to you. Every sortie is a saga. You go to the car wash, the bank, and the laundry and head home with this incredible experience where you were shocked or amused. And you have to tell your closest friend immediately. She'll be happy to listen because your tales are always interesting and often funny. Sometimes, though, she wishes you wouldn't call during dinner. She tried telling you once, but you felt so hurt, so criticized, it wasn't worth pushing it.

You are attractive and animated, apt to look younger than your years. You are fashionably stylish because you put considerable time and effort into your appearance. You know intuitively that if you want to be center stage, you've got to give the folks something to look at. You're perfectly happy to do so.

You are extravagant in word and deed (and probably in spending, too). People tease you about your habit of hyperbole—everything is the best, the most fabulous, the worst, the most depressing. (To your companion, it was "a nice day." To you, it was "the most perfect afternoon.") There is no middle of the road.

When you speak in superlatives, you are faithfully describing your own intense emotional reaction to an event. You describe yesterday's haircut as the worst experience of your life in order to convey the force of your feelings. To people who don't have easy access to strong emotion, your descriptions may sound like foolish exaggeration. For you, they are a simple statement of inner truth. That truth is, you need to live big.

You feel most alive, most like yourself, when you are in the grip of a strong emotion. Without this powerful force, life pales for you. You are easily bored and seek to escape apathy through intense, emotion-packed situations.

You are drawn to love triangles—your own or someone else's; you adore romances, complete with sexy heroes and damsels in distress. If you can't make the drama occur in your own life, you long to escape to a world where it's happening with some regularity (*People* magazine is published for you). But when you can make it happen in your world, you do, whether through gossip, intrigue, physical risk, fantasy, dress-up, confrontation, financial excess, drugs, alcohol, or middle-of-the-night analyses of the Relationship.

Sometimes your body is a source of major drama. You present minor illness with flair and color. This does *not* mean that you are necessarily hypochondriacal. Nor do you necessarily use your exaggeration to get sympathy or avoid work. It's just that you love to paint life's events with a wide brush, and your body provides you with an opportunity. One woman describes it perfectly:

"My girlfriend and I love to suffer. We can't help ourselves. We don't get headaches . . . we get early signs of a cerebral hemorrhage. We don't get stomachaches . . . we have a possibility of pancreatic cancer. We're never thirsty . . . we're soooo dehydrated. You want some more examples? Wait a minute, I'll ask my husband—he's heard it all for years."

You celebrate life—your own and other people's, too. You would appreciate it if they would return the favor. You could discuss a friend's wedding in infinite detail, take great delight in planning a surprise party for your lover's birthday. Likewise, you expect a similar celebration from your loved ones for your special occasions. You would be deeply hurt if they were casual about it, upset if a child away at college merely sent a birthday card, and outraged if your mate forgot your anniversary completely.

Sometimes you become anxious several weeks ahead of an event, concerned that people won't make enough of a fuss, won't understand how important it is. You see it as a test of your value to them. If they love you, they will pay special attention on this special day, just as your mom probably did. You don't want them to fail this test; it would hurt you very deeply. But you can't seem to call the test off. So you help them out as best you can. You mention your birthday a few weeks ahead of time. You make sure to recognize your friends on theirs. You hint about desirable gifts or festive restaurants, all in hopes that you can make it easier for them not to disappoint you.

The hardest thing you have to do: The mundane, the routine, the unrecognized, unappreciated tasks of life.

When there is no possibility of celebration or appreciation, you find it very difficult to be motivated. If your boss gives you a special filing project, assigned because of your expertise, which will be held up as a model for future endeavors, you can show amazing perseverance, diligence, and organizational capacity. But day-to-day filing? A deadly bore.

Since the bulk of domestic life is maintenance, you may have difficulty running a smooth, untroubled home. It's likely to be messy—unless you've hooked up with a stern parental figure who "forces" you into tidiness (a parent with whom you live? a mate? a roommate?). You find it loathsome to tidy every day on your own behalf, though you might launch yourself into a major weekend cleanup from time to time— complete with newly purchased cleaning products and, with any luck, the aid of a friend who was lured somehow to help you. ("Would you mind just lugging the really heavy boxes? Oh, thank you, thank you. I'd put music on to make it more fun but I don't know how to hook up my new CD. . . . Oh, you could? You are so wonderful. I'm going to make you the best lunch you ever had.")

Your casual disregard for the daily "requirements" of life are both astonishing and irritating to people with a keener sense of "should": "She lets the mail pile up on the couch day after day—without opening it." "She sends her dog to the groomers in a cab!" "He eats when and if he feels like it—usually standing up or lying down."

Your psychiatric label would probably be: Histrionic personality.

You Have a Wonderful Capacity to Feel—and to Express These Feelings

You are the person who feels the rush of love for a friend, while the rest of us just think highly of that person. You laugh until you cry over the joke that made the rest of us smile. Christmas morning is still a thrill, vacations still excite you, and you can still enjoy a bouquet of roses, a Hallmark card, an unexpected love note. As we get older, it takes enormous stimulation for the rest of us to feel much of anything—except stressed, spaced out, contented, or cranky. You still feel it all.

You feel it sweetly, and you savor the feeling. You are sentimental. A Budweiser commercial can make you tear up if it plucks the right underdog heartstrings. You are moved by the national anthem, by Norman Rockwell's rendition of the Four Freedoms, by Andrew Wyeth's "Christina's World" (no matter what you may think of it as art). You love to reminisce. "We used to have breakfast on the balcony every morning," you'll sigh with a smile, transforming a five-day vacation into a stage of life.

You feel it intuitively as well. You get hunches, "feelings," and you take the risk of trusting them. While this is irritating to more logical, data-oriented folk ("He bets on horses because he likes the name! It makes no sense at all"), they learn to value you ("I have to admit, he sometimes wins").

You are intuitive about other people's emotional reactions too. You can sense a parent's extra interest in a brother's accomplishment, no matter how evenhanded that parent tries to be. You know when an audience of friends is appreciating your story and when you have to step up the pace. Above all, you pick up on a lover's lapse of interest, however momentary. You feel it even when he or she denies it. You feel it, you believe it, and you suffer over it.

You are not just a sophisticated barometer of other people's reactions to you. You also get a perceptive reading of *their* emotional states.

"My family calls me the emotion police. I'm always patrolling to make sure they feel O.K. Then it bothers me because they don't pay the same attention to how I feel."

You "feel" for people. Sometimes they appreciate your extraordinary awareness. (Sometimes they hate you for it.)

At work, you'll be the one in staff meeting who is most conscious of the impact of a decision on others. "But won't this mean the front desk women will be stuck in the building on Tuesdays at lunch?" you'll point out, quick to see the flaw in the new message system. "They could bring a brown bag one day a week, or rotate, or work something else out," your boss says dismissively. He is focused on the efficiency of the system being proposed. You are focused on how it will feel—naturally.

Everyone tells you everything, partly because you are intensely in-terested in hearing it. But it's a risk because you are a sponge, literally soaking up everyone's emotional life. An afternoon spent listening to a parade of girlfriends with uncommitted lovers or obnoxious husbands can leave you too limp to live your own life.

Your secret brag: "I'm too emotional."

What you really mean: "I should just be cold, selfish, or controlling like them, instead of being the warm, feeling, loving, caring person I really am. It would serve them right."

The exhaustion you sometimes feel from assuming other people's emotional burdens is not the only cost of your extraordinary access to emotion. Because you are in touch with your every emotional shift, you can take yourself on some very uncomfortable roller-coaster rides. If you are in a rapidly evolving situation like a new love affair or new job, you can rocket from low to high with a phone call, then plummet again after an unfortunate conversation.

Because you feel so strongly, you are also apt to express yourself strongly, or at the very least freely.

"Usually, it goes from my gut right out of my mouth. I wish I could get my brain engaged."

When you feel it, you probably say it. It's hard for you to engage your brain because the feelings are so strong they overwhelm your thinking. You are much more likely to act on impulse. Sometimes this makes you disarmingly and charmingly honest. "I have to tell you I think you're the smartest supervisor I've ever had," you blurt with complete sincerity.

At other times your impulsive speech is a chore and a bother. Every time your boss gives you an assignment, she has to hear how you feel about it, both positively and negatively. Frankly, she doesn't care how you feel about it. She just wants you to get the job done.

When you're angry and/or upset, you'll not only say it, you'll show it. You are likely to:

- Cry, if you are female. Hit a wall and hurt yourself, if you are male.

- Storm, leave, threaten, say something outrageous.

- Wake someone in the middle of the night because you have to tell him how you feel.

When you feel strongly, you tend to speak very rapidly, very loudly, and very passionately. You communicate your feelings clearly, but you have difficulty waiting for the best moment to be received. And once you get going, you need to go on a long time before you are satisfied and ready to stop. From your viewpoint, urgent feelings require instant and complete expression, whether they are yours or someone else's. You'd be happy to get up in the middle of the night if *he* needed to talk.

You Hate to Admit It, But You Catastrophize

Your great capacity to feel and to express those feelings becomes a problem because it becomes a part of your dramatic baggage. You make an event more dramatic, bigger, more negative, more threatening than it has to be. In other words, you catastrophize.

When you entertain a new lover and his friends, you aren't just giving a dinner party. You are being tested as marriage material by the last man on earth in an area where you are sure to fail because his friends obviously hate you.

You aren't just staying late at work. You are locked in a vacant building long after dark, toiling for a miserable despot of a boss who would be home herself but for the fact that her husband is having an affair and she has to make everyone suffer.

The effects of your catastrophizing are costliest to you. Friends and family soon learn that when you say you are having a heart attack, that probably means heartburn, and when you say you're going to be fired, it means your boss spoke sharply today about your lateness. But you don't always make this translation yourself. Often you believe that things are as bad as you say they are. Then you feel even worse.

"My husband and I gave a dinner party last night and Cindy came. It's not that she isn't fun—she is. She tells a great story. Her energy is enormous. But we wouldn't want to see her today. We were over-Cindied."

Your dramatic flair is so natural that you lose sight of its impact on other, more sedate folk. The more retiring of your friends feel unable to compete, and the more rigid wouldn't deign to. You tend to bombard people. Your own dramas are so colorful that friends and family can feel they are reduced to audience and only you are on center stage. (It's not your fault they feel this way. The truth is, you'd be happy to hear their dramas and doings. Some people just don't seem to have any.) Sometimes others find it tiring simply to be in the same room with all that emotion. It's difficult for you to be empathetic to their sensitivities, because you're *always* in the room with all that emotion.

Other people who are emotionally expressive like you—warm and intense—aren't usually overwhelmed by your outpourings. Instead, they receive them as a signal that their own would be welcomed when their turn comes, as indeed they would be.

Still, the overall force of your reactions often unnerves other people. You are all too well aware of the problem, because you are used to people complaining: "Why do you always make such a big deal out of everything?" "I don't tell you things, because I know you'll get hysterical." Or worst of all, "I think you're crazy."

"We think by feeling. What is there to know?"
    —e. e. cummings

Feelings form the basis for much of your thinking. The information you draw from a situation tends to be highly impressionistic and subjective ("Tell me about the movie." "It was fantastic. I cried right through it"). You won't get much detail, though you won't miss the essence.

Areas of pure information, without emotional content, tend to be of little interest to you. You are not likely to be well informed on politics, world affairs, or advances in technology and science. You are far more apt to be drawn to art, culture, and the continual human drama of who-did-what-said-what-bought-what-with-whom.

Your decisions are based on gut emotion as well. You are guided by what "feels right" or "feels comfortable" to you, even if you can't precisely articulate the cause of these feelings. Your choices might be motivated by a desire for a thrill as much as anything else. This can be a problem for you if your partner chooses according to "logic." You want the sexy car; your mate wants the car with great gas mileage and air bags. Or your mate wants the house in the best location, with the best dollar value, while you argue for another house because it "feels like home."

Relationships Are the Center of Your Life

Your emotional gifts enable you to connect with other people. Your warmth magnetizes colder, tighter people. You lavish them with attention, nudging or crashing through their psychological barriers. You home in on someone else's heartstrings and automatically pluck the cords. You make people feel things.

You are at your best in social situations. Though inwardly you might think of yourself as shy, it doesn't show. (You tell your friends that you are actually quite timid. They laugh at you.) In a party of strangers, if you are in your customary, outgoing mood, you can create instant rapport. "How do you do—I'm Myrna," you assert with great warmth, reaching across the table to send a smile and a handshake. Five minutes later, the whole group is chuckling together. You made that happen.

When you enter a room, the group invariably stops itself and shifts course, addressing you, incorporating your presence. You are so accustomed to your entrance having impact that you may be completely unaware that you are interrupting. Instead, a group that does not change course may hurt your feelings unintentionally. "How come they ignored me?" you wonder. Or, "Obviously Max is mad at me," you'll think. It will be difficult to persuade you that these interpretations are only your projections. After all, you felt ignored. Something must have happened.

You hate to miss a social opportunity, think nothing of stopping at more than one party in a night rather than turn down an invitation. You might agree to be three places at once, keeping your options open until the last minute. More often than you admit to yourself, you're a no-show. You break plans, arrive late, or keep your social commitments irritatingly tentative.

You don't consciously intend to be rude. It's just that you are impulsive. If you run into someone who interests you, it's impossible to tear yourself away just because your sister expects you for dinner. You could never comfortably confine yourself to one invitation, one plan. It's unrealistic for you because *what if something better comes along?*

Because you do whatever is most interesting at the moment, inevitably you disappoint people. Because you like to keep your social options open, you leave people hanging. And because you respond to immediate suggestions, long-term plans are easily disrupted.

If your phone rings as you are walking out the door, you have to turn back and answer it. Even if it means you'll be late, you feel you have no choice—what if it's important? Besides, you love the feeling that somebody wants you.

If a friend invites you to dinner, you say, "Maybe, we'll see, call me later." You don't want to say no—you might be free. You don't want to say yes. After all, there are several people, several possibilities you haven't checked out yet. "Maybe" seems like a fair enough response. (Actually, it took you a long time to learn to say "maybe." You used to say "yes," and then change your mind.)

You don't always agree with people who see you as "unreliable." Aren't you the first one to call if a friend is sick? Don't you always send a nice note after a party or a present? Besides, you figure people who are always where they said they'd be, pretty much when they said they'd be there, might be so reliable because they don't have much going on in their lives.

People feel they've known you forever. You have a wide circle of friends, many of whom know the intimate details of your life. These friends are crucial to you as a support network. They are to you what the computer is to the person who needs to be right—the necessary adjunct without which life would be too overwhelming.

A select group of friends or family form a board of directors whose consultation is required for the proper running of your life. You would not seriously consider a major life move—or maybe even a minor one—without running it by the board. Is this the time to make it a sexual relationship? Should I volunteer for the project, or will my supervisor think it's pushy? Should I start nighttime toilet training or let it go for a while? You frequently disagree with the board's rec-ommendations arguing, "Yes, but . . ." to any advice that wasn't what you were hoping to hear. But you will still put in the effort to get them to endorse your choices. The review process itself makes you feel comforted and cared for.

You might have chosen your board members from the friends whom you most idealize or respect. These people are significantly more in-dependent and autonomous than you, and the advice giving is a one-way street with you at the receiving end. Often, however, your friends create drama too. Then you serve on their boards, happily provid-ing the same inexhaustible audience, advice, and opinions that they provide to you. You derive pleasure, and comfort, from these friend-ships. Many of your experiences can only be fully appreciated in the retelling.

You may seek guidance from friends, but they are still friends and therefore relative equals. Once someone is identified as an "authority," you are unconsciously apt to assume a different posture.

You are willing to be cute or boyish, vivacious and engaging, sexy, sweet, or whatever else is called for. In exchange, you have an unspoken pact with the authority figures of the world to notice you enough and be delighted with you enough to take special care of you.

You flirt a bit with your boss and he overlooks your extra-long lunches. You compliment a supervisor, who can't help but soften your annual review, even though you slipped up on that one conference. You have a way of creating a ripple of excitement in the boring slog of office routine. You push the limits, just to see what you can get away with. This behavior might hark back to the days when you were the naughty little minx or cute little scamp who pushed Dad or Mom to the limit and then charmed your way back into his or her good graces.

When you run into an authority who isn't buying the deal, you feel anxious and angry. This is most likely to occur when you have a same-sex boss. You can't flirt under those circumstances, and your boss may not be interested in being in a naughty-girl or -boy/-forgiving parent relationship. She may only be interested in competent work. You'll be unnerved by her demands, think of her as a bitch, wonder if she's harsh with you because she's jealous. An authority figure, male or female, who doesn't want an important emotional connection with you presents a problem. You want to be close. Your boss may want only performance—instant insecurity for you.

You enjoy most relationships with authority because you can simultaneously get a rise out of them and feel taken care of. In fact, you'll make other people into authorities whether they are or not. You often don't wear a watch, but you'll frequently ask what time it is. Sometimes you'll ask even when you're wearing one yourself.

Variation on the theme: You might create drama through rebellion.

You'll skip the winning dependency dance entirely and get your inner rush from flouting the rules. You'll be a lot angrier than the other person just described and a lot less popular. But you'll get all the attention you are craving.

▪

Family and friends and authority figures are very, very important to you. But their importance pales beside the emphasis you place on your romantic relationships.

"It's kind of like I don't have a self-concept when I'm not in a relationship. When there's a man in my life, a spotlight goes on and I'm tap-dancing like crazy. I'm funny and exciting and interesting and full of great plans. But when it's over, the light goes off and I burrow into myself. I stop exercising. I stop trying to look good. I stop reading the paper. I lose a grip on my life."

Your Belief Baggage: "If you loved me, you'd . . ."

Your belief baggage reflects the amount of reassurance and attention you require to feel satisfied and happy in a romance. (Your beliefs center around romance because this is your most important relationship.) This need is expressed in a list of rules you have for how a lover should or would act. You may subscribe to some or all of the examples of dramatic belief baggage listed below.

"If you really loved me . . ."

- You wouldn't walk out of the room when I'm talking.

- You would let me have my way ("If he wants to rent a samurai movie and I want *Gone with the Wind* and he wins . . . I feel like he doesn't love me").

- You would know what I wanted for my birthday. You wouldn't have to ask.

- You would take my side against the kids.

- You'd deal with my family for me.

- You'd deal with your family for me.

- You'd let me stay in bed, or you'd come to bed, or you'd get out of bed.

▪ You would worry about me. (You wouldn't let me drive at night, you'd make me stay home from work when I'm sick, tell me to slow down, I'm doing too much, I could wear myself out, and so on.)

▪ You would spend money on me!

▪ You would talk to me, say "I love you," compliment me, say nice things.

▪ You would spoil me.

▪ You would be jealous.

Your appetite for fantasy, fairy tale, and romance has helped you to create a detailed template of the proper hero or heroine. Where your current partner doesn't match, you are outraged. S/He broke the rules!

Your ideal gift: A surprise public demonstration of how much you are loved.

In the middle of the Thursday lunch conference, a staff of waiters wheels in a gourmet meal your lover sent over. In the middle of the soufflé a note is tucked: "I don't want you hungry for anything but me."

In fact, any surprise planned for you, about you, featuring you as the recipient of applause or attention seems like a great way to spend an evening. You dream that a skywriter will spell out your marriage proposal. You'd love to be handed a kitten wearing an emerald bracelet at the New Year's Eve party.

Your best fantasy: Someone wealthy and wonderful-looking is leaning over you saying, "Don't worry, darling. I'm going to take care of everything."

Your worst fear: Being alone.

On a more somber note, your need for stimulation might partly be a consequence of the uncomfortable feelings you experience when you are alone. You tend to overbook yourself, to schedule every minute in order to avoid your empty apartment or your empty marriage. You may drive yourself to physical or emotional exhaustion, but you can't allow yourself the necessary down time for refueling and reflection. To sit home makes you too anxious. You mean to think things over, to reflect on your goals, but you procrastinate.

It may be that the fear of being alone does not affect you on a day-to-day basis. Perhaps you can pass an evening in solo contentment—as long as you have a lover stashed somewhere. Some of us go from relationship to relationship as if with hands reaching out to steady ourselves on life's balance beam.

Your Marriage

Of all the relationships central to your life and sense of self, your marriage is the most significant. You focus a great deal of energy and emphasis on this marriage. You may well have been envisioning your mate since childhood, though you have adjusted the details with maturity. Sometimes you do marriage over and over, trying to get it right.

Often when you choose a mate, you tend to marry someone who will do your thinking for you (the person who needs to be right and/or feels superior, for example). You hope to marry the strong, solid, materially successful partner who will be able to take care of you, both financially and/or intellectually. Having attached yourself to him because he can care for you materially, you then battle with him endlessly because he doesn't take proper care of you emotionally. He's cold, he won't talk to you, and he tries to control everything you do. ("He even orders for me in a restaurant. If I don't feel like the lamb chops, he's annoyed because he knows it's the best thing on the menu.")

If your need for drama is strong, your marriage could be a theatrical event, full of scenes and crises. You will go to great lengths to get a rise out of the stoic you married. You are ripping up the wedding pictures and flinging shattered glass. He has retreated to the den, where he calls a mutual friend, reporting that you are crazy again, that you've had a tantrum out of nowhere, that he has not, to the very best of his knowledge, done anything to precipitate it. "I think she's emotionally disturbed," he is commenting with great seriousness. You are sitting in a heap of broken glass unable to get him to listen to you.

You know why you lost your temper. It was because he announced plans for a summer vacation without even consulting you. And when you tried to rearrange the vacation more to your liking ("Honey, how about three days camping and three days in a hotel?"), he shut down. "The hell with it," he said. "I wouldn't enjoy a vacation with you anyway. Nothing pleases you." Then he quite calmly turned on the TV and tuned you out. That's when you started ripping up the pictures.

Eventually, when you are calmer and he is less frozen, you two try to talk. "Peter, you try to control everything I do. You decide what I wear, when we go, when we eat, where we live. The vacation was the last straw." He replies in great frustration. "I didn't decide. Our budget decided for us. You can't accept those financial realities. All you can do is complain about them."

She complains: "He won't listen to me. He has an answer for everything. It all has to be his way."

He complains: "She won't listen to me. She takes everything so personally. When I try to talk to her, she curls up in a little ball and cries. I end up standing over her and lecturing."

If you are a man who creates drama, you might make exactly the same kind of marriage as your female counterpart—to the solid, strong woman who will anchor you, with whom you struggle because she tries to control everything you do.

On the other hand, you might marry the quiet, self-effacing partner who is charmed and excited by your drama. You'll be irritated because she's so boring. Or, male or female, you might marry partners more like yourselves, exciting figures whose styles are very attractive to you. If you do pair off with an attention getter like yourself, you might be able to put together an intensely stimulating life. You will appreciate this person's charm and adventurousness. It will make you feel special. Still, when you are feeling special, you do not necessarily feel secure. If your partner has problems with commitment and responsibility, you will be flooded with anxiety. Who will keep the bogeyman away? You may be jealous of the effect his flair has on others even as you revel in its effect on you. If your partner has great flair, which of you will get the attention? You are both likely to compete for the goodies and resist the chores.

Sexually: You could be a very responsive man or woman.

If so, you are apt to enjoy great sexual variety. You want to try every position you ever heard of, and you'd love it if someone suggested one that hadn't crossed your mind yet. You enjoy variety in your sexual partners, too, though you *try* to inhibit your impulses according to your relationship status. (You are not always successful.)

If, however, you have a sexual problem, it is most likely to be an inhibition of your ability to have an orgasm. Your sexuality can get tied to the cute-little-girl identity to which you cling. That little girl loves to be kissed and cuddled, but she might be uncomfortable being fully sexually developed.

Vanishing romance, a side effect of the stable marriage, is a source of great pain for you. So much of your fantasy life has revolved around love, conquest, excitement, and sexuality. Now you've committed to the guy, or you got the girl, and the whole reason for wanting them in the first place seems to have disappeared.

"You've changed!" is your great marital accusation. "You take me for granted." "You aren't nice anymore."

So the fights begin. Some, as we described earlier, are caused by your partner's need to be right and your own refusal to have your desires canceled out by "logic." And some are sad substitutes for passion. Where once we connected in a frenzy of desire, today we connect in a storm of rage. It's not an improvement, but it beats talking to each other only during the commercials.

Some fights may be about monogamy. On the one hand, you need a faithful mate. A relationship for you is a matter of dependency and security. You cannot feel safely dependent on a partner who is sexually fickle. Period.

Yet, as deeply as you need your partner's fidelity, you might find your own sexual faithfulness a chore. You don't necessarily need to be sexually active with other partners. But you *do* need the fantasy. You need to flirt, and you thrive on the attention, appreciation, and excitement such flirtation stirs. You like to go to a party, look your best, and stir a little ripple of sexual arousal in those around you, as well as in yourself.

This might pose no threat at all to your mate. You might be attached to one of those treasures whose self-confidence is relatively imperturbable. He or she might watch you flirt and enjoy the performance, perfectly secure in the strength of your bond together. It might even be a source of sexual excitement. Look how many people want you. Look who has you. Let's go home and enjoy it. He might even play the game himself, flirting and glancing sideways to see if you notice.

Your mate *might* experience your flirtatiousness in this benign light, but he or she might not. Some of a partner's reaction depends on how far you take it. Anyone can be jealous if sufficiently provoked. (Sometimes you overdo, necking on the dance floor with a friend of his, and disappearing from a party, just to keep an exciting edge on things. It's drama very much at the expense of stability.)

But some of your partner's reactions depend solely on him, on his or her degree of security, need to control, to be possessive, to be special. To the degree that your partner is upset by the fact that you crave the attention of others, you will have a second front in your marital struggles.

$! $! $! $!

Your most likely professions: performing artist, teacher, wife of . . . ; salesperson—for women, especially sales of clothes, beauty products, and other items where you can act as a personal display case; for men, the choice of product is wider.

The power of your emotional life, combined with your intuitiveness and spontaneity, makes you a more creative person than most. You might be one of the fortunate few who are able to earn money through their creativity—an artist. Your work is one of your prime sources of excitement and attention.

But few of us are artists. Most of us work at jobs that are not vehicles for our creativity or emotional expression. If you are in this large group, then earning money (though necessary) is probably not one of your prime sources of passion.

Work does not interest you nearly as much as love, though some of your greatest successes are at the office (or were, before you quit for the sake of love). The difference in your styles of functioning in these two arenas may be striking. People are always wondering how someone "as smart as you" could choose your lovers so poorly. How could such a savvy real estate agent negotiate such a bad deal for herself in marriage? How could such a talented filmmaker let himself get taken by one calculating wife after another? The answer is that in your work life, you give greater credence to your judgment and your critical sensibilities.

Contrary to the dizzy, excitable social impression you may make, you are quite capable of sound judgment. It's just that you are so frequently swamped by emotion that it clouds your ability to be guided by that judgment. When you "think by feeling," problems that evoke strong emotion make more logical thinking difficult. But work problems do not necessarily evoke strong emotion. Then you can use your other strengths to great advantage. For example, your warmth, interpersonal ease, and keen intuition can make you a terrific salesperson. You can cut a brilliant real estate deal in the morning and still go home that night to sob over a married lover from whom you can't separate. In the morning, you relied on your judgment, your capacity to "read" a buyer, to play a seller, to make people trust you and talk to you. It worked for you. At night, that judgment is swamped by passion, by the emotional power of your attachments, and by the dramas you create.

If the way you earn your money does not especially excite you, managing that money is even less interesting to you. You don't balance your checkbook, because, after all, who is more likely to make a mistake—the bank or you? You figure it's their job to keep track.

Likewise, someone else probably decides on and monitors your investments. (You probably don't follow the stock market unless you are interested in developing a relationship with someone who does.) Somebody else organizes your taxes.

Whether you are a salesclerk whose greatest financial reward is in the discount he gets, or a real estate tycoon in a hot market who is earning more than she ever imagined, one fact still holds: your satisfaction does not come primarily from earning the money.

That is not to say that you don't enjoy the money or the things money buys. It's just that earning the money is not your primary motivator. For you, money is a reflection of how loved and valued you are. The thrill is in the attention you get because of your work. Money is the by-product.

Here is where the traditional female job "wife of . . ." fits for you. Earning money is usually a bore and a chore. But having someone else earn the money and spend it on you can be a heartstopper. It's a thrill because of the excitement of what it buys, and it's a thrill because of the love and attention it represents.

So you tend to use all your flair, style, warmth, and sexuality to hook up with someone who will handle the deadly responsibility of earning a living for you. Oh, you might work, of course. No amount of affect can get you past the economic harshness of our times. But you work to "help out." You work to provide yourself and your family with "extras." Isn't that your role in life, after all—providing the icing, the dramatic delight? This drama is played out financially in one woman's marriage after another, despite the fact that it frequently results in disaster.

Whether you think financial dependence is a good deal, an enviable luxury, or a prison, one problem remains: quite often, the deal falls through. If the marriage dissolves, or a mate dies, then the dependent partner ends up in financial and emotional trouble at the same time. She is *not,* as she had enjoyed feeling, a financially secure woman. She's just a woman who was married to a financially secure man, or at least a man with the skills to build up his financial security again.

At this moment, the woman who craves drama is hit with every mundane maintenance assault she's been protected from her whole life. What should she do about insurance, investments, the rear brakes? The catastrophe of having been financially dependent and then having that prop suddenly and irrevocably removed is one from which many fail to recover.

Earning and managing money are not your particular financial focus. But spending it could be one of your real joys.

People with dramatic baggage love to shop. It's a voyage to the fantasy land of who you might be and how you might look. Shopping, spending are not solely a self-interested process. You can be generous, even extravagant in your purchases for others. You want everyone you love to have wonderful things and you feel terrific buying them. You love to give great gifts and you'll put the time and energy into finding a perfect expression of sentiment for an occasion.

If you have plenty of money, your spending will be a source of pleasure for you and for everyone lucky enough to be on the receiving end of your generosity. If your resources are limited, you could have some serious financial problems. You may incur huge debt and high interest obligations because it's hard for you to balance the impulsive satisfactions of the moment with the dreary reality of your financial limitations.

More seriously, you might shoplift or gamble. Both of these create an intense excitement, and both are signs that your need to create drama is out of control. You may have thus far been spared the shocking humiliation of arrest, or the sharp awakening of a gambling debt. But you know your secret. If this is you, get help to get back on track.

THE INNER PORTRAIT

What could make an emotional rush so important? Why would you chance getting fired just for the thrill of sneaking out early? Why does a difficult lover exhilarate you more than an equally passionate but available one? Why do you go to such lengths to create a drama, especially when some of those dramas are so unpleasant?

The first hint of the answer is in your theme song.

Your Theme Song: "I Feel."

You have an ongoing unconscious assessment of life, always organized around one point: "I feel." Feelings are both your source of information and your "reason" for reacting to information, for handling it one way as opposed to another. You trust these feelings and believe in them. "I don't know why, but that's just how I feel" is basis enough for you.

Feelings are your driver. You don't "control" your feelings. You don't believe they *can* be controlled. Instead, you are controlled by them. They steer you. They tell you what's good, right, imperative, intolerable.

Your bottom line is this: If you don't feel, you don't know where you are. You don't know what to do. In a way, you don't know who you are. But—it's not a problem. You always know how you feel.

You always know how you feel because you're always checking in with yourself. You're always taking your emotional temperature and guiding yourself according to how it reads.

You always know how you feel because you feel things more intensely than other people. Emotionally, you are like a car with a high idle. Stopped at a light, that car continues to rev although you aren't giving it any gas. Sometimes you have to stand on the brake in order to keep it under control. When your own idle runs high, more emotional gas floods your system. (This is probably a basic biologically determined part of you, though no one knows yet exactly how it works.) You have more juice available to you—more juice for you to enjoy and more juice for you to cope with.

And finally, you always know how you feel because you go out of your way to create a situation that will evoke a feeling. In other words, if you have no other way to evoke feeling, you will create drama.

Remember this: A part of you is always oriented to feeling—to feeling more, to wanting to feel, to wondering how you feel—until your feelings are so loud, so strong, that you don't have to wonder anymore. When that capacity for feeling serves you, it makes life the kind of joy for you it could never be for the rest of us. But when you live to serve the emotion, it leads you into chaos. Whether it works positively or negatively, your theme song has one main effect: It connects you with people.

Your Ruling Passion: Attachment

What are you trying to *get* with all this emotion? What drives your expressiveness, other than the sheer, overwhelming force of the feelings themselves?

You are trying to connect. The dominant need around which your personality is organized is your fierce desire for attachment. Attachment comes in a hundred and one flavors, but at the heart of each of them is the same theme: To you, attachment means intense emotional connection to people. Attachment is your ruling passion.

On a minute-to-minute basis, you unconsciously attempt to connect with the people around you by commanding their interest. There is no such thing in your book as *too much attention*. It's like too much air to breathe. Your color, your warmth and physical appeal, and your energy are all successful beacons for the attention of others. When someone is looking at you, smiling at you, sympathizing with you, appreciating you, you are rewarded with a strong emotion. Your reading in the "I feel" meter is excellent, because you've made contact.

On a deeper level, your desire for attachment is reflected by the central role of relationships in your life. For example, you are not just looking to get married. You are looking for an emotionally charged marriage, one where you can feel the love, the concern, the sexuality. This relationship, its ongoing development, and your disappointments and delights within it could become your life's work.

Your passion for attachment is so powerful that endings—even trivial endings, even longed-for endings—are awful for you. You suffer acute separation pain. You'll miss the characters in a good book for several hours after you've finished it. If your favorite TV show is preempted, you feel stood up. To leave friends or family, if only temporarily, is a wrench. And to break up a relationship permanently, even an unhappy relationship, may feel unbearable.

It may be that when something bad has happened, it's hard for you to let that go too. A lover rejects you and you find yourself rereading his old letters, though it hurts you. A colleague embarrasses you and you play the scene over and over in your mind. When an event stirs an intensely negative feeling, you might still cling to it. You'd rather feel something—even a negative something—than nothing at all. And you'd automatically stay attached rather than separate and move on.

You can see by these examples that your passion for attachment and the emotional focus of your theme song feed on each other:

On the one hand, deep attachment is your anchor, your "still point of the turning world." The more deeply attached you are, the more emotional you can afford to be. You can ride the tides of your inner life, secure in the sense that stable bonds ground you and solid people watch over you.

Attachment makes your emotional intensity easier to handle because you always have someone there to help you sort through the feelings. Connect with someone—friend, lover, the stranger on the bus with whom you were able to establish an instant rapport—and you can present your feelings on any given issue. The other person can then help you analyze those feelings, help you plan a course of action, suggest alternatives you may have overlooked because strong feelings can easily drown out options. Furthermore, the attention can make you feel better. This attentive person can listen, he can sympathize. He can "understand how you feel." Attachment soothes your stormy inner state because it makes you feel loved, or important, or powerful, or best of all, all three.

So your passion for intense interpersonal contact serves as a guide, an emotional stabilizer. Paradoxically, your passion for attachment can create arousing experiences, too. For you, that's a second payoff. Work might occasionally be exciting. Art might, in a rare instance, move you to tears. But for a regular hit of emotional juice, nothing is as reliable as an important relationship. You are most yourself feeling love, affection, and sexual longing. You will turn to a relationship to deliver these inner jolts over and over. So attachment can anchor you *and* it can excite you. No wonder you have a passion for it.

Finally, to complete the circle, your emotional range makes it far more likely that you'll attach to people. You are an emotional heat-seeking missile aimed at the hearts of those around you. We connect to you because you show us how, you make it easy, you take the first step. You need to attach, and your warmth and enthusiasm is the bait. It's a powerful lure.

The passion for attachment is the source of your strength and your contributions. It is also, of course, the source of your baggage.

WHAT'S THE BAGGAGE?
YOUR NEED TO CREATE DRAMA

I worry that the idea of having baggage might make you feel bad. After all, you feel things so acutely that you are apt to suffer unnecessarily over a portrait of your liabilities.

You'll feel best while you are reading this if you keep the big picture of *Excess Baggage* firmly in mind: Every one of us has baggage. It's our ruling passion run out of control.

If you could see how your need to attach goes out of bounds, how it stops working for you and starts getting in your way, you could rein it in. Yes, that takes a certain amount of effort, concentration, and maybe even a momentarily painful self-awareness. But the benefit is huge. For you, the reward is not that you'll feel less but that you'll feel better—happier, more relaxed, clearer, more confident—than you have before. You won't need to give up any of your enthusiasm for life. But you will free yourself from much of the troubling chaos and confusion your enthusiasms bring in their wake.

Some might say that your entire personality is dramatic, and in a way, that's true. Your presentation of self, from your speech to your style of dress, is certainly more "dramatic" than most, and your inner life hits more of the high (and low) notes as well. But none of this is necessarily dramatic baggage.

Your baggage, in a nutshell, is this: Sometimes you go beyond warmth and energy in your desire to attach. Sometimes you go all the way to the point of creating a drama in order to make contact.

Dramatic baggage means that you might unconsciously create conflict, crisis, or helplessness as a way to attract attention and make an emotional connection. You create risky or dramatic situations because:

a. You want to keep your inner emotional tide high. It is your most familiar, most comfortable inner state, so you automatically seek to reestablish it, and/or:

b. Your emotional flood is so automatic and so powerful that you are drawn to dramatic situations in order to discharge some of your emotional buildup. You turn to situations where you can scream or cry or pace or laugh and so relieve some of your inner storm.

If life becomes too stable, too mundane, too predictable to stir much feeling, you will create the stimulation, staging dramatic family battles, choosing impossible partners, risking your job, flouting the social rules, just to get a rise out of yourself.

THE STRENGTH: You Can Make Day-to-Day Life
a Compelling Experience.
BUT
THE BAGGAGE: Sometimes You Create This Sparkle
at Your Own Expense.

Ho hum, my mate, my job. For most of us, these two essential elements of life are, well, real life: sometimes stirring, sometimes dull, sometimes disappointing, sometimes surprisingly sweet. Always very important, but certainly not always thrilling, at least not after the first few months.

But your dramatic baggage might mean that you must get a thrill. And in order to get one, you can develop some difficult patterns:

The Drama of the Deadline

You've discovered a magically efficient way to add excitement to your daily work life. Just don't leave yourself enough time in which to do it. If you leave everything to the last possible minute, you can make even the most humdrum report a source of emotional theater.

You can create a pressured, even frenzied situation in a very stable work environment simply by not doing the work until very shortly before you will get in trouble if you don't. Then you will need to disrupt your family life so that someone can fill in for you while you do your work. This will add a little steam to these normally routine relationships. Your spouse might be moved to yell or point out your deficiencies. Your friend might be drafted to devote time as typist or proofreader, thereby proving her devotion. Your sister could be provoked to jealousy because, once again, the family stops everything to help you with a crisis. You will get to stay up later than usual or wake up earlier or drink more coffee. All this will induce a body state more consistent with, say, a foreign correspondent than with a graduate student.

The problem is that while the deadline drama does serve as a relief from the drudgery of day-to-day compliance with obligation, you don't do your best work under these circumstances. Oh, I know you've convinced yourself that you do. You believe, "I can only work when the pressure is on," or, "I do my best thinking at the last minute." But reality disputes this. You may only be willing to work under pressure. But quality work requires reflection, organization, review, and revision. All of this is, by definition, a lot less likely when there's a lot less time.

Not only is the quality of your work limited by deadline drama but the quantity and level of responsibility of your work are severely handicapped. If you can work only in spurts, when time exerts immediate pressure, you can produce only a limited amount. And that work must be directed by someone else. The deadline drama is most often played out with a deadline imposed by external authority. It's very difficult to work up the same sense of pressure from a self-imposed time limit. If you need the threat of punishment or disapproval by a boss to motivate you, you'll always seek the subordinate position, long after you are competent to be a boss yourself.

The Drama of a Broken Heart

"I've let this relationship take over my life. I'm totally wrapped up in it. I don't think of anything else. I get a sexual rush just hearing his voice. You might say I'm obsessed."

Your need to create drama can be satisfied through a series of rocky, misery-inducing, but undeniably dramatic romantic episodes—either with a series of partners or in one long-term love affair.

"Obsessed" and "addicted" are two fashionable and not inaccurate ways of describing the intensity of these romances. You are the woman with the long-distance passion against whom none of the local boys can compete. You are the man deeply in love with a woman who embodies your sexual ideal, though she is available today, uncertain tomorrow, and always a bit disparaging of your worth. Your lovers are terminally married men or bitchy, difficult women. You are aroused most easily by Don Juan womanizers or cold, pure madonnas who are available only as objects of unrequited adoration.

You suffer deeply in these affairs because the relationship never becomes secure. You sometimes rationalize that you'll bring yourself to end it "when the pain outweighs the pleasure." But the truth is, you stopped keeping track long ago.

The "pleasure" is in the intense emotion these affairs arouse. They cycle around the agony of rejection and the exquisite relief of reconciliation, cemented by the exalting glue of sexual passion. A solid, serene, contented love (the kind where you amaze yourself with the amount of work you can get done, as opposed to the kind where you can hardly eat, much less work) does not sustain passion as long or as deeply as a dramatically uncertain love affair. This is one of the great trade-offs of adulthood with which you have yet to come to terms.

Not everyone with dramatic baggage is equally vulnerable to creating drama through the misery of an uncertain love affair. If your family was abusive, alcoholic, or erratic, if your early emotional life was colored by the bitter push/pull of divorce, by deep loss or enormous conflict, you are at greater risk of re-creating this emotional climate as an adult. After all—however noxious, in a sense it is home.

The highest cost for these exhilarating love affairs is the price you pay in self-esteem. Your pride and judgment erode. You tolerate lies, refusing to confront deception for fear of alienating your elusive partner. You endure days of uncertain waiting, punctuated by bursts of brief, exalting reassurance. But the reassurance is never enough, the dread is all-consuming.

You suffer the daily drip of rejection, the steady erosion of self-worth. In the end, your dramatic baggage pushes you to trade yourself for sparkle. That you could call the pain "love" is proof that you have a blind spot.

THE STRENGTH: You Are Both Perceptive and Intuitive.
BUT
THE BAGGAGE: You Overreact to the Information
You Sense.

Dramatic baggage turns up the volume on all your fears and anxieties. When you think by feeling, you have no particular check for accuracy.

If you feel it, it's so. That's a serious problem because in fact, sometimes it's so and sometimes it's not and you don't get much practice telling the difference.

For example: Your boyfriend is watching a movie intently. Usually you hold hands, but tonight he's focused totally on the screen. You feel ignored. You begin to get anxious. "Why is he ignoring me?" You try to talk yourself out of the feeling. "Maybe he loves the movie. He's allowed to pay attention to a movie. He doesn't have to hold my hand every minute." But the feeling won't go away. You definitely feel ignored. You get upset, can barely wait until the end of the movie to discuss it with him. Why is he ignoring you? Is something wrong? He is perplexed. What are you talking about? Nothing's wrong.

Now, it is possible that he was ignoring you—just a little, just slightly, just backing off a bit—and he doesn't even want to acknowledge it himself. Naturally, your emotional radar picked up this smidgen of a blip on the screen. You felt ignored, because you were ignored. Unfortunately, you are apt to create a storm over this small lapse of attention. Your dramatic baggage inflated your small disappointment. It turned the momentary loss of his attention into a major emotional assault.

It is equally possible that he wasn't ignoring you. He was just losing himself in a particularly great film. There was no message, intended or otherwise, about you. It wasn't about you at all. (Which, in a way, makes you feel even worse.)

By now your dramatic baggage has amplified your hurt feelings to such a degree that you'll probably have trouble believing him. If your need to create drama is great, this situation will climax in a scene or a fight, which will serve to regain his attention, though in a negative way.

Without a rational check for accuracy to curtail your tendency to drama, your painful interpretations of the world are allowed free rein:

Your boss is short-tempered today and that feels scary. Therefore, he must be mad at you.

You felt stupid playing Trivial Pursuit. Therefore, you must be stupid, and everyone else thinks so too.

You felt criticized when your manager reviewed the project in detail. Therefore, he must have been critical of you.

You felt belittled when your friends teased you about your cooking. Therefore, they intended to demean you.

In each of these examples, your emotional intuitiveness may or may not have picked up a subtle message from someone. Unfortunately, your dramatic baggage makes you (a) assume your interpretation is true, because it feels true to you, and (b) interpret the message as dramatically as possible, increasing your suffering and eventually making the other person suffer too.

As a final note, dramatic baggage does not just amplify the negative messages. It makes you vulnerable to overreacting to small positive signals as well. In general, feeling unrealistic joy is a small problem. But it has its costs too.

For example, you have the capacity to be elated for a week over a postcard from a man you hope to date when he returns. The elation is marvelous, energizing, and sincere. But when you realize he sent postcards to everyone, you are apt to suffer a severe emotional thud.

THE STRENGTH: You Are Joyfully Spontaneous Long After
the Rest of Us Have Frozen in Place.
BUT
THE BAGGAGE: You'll Act on the Spontaneous Impulse
Without Thinking. It Can Land You in Misery.

If you feel like it, you are very apt to do it. And you'll skip the step where you wonder if you should do it or not. In many ways, this impulsiveness is a gift. You can take advantage of the opportunities the rest of us miss because we are too busy weighing the pros and cons. You don't miss out on much.

Yet a lot of what you don't miss out on you might wish you had. When you act dramatically, lavishly, impulsively, you are not acting thoughtfully, deliberately, or, necessarily, wisely. Your impulsiveness may create two kinds of problems for you: you risk venting your inner conflicts instead of resolving them, and you risk self-destructive highs and bitter lows.

When you discharge strong feelings by acting on them instead of thinking about them, psychotherapists call this "acting out." "Acting out" is not conscious; that is, you don't say to yourself, "I feel angry, so I'm going to be late and make her wait." Instead, possibly without even being aware that you are angry, you are "unavoidably" late. The problem is that you act on your anger without acknowledging it, even to yourself. How can you resolve a problem you haven't acknowledged? We all act out some of our feelings, leaking anger, sexual desire, competitiveness, disappointment, in ways we are not at all aware of. But those of us who create drama are vulnerable to serious disruptions of our lives because we act on our impulses instead of evaluating them.

For example, Wendy's husband is glamorous, rich, poised, and very, very busy. Until Wendy got caught shoplifting, they hadn't talked about her life in months.

Greg never wanted his wife to know about his affair. It could only hurt her and their family. He says that when he left the love letters at the bottom of his bureau drawer, he "never expected her to look."

Vicky wasn't aware of any envy when her younger sister became pregnant. After all, her sister is married, Vicky is single and in no position to have a child. When she found herself pregnant six months later, she was devastated by her dilemma.

When you act on feelings, you skip the step of speculating on and being responsible for the consequences of those actions. If the consequences are negative, you are apt to feel victimized. "Why does everything happen to me?" is the heartfelt cry of the person who makes things happen behind her own back.

The second risk of acting spontaneously on your feelings is all too apparent in our culture. What feels good at the moment often has a long-range payoff in misery.

You might be a binger—eating or drinking out of control from time to time (or worse, most of the time). You might spend impulsively, enjoying the high of the moment at the expense of your financial stability. You might give in to a sexual impulse that leaves you guilty, embarrassed, or at worst, diseased. You might discharge feelings in a rush of temper without regard to the long-term consequences in the relationship.

All of these problems of impulse control are the consequences of the dramatic, emotionally driven life choices you've made. And they all deliver long-term suffering right after their short-term high.

Rx: TONE IT DOWN AND THINK IT THROUGH

If you are a person who creates drama, you are probably also a person who creates warmth, creates joy, and creates relationships. The problem is that you also create conflict, catastrophe, and confusion, each of which makes your life harder than it has to be.

You can reduce the impact of your dramatic baggage by learning in small, significant ways how to *tone yourself down and think life through*.

"Tone down" means that you consciously decide to curb the power of your feelings. Essentially, it means that you need to tone down your emotional excesses in order to hear yourself think. The more time you give yourself to think, to judge, to decide, the more opportunity you have to improve these skills.

None of this means a fundamental change in your passion for attachment. Meaningful emotional attachments to people will always be your core motivation. But when you reduce your need to create drama, the kind of relationships you form will be significantly different. Drama makes your attachments stormier and more stressful than they have to be. Your emotional flooding makes your relationships more dependent than they have to be. And your overall frenzy for attachment makes your relationship with yourself—with your own goals, with your spirit, with your identity—less developed than it might be.

When you are consciously controlling your impulse to create drama, you will:

■ Choose more wisely the people to whom you attach. You won't react solely to how you feel about them. You'll also consider what you think about them.

■ Sometimes resist the impulse to attach, leaving room to develop self-reliance and with it, self-esteem.

■ Challenge your own emotionally based interpretations of events.

■ Add a third step to your current two-step process of (1) Feel it, and (2) Do it. The middle step will be: Think about it. Then maybe you'll do it and maybe you won't, but you'll be acting on decisions instead of on urges.

The goal of each of the following exercises is to increase your opportunity to think. The exercises are basic, but they require a surprising amount of energy. Your powerful emotional life is the star you steer by, and your course is set on intense emotional connection. These exercises provide an opportunity to ignore your automatic inner urging and so leave room to develop some other strengths. But the magnetic force of connection is compelling, and resisting it is uncomfortable, even in as simple an exercise as not answering the phone.

It may help you to remember this goal: The best reason to tone yourself down and think life through is that it *feels better*. In the beginning, you will wonder if you will feel anything at all, or anything but the inevitable anxiety that accompanies change. Persevere. Eventually, what feels strange will become comfortable and what feels flat or boring will take on a surprising, subtle flavor of independence and self-respect.

Independence Assignments—Part I

The simplest way to gain control over your passion for attachment is to pick things for which you usually depend on other people, and deliberately do them yourself.

This exercise is based on the idea that you need to create drama in part because you need people to take care of you. Drama, as we said, is one of your survival skills. Of course, this works in reverse too. The more self-reliant you are, the less you'll need to create drama in order to seek attention.

The following is a menu of tasks to facilitate independence and decision making in your life. The more frequently you take the opportunity to cope in a nondramatic, nonhelpless way, the more comfortable you become with this self-image.

You may find yourself well beyond some of these tasks, while other items may be beyond you at the moment. First, mark each item 1, 2 or 3:

1 = I already do this on a regular basis.

2 = I don't do this very often (or maybe not at all) but I would try it.

3 = Who me? *Never.*

There is no score for this test. But you can look at your number of 1s, 2s, and 3s and get a better feel for the level of adult responsibility you've taken on, the amount you'd be willing to take on, and the degree to which you resist taking it on.

Manage your money by:

- balancing your checkbook

- preparing your tax return

- selecting and monitoring an investment

- choosing insurance

- setting up a retirement program

- applying for a bank loan rather than relying on family or friends for help

- setting a financial goal and *writing* your own plan for accomplishing it

- making a major purchase—a car, a house, a coat, a computer —relying solely on your own judgment and research

Manage your career by:

- initiating a meeting with your boss to discuss your future

- asking for a raise

- meeting with senior people in your field to help you create a long-range plan

- taking a refresher course, or improving some specific skill or credential, just because you think it's wise, not because someone told you to

- starting your own business instead of waiting for a partner who would motivate you

Manage yourself by:

- deciding what you want on the menu—order it without consulting a friend

- going clothes shopping alone—don't turn the salespeople into surrogate girlfriends.

- disciplining your child on the spot—don't turn it over to your spouse.

- telling the friend who hurts you what's wrong directly—don't tell a third friend and trust the grapevine to take care of you.

- changing a fuse or flat tire, fixing a toilet, planting a garden, painting a room—doing for yourself any manual job you would ordinarily have someone else do

- doing the driving

Put yourself in charge by:

- planning the party on your own

- volunteering for leadership of a committee, a project, a program

- being well informed on a specific local issue or political event and offering your information and its sources publicly

- discussing the issues of an election before you vote, researching the pros and cons on your own, and voting

- calling, hiring, and coping with a contractor

- planning the trip—making the hotel and travel arrangements, deciding the itinerary (this does *not* mean that you just do the clerical work of carrying out someone else's decisions—you make the decision *and* execute it)

- reading up on any illness you and your family might experience; taking charge of your treatment with your physician in the role of respected consultant

Now that you've rated yourself on each of these items, pick several you've scored "2" and try them on a consistent basis. (You might pick one a week, or you might commit a month or more to a complicated project like researching a disease or a political issue.) If you want to take a real risk, try a "3."

When you accomplish any of these independence assignments, your reward will be twofold. The assignment itself may have been surprisingly interesting. Maybe you thought you were awful at math and the stock market was over your head. Now you've discovered it's just a form of offtrack betting and you have a knack for it. It's always possible that when you put yourself in charge instead of depending on an expert, you'll discover a strength.

But then again, you might not. You might find researching a political issue a tiresome bore and changing a flat even drearier. It doesn't matter. Self-respect and self-reliance come from what you *know* you can do, not from how you *feel* about doing it. Choosing your own clothes may be no fun, but knowing you can have confidence in your taste is a source of strength. It's also a freedom. You no longer need to create a crisis in order to get a friend to come with you.

Independence Assignments—Part II

Drama is created with an audience in mind. One way to curb your dramatic impulses is to cut down the size of your audience, and the frequency with which you consult it. This section includes four exercises to accomplish these goals, including techniques to reduce both the likelihood of your creating an audience and your reliance on the audience you have already created.

1. Make an important decision and don't ask anyone's advice!

That doesn't mean that you must act blindly. You can avail yourself of any source of research or information that will allow you to make an educated decision.

If, for example, you are considering a career decision that involves financial sacrifice or long-term time commitment, you'd be foolish to make this move without investigating income potential, sources of financial aid, program options, and so on. But that is not the same as calling your family and hoping you can get them to decide for you.

Remember, this is very new for you. You will only be able to have this independent experience if you force yourself to avoid the people who usually do your thinking for you. Oh, even without an audience, you'll automatically stir up some drama by initially feeling overwhelmed or miserable. But with no audience for these emotional states, you'll tend to stop paying them so much attention. And you'll move on to information gathering because it's the only way to make yourself feel better. As you gather information, you'll find the fog of confusion and uncertainty begins to lift. Issues fall into place. Choices emerge. When clarity replaces chaos, we don't simply think better. We feel better too.

The payoff for making decisions on your own goes beyond the self-esteem we all enjoy only when we stand by ourselves. A decision you make is a decision to which you can make a commitment. When someone else urges a decision (a friend insists the dress looks great on you, a colleague insists you should talk with the boss directly, your mother feels this is the woman you should marry), we often simply go along for the ride. We agree, but we agree halfheartedly. Or we agree, but we tag on an unspoken "Yes, but . . ." which encompasses all the reservations we don't know how to sort through on our own. We carry out the decision, but balk at the first sign of difficulty. If the dress is expensive, the boss is testy, or the girlfriend is irritating, we find these setbacks hard to overcome. Without wholehearted commitment, most goals are more difficult to achieve. And how can we be wholeheartedly committed to a decision someone else made?

This is a high-risk exercise, but it pays off twice: it makes you feel good about yourself, and makes you more likely to succeed when you want to.

2. Sit on the sidelines.

If you move to a new position in a group, you will experience your social world afresh. It can be a lively, if initially awkward, change of perspective.

Your goal is to move from the center of attention to the sidelines, to become a part of the audience. This is not that difficult to achieve. Force yourself to sit quietly through the next several social gatherings. Resist the temptation to do it with an air of mystery or preoccupation, or your silence will attract as much attention as your more usual enthusiastic chatter. Don't tell even one funny story. Simply let yourself fade from center stage and observe the parties from that perspective. Practice listening. (Remember, silence is not the same as agreement. You don't always have to register your dissenting vote.) You may notice how people look to you to keep them going. You may discover how responsible you feel for entertaining others, or how uncomfortable you are with silence. Or you may be surprised to see that the group flows on without you to stoke its energy level. Perhaps someone emerges to replace you. That might explain some of the subtle tension that has always existed between the two of you.

You might discover that you loathe the sidelines, that it's suffocatingly boring to sit back and listen, to observe instead of to participate. But some people experience an enormous sense of relief when they move out of the spotlight. There is less pressure on the side, less anxiety. It's an option that is scarcely available to the person toting dramatic baggage.

3. Change your relationship with your telephone.

Since the telephone is one of the umbilical cords to your audience, cutting the cord will magically cut down your reliance on an audience. Here are three ways to cut the cord:

▪ Don't answer the phone. You treat a ringing phone like a royal command. It's impossible to ignore the ring, no matter what you are doing (with the *possible* exception of making love). But how can you think through a complicated task if you're interrupted regularly? For the sake of your thinking, buy an answering machine—one on which you can turn down the volume.

▪ Cancel your call-waiting service. You love call-waiting. Your need to know all, be involved everywhere, talk to everyone and generally stir up drama knows no technological bounds. Call-waiting increases the amount of time you spend on the phone, talking about your life, as opposed to the amount of time you spend off the phone, actually living it.

▪ Put a time limit on your calls. The phone is a wonderful opportunity to procrastinate. You have tasks to accomplish and you mean to do them, you really do, and so you mention them to your friend several times during the conversation. Yet the talk goes on and the work, which you were never dying to do in the first place, somehow does not get done.

If you need time to think, to plan, and to produce, you'll deliberately have to limit the time you spend connecting to people—even though it feels good.

4. Increase your solo activities.

One excellent way to cut yourself off from your audience is to increase the number and regularity of activities you engage in without one. Stretch your limits. You may discover you don't need an audience as much as you thought. Regularly schedule a movie, ballet, exhibition by yourself. Spend a weekend out of town alone. Take a class where you don't know anyone. (Don't instantly make friends the way you usually try to do. Make it a purely intellectual experience and concentrate solely on the work.) Go somewhere new and walk. Look at the architecture, the shops, the people. But don't diffuse the experience by sharing your impressions. Just absorb them.

Plan, Plan, Plan

Planning, for both immediate issues and long-term goals, is an excellent counterbalance to the emotional impulsiveness that causes you such pain. In fact, structure is *the* antidote for the more extreme abuses of dramatic baggage. Structure is simple: Write a plan. Follow it. This is the easily stated but exquisitely difficult-to-adopt core of every recovery program. If addiction is part of the drama you've created—whether to drugs, alcohol, food, sex, or gambling—structure is the essential tool you'll need to heal.

If, like most people who create drama, you struggle with goals that require discipline or delay of gratification, structure is your best hope too. When you create drama, it is impulsiveness that frequently gets you into trouble. Structure protects you.

Structure and planning include

- anticipating a problem *before* you are faced with it

- having alternative solutions to that problem in writing

- having the means at hand to execute the solutions

Planning is something you can get better at. It takes practice. Remember, curbing your impulse to act and giving yourself opportunity to think is the medicine for dramatic baggage. Planning is just a specific form of thinking.

The following strategies and techniques help to strengthen your capacity to plan. It is more important to do a small part of one of these techniques over three months than to try all of them for a week. Pick one suggestion, or part of one suggestion, and commit yourself to doing it for some specific period of time. If you succeed, reward yourself by gratifying an impulse—but decide in advance what impulse you could gratify without triggering a binge.

Here are the possibilities for practicing your capacity to plan:

1. Instead of a diary, keep an appointment book. Keep it religiously, every single day, weekends included. You see, a diary, like the one you may have kept in adolescence, or a journal, like the one you may keep on and off in adulthood, celebrates the thoughts and feelings of the life you've lived. But a daily appointment book records the life you plan to live.

2. Schedule several events that you would ordinarily do spontaneously. For example, decide what day you'll do the laundry or go food shopping.

3. Sit down and make a monthly budget. Try it for three months and see what it feels like to plan your spending. Decide exactly how many dollars you can spend "on impulse."

4. Make a weekly appointment with yourself. Respect the time in the same way you would honor an appointment with your doctor or your lawyer. Decide in advance how you'll use the time. A chore? A treat? A time for creativity?

5. Make a food plan, a menu of what you plan to eat in the week ahead. Stick to it.

6. You know those five-year plans you hear other people talk about? Take the time to write your own. There are any number of workbooks to assist you. You may find it fascinating to think ahead about your life before you live it.

Written plans, whether they refer to a To Do Today list, a topic like food or money, or a long-range perspective like a decade, are an antidote to impulsiveness. They also help you focus your enormous energy and enthusiasm. When your emotional idle runs high, you have the fuel to get you where you're going. Planning is what steers your course.

The Challenge

When you feel things intensely, you come to trust your feelings too much. What you need to do is learn to think instead. You need to call into question your emotional responses and evaluate them by various rational standards. Essentially, you need to adopt the following maxim with utter conviction: *"Just because I feel it doesn't make it so."*

It's both simple and very difficult. The problem is that strong feelings *feel* true. And it's very difficult to question what feels absolutely true.

This exercise suggests that each time you interpret an event according to how it made you feel, you *stop*. Then you remind yourself, "Just because I feel it doesn't make it so." Follow that mental reminder with a written list of all the other possible interpretations you might make of the event if you weren't being unduly influenced by your feelings.

For example, you have a telephone conversation with your mom, who asks if you'll be coming for dinner Sunday evening. The question infuriates you. You're angry, and if pressed, you'll explain that you feel angry because she tried to make you feel guilty by bringing up Sunday dinner. How dare she try to manipulate you with guilt! Of course you're angry.

Here's where you stop yourself and repeat—"Just because I feel it doesn't make it so." Just because I'm angry doesn't prove she tried to make me feel guilty. Then you make your written list:

1. Maybe I'm guilty about not going and it's just more convenient to blame her.

2. Maybe she mentioned Sunday because she's secretly hoping I won't come and that makes *her* feel guilty, so she bends over backward to sound welcoming.

3. Maybe she mentioned dinner because she never knows what to say to me, so she burbles.

4. Maybe it was a purely benign inquiry prompted by the need to write a grocery list.

The point of this exercise is not to discover the "truth" about Mom's motivation. It is to help you think about events instead of relying on how that event made you feel.

The process of thinking this through, however, might change your feelings considerably. You might feel better, less angry, because you considered an interpretation you hadn't thought of before. Or you might hold fast to your original conclusion. (After all, she's your mother. You believe you know when she's trying to make you feel guilty.) But the simple process of thinking through the situation helps you to see the other person's point of view.

Here's another example. You lock your keys in your car and you feel stupid and frustrated. *Stop.* Repeat to yourself, "Just because I feel stupid doesn't make it so." Then write down a list of alternative interpretations.

1. Maybe I have too much on my mind and I got distracted.

2. Maybe the mornings are too much of a rush for me and I should get up earlier so I can calm down.

3. Maybe I'm not stupid. Maybe I'm trying to tell myself that I don't want to go to work! Maybe I'm just cleverly letting myself know that I need a vacation and I'd better stop in my tracks and make plans. That is, even if I feel stupid—that doesn't mean I am.

Drama is created out of emotion. When you learn to rely on your emotional reactions less, you are apt to create fewer dramas. And when you create fewer dramas and think things through more, you feel better.

You'll feel better because your life will run more smoothly. You will act less impulsively, having slowed yourself down long enough to consider the consequences. You will suffer less because feelings don't get hurt as easily when you can see things from someone else's point of view. And you'll feel better about yourself because you will have proved that bit by bit, step by step, you can handle life on your own.

Independent assignments are a beginning, planning is a tool, and challenging your own emotional interpretations of life is a major step along the way.

If you create drama, you also generate enthusiasm and excitement. We're lucky to have you in our life, and you are fortunate to have access to an emotional range denied most of us. Your intensity and warmth make life a richer, more vivid experience. You could never lose your love for the colorful in life, or your capacity to create color yourself. You need only tone down your emotional excesses and leave room to develop sounder judgment. When you do, your reward will be fewer wrenching love affairs but more love, fewer exhausting highs and pulverizing lows but more happiness. You will have more responsibility, it's true. But with it, you will have the intoxicating conviction that you can handle it. That is the best feeling of all.

As your sense of self develops, as you are able to set aside your need to create drama, you'll be ready to confront head-on what may be your last piece of baggage. If self-love and self-respect are what feel the best, rage is what feels the worst. If you are holding on to the pain and poison of an old injury, it will stir up an emotional storm that gets in the way of everything else you are trying to accomplish.

Rage is not just a problem for someone with dramatic baggage. Anger is potentially baggage for every one of us, no matter what our personality, no matter what our ruling passion. Every one of us is vulnerable to injury. Sometimes, without realizing it, we let the pain from that injury dictate the rest of our lives. The next chapter tells you what makes you likely to hold on to rage, and how you can start to heal.

Chapter Seven

■

YOU CHERISH RAGE

"Sometimes, I'll blow a hole in the ship, just because someone gets ahead of me in line for captain."

Bile, venom, jealousy, fury—all the toxins of the spirit are the stuff of your day-to-day experience. Why?

Because once wounded, you cannot heal. Because once offended, you cannot forgive. Because once your anger is stirred, it doesn't seem to dissipate. It becomes an extension of yourself, an appendage to your personality, and very weighty excess baggage indeed.

Anger itself is a normal and necessary part of the human experience, a survival signal alerting us to the fact that something is threatening your well-being. It's easy, however, to miss the price you pay for your anger when you view it as healthy and inevitable. Anger is normal, *to a point*. Past that point, it is pure pain, for you and for everyone touched by your churning spirit.

Anger becomes excess baggage when:

■ you are so sensitive, so vulnerable, that you feel constantly offended, or

■ you cannot heal from an old injury and it continues to be a dominant theme in your life.

Most of us who cherish anger are people who had one or, worse, a series of intensely wounding life experiences—a mate who left us, a child who exploited us, a partner who cheated us, a parent who failed us—and the wound never healed. Without our realizing it, the bellow of rage from these wounds remains a powerful force in our present.

That rage is different from day-to-day anger. Anger is a response to an immediate and specific event. Rage is a feeling that lives at your core, a hardening of overall hostility into one laser focus. The frustrations of daily life might make any of us angry frequently. That does not have to mean that you will cherish rage after these experiences. You might be one of those people who get angry, let it fly, and smile benignly at a person you hated two minutes ago. Whatever problems this may cause, the burden of harbored rage isn't one of them.

The baggage of rage is a little bit different from the other categories of baggage discussed so far. Like each of the others, rage is *most likely* to be present in a particular personality type. But unlike the others, rage might be a burden to anyone if he or she is sufficiently wounded. Your other baggage makes you especially susceptible. Specifically:

If you need to be right, it's hard to let go of a past injustice, because forgiving a wrong feels like being wrong yourself. You are a black-and-white thinker. If you were wronged—you are angry. If you stop being angry, maybe it means you were wrong to have reacted with anger in the first place. Besides, you are not forgiving of your own transgressions. So it's doubly difficult to give someone who hurt you the benefit of the doubt.

If you create drama, you'll find that fury satisfies your needs all too readily. And nursing your fury gives you access to drama at will. That can make rage very tough to part with. Since a dependent attachment can be a big part of your baggage, you are most likely to be seduced by rage when someone important does not do a good enough job of taking care of you. A mate or a mom who disappoints you or leaves you could trigger a bitterness that will dominate your thoughts, your decisions, and your dreams for the rest of your life.

If you need to feel superior, you are most likely to get stuck in a fit of rage when you've been struck in the ego. For example, if your friend dates an ex-lover of yours, you might end the friendship. You didn't want him, but that doesn't make it O.K. for her to take him. Or an actor might never forgive a close friend who gets a part he coveted. It does not necessarily matter if the ego blow was unintentional. If it made you feel demeaned—somehow, some way, someone should pay.

If you fear rejection, you are likely to feel a suppressed rage in direct proportion to the degree of self-sacrifice you have endured. When you bury yourself—your needs, your opinions, your true feelings—in order to keep an important relationship stable, rage builds like interest in a psychic bank account.

Any of us might stay angry too long because our other baggage makes it difficult to heal from a serious emotional injury. Angry baggage is most common, however, in the man or woman whose psychological radar is on automatic pilot, continuously scanning the world for potential offense. Naturally, this person finds such examples with amazing frequency. You might recognize yourself below.

A PORTRAIT

You Are Hypersensitive and Hypervigilant

"How dare that woman point at me!"
"Honey, she's trying to tell you your engine is smoking."

You notice anything out of the ordinary and wonder what it means. Usually, you assume it means something negative. When your mother-in-law sat you at the table with the out-of-town relatives last Thanksgiving, you understood it to be an exquisitely subtle insult. When your ex's name showed up on a charity list for which you were stuffing envelopes, you felt sure she had joined just so that you would have to be sending her things. You feel ganged up on a lot.

You hold grudges. It's something you've always known about yourself. You don't necessarily think it's a good thing to do. Maybe you've even decided that, in principle, you aren't going to do it anymore (except in the case of your former best friend. Given his betrayal, you could never let go of your grudge).

Actually, a grudge serves a deep need of yours. It keeps you alert in the presence of a potential enemy. After all, you reason unconsciously, someone who hurt you before could hurt you again. A grudge serves as a constant reminder of the injury so you won't be lulled into closeness and trust.

But this vigilance makes it difficult to relax. If someone put an unexpected hand on your shoulder, you'd jump. Your body is usually in a state of tension, though you are so accustomed to your wariness the tension is barely perceptible to you.

Your spirit is tense too, cautious, guarded. It's rare for you to be playful or sentimental. Other people's giggling or clowning, especially at the office, irritates you. You think it's a foolish way for adults to behave, and you won't be lured into it. Usually, colleagues get the message and give up trying to make you part of it.

Sometimes you are bothered by this isolation. But basically, you don't mind being set apart, at a safe, dignified distance. You get to observe and figure things out from there, and that's a comfortable feeling.

At the Congress of Vienna, when the Russian ambassador died, Metternich, master of political nuance, supposedly said, "I wonder what he meant by that?"

You are hypersensitive to motive. Vigilance makes you look below the surface constantly for potential exploitation or offense. You proceed very cautiously in relationships, feeling your way toward trust across a proving ground of possible hidden agendas.

On the one hand, this hypersensitivity is a tremendous asset. It helps you to see the world from a keenly perceptive and sophisticated point of view. People often *do* have covert motives, unarticulated goals. An appreciation of someone else's unexpressed motives helps you to protect yourself, should these motives threaten you, or to relax, if these motives reassure you.

Unfortunately, though your perceptiveness *could* make you closer to other people, it hardly ever does. This is the serious downside to your hypersensitivity. Not everyone has a hidden agenda, and even those people who often do, don't have one all the time. Some people really are direct, up-front, and honest. Some invitations really are straightforward expressions of the desire for your company, not simply the hidden hope that you'll become a customer. Some compliments are honest expressions of admiration, not covert attempts to woo you sexually.

When you are hypersensitive and/or hypervigilant, you find it difficult to be comfortable with these surface explanations. You'll put a lot of energy into looking for something that may not be there. And when you can't find it, you'll be uneasy. In a way, honest people are more unnerving to you than manipulators. At least the Metternichs and Machiavellis make sense to you.

Your hunt for motivation might distort your relationships in another way. When you "find" the hidden agenda, you tend to overreact to it. Aha! He's being nice to me because he'd like to get a job with my father. Aha! She invited me over because she thinks I know interesting people and she'd like an introduction. Aha! He's being so sweet because he wants to go to bed with me. When you find the motive, you automatically assume something negative about the person. But really, what's so terrible about any of these motives?

Is it always insincere to be positive, pleasant, or to extend an invitation because one has hopes of a job, an introduction, or a sexual encounter? Is a compliment automatically false because the flatterer is sexually attracted to you? Is warmth automatically phony simply because knowing you might do someone some good?

Your hypersensitivity makes you cancel out everything *but* that hidden motive. That automatic process, where you cancel out the positive by speculating on a hidden negative, naturally makes you angry. After all, you were looking for something to take offense at. You found it and you're mad, just as you expected to be. "Angry" is comfortable for you. When things are warm, friendly, positive, you are suspicious. "Watch out," you remind yourself. "Don't feel good. This could be a trap." Then you hunt until you find the pitfall and you are able to relax into anger. It's your most familiar, safest state of mind. They can't hurt you now. You're "on to" them. If you had a psychiatric label, it would be: Paranoid personality.

Your secret brag: "I'm too suspicious."

What you mean: "I'm not one of those naive fools who let people take advantage of them. I know what's really going on."

You Hate to Admit It, But You Might Be a "Grievance Collector"

"They are the beachcombers of misery, who see each grievance as a treasure to add to their collection."

—WILLARD GAYLIN, M.D.

Gaylin goes on to describe the person whose black cloud of baggage is the pervasive sense of himself as unutterably and eternally deprived. Life for this "grievance collector," as Gaylin has termed him, is a series of events each of which "proves" his state of deprivation.

When you are a grievance collector, your anger is ever present because you find evidence of life's unfairness to you everywhere. You live in a state of bitter envy because any other person's good fortune is proof of your relative deprivation.

Pathological envy is a matter of degree. For example, when your girlfriend gets engaged and you just broke up with your last best hope for marriage, nearly anyone would be flooded with envy. Her engagement feels like it should have been yours. This intense envy and self-pity is not grievance collecting. It is the pain of your loss acutely triggered by her gain. But if you experience any couple as evidence that life is unfair to you—you have a hint of the depth of your sense of deprivation. No matter what comes your way, it signals to you second best, unfair, or not enough. That is the thinking of a grievance collector.

When other people have bad luck—they miss the train, get the flu on prom night, sell just before the stock doubles—they are certainly disappointed. Each will handle the disappointment depending partly on his or her excess baggage. (The woman who needs to be right might curse herself viciously for the stock misjudgment, the man who creates drama might turn a missed train into a life catastrophe, the person who needs to feel superior will assure you that he never wanted to go to the prom in the first place, while the person who fears rejection will worry about who might be mad at her for suffering such bad luck.)

But the grievance collector will use these all-too-human experiences of misfortune as evidence that he and he alone is singled out in life for special harsh treatment. How could he not feel angry about it?

You are often unaware of your anger. You experience anger as coming back *at* you instead of coming *from* you. It seems as though cars almost bump you, lines you happen into get longer and slower. Your boss picks on you, your friends laugh at you. You feel the need to be constantly on guard lest someone take advantage of you.

Your strongest defense mechanism is projection ("I'm not angry. *You* are!").

The hardest thing you have to do: Forgive or forget.

Your best fantasy:

You hear semibad news about someone with whom you are angry (for example, a divorce in embarrassing circumstances, but not anything like the loss of a child where you might feel sympathy.) You don't want the guilt or punishment associated with actually retaliating. But you wouldn't mind the reward of learning that it had occurred all by itself.

Your likely relationship role: Victim!

Other people might not automatically see you in this role, because they think of you as more combative than passive. And you'd agree. Nonetheless, you usually see yourself as the victim. You are combative *because* someone provoked you. You bristle quickly, but only *after* you are insulted. You feel you are aggressive only because you've been victimized. After all, any victim who seeks justice has to fight back.

Your motto: "Don't get mad, get even!"

From your beliefs to the defenses on which you rely, from the role you assume over and over in your relationships to your greatest struggle—each is consistent with your central perception of being the done to, not the doer. For reasons you have never precisely understood, life is unfair to you in great and little ways. Yes, you recognize that you are angry about this injustice, but you believe that the wounds precipitate your rage. You are blind to the ways in which the rage itself creates your wounds.

Money and Rage

Your likely profession: Whatever your field, you work best under your own authority or under the lightest of management direction. Because you are so sensitive to exploitation, it's hard for you to be bossed around, however legitimate your boss's authority. You are perfectly willing to work hard, but you prefer to do so because *you've* determined it is appropriate. When someone else drives you, you always feel a bit like he did it to belittle you, not just to get the job done.

If you do work for an organization, a good boss is one who shields you from the ordinary jockeying for power that is part of organizational life. You might be outstanding at what you do, but you are apt to be clumsy if not downright self-destructive at office politics. Chronic anger is not great fuel to get you up the corporate ladder, because it either scares or offends the people above you. You can work in a company, if the company leaves you alone and respects your work.

If you experience a chronic low-grade anger (which occasionally flares to fever pitch), you might choose to channel that anger into a cause. Causes have bad guys who are then convenient and legitimate targets for anger. The cause becomes a life's work and serves multiple psychological, economic, and social purposes. Depending on one's political or social persuasion, you do either great good or great harm to the society in which your crusades are staged. The point is that independence, hypervigilance, and unacknowledged internal anger make it easy for you to be the crusader.

Some people with angry baggage get in their own way every time they have to spend money. (The emphasis here is on "some." Others confine the impact of angry baggage to stormy social relationships.) Spending money can become the ideal vehicle for expressing your feelings of deprivation and victimization. You get caught in a frighteningly stable circle: "I'm deprived and angry. I don't have enough, so I have to hang on to what little I do have. Therefore, I can't spend what I have, the way other people can. So I buy less than they do, have less than they do. So I'm even more deprived and angry." If you are one of these people, you know the agony each financial transaction can provoke.

One part of this agony comes with the torturous necessity of spending anything at all. At the very center of your being is the feeling of not having gotten your fair share. Spending money is a form of giving. When you did not get enough—it is hard to be asked to give.

At the very least, you'll need to feel that what you get back is equal to what you give. That's part of why if you overpay for something, it can make you almost physically ill. Usually, you need to feel that what you get back is worth more than what you gave. A bargain, a sale, a find—all give you a triumphant kick.

Your inability to spend money might make it difficult or even impossible for you to enjoy normal daily pleasures. You can't buy clothes that are not on sale, and you'll wear a great bargain no matter how it looks on you. You can't enjoy a meal in a restaurant unless you get the Early Bird Special. You wouldn't take a trip that wasn't a tax write-off, no matter how badly you wanted to go. Hobbies that interest you cost too much to learn. In general, life's pleasures are not available to you because if you have to pay for them out of your own money, they are no pleasure at all.

Your views about spending can bring you into conflict with the other people in your life. If they aren't people with whom you must share money, they may confine themselves to pointed comments. (Why does your roommate tease you as you rush to the video store before closing to avoid an extra night's charge? It doesn't make sense to you to pay late charges if you don't have to.)

But when you share money, it can become a raging battle. You can't imagine why it bothers your wife when you use the two-for-one coupons at a dinner out. You think your husband is being impossibly shallow to want a status watch when a drugstore model will tell time just as well. You will do everything in your power to control the money, to nurture it, shepherd it, and in all other ways protect it from a partner who doesn't share your degree of concern.

Your financial arrangement with your spouse serves your idea of what is good for your money, even if it is not good for your marriage. You might keep a mate on a strict budget and hold him or her accountable to you (instead of a marriage, you have a military relationship). You might give a mate an "allowance" and invite personal requests and sweet bargaining for special financial privileges (this is less a marriage than a parent-child relationship, however benevolent you may be as the good daddy). You might feel comfortable financing your own hobbies, interests, wardrobe, but balk at paying for these luxuries for a mate. ("He's always happy to buy himself a computer gizmo. But I have to justify every sweater.")

The inability to spend money confirms your inner feeling of being deprived ("See. You can go on a vacation and I can't because I don't have enough money"). What you have labeled as "prudent budgeting" might actually be a dangerously self-fulfilling prophecy—a way to keep feeling bad about yourself, a way to keep feeling angry with the world for treating you badly.

In the Social World

You are highly independent. You don't feel comfortable needing other people and you wonder what it is they really need from you. Independence serves to avoid both these dilemmas. Privacy makes you feel safe from exploitation. But it also makes you feel lonely.

> *"I was invited to a wedding, but I knew that my boss was also friendly with these people. I couldn't imagine seeing my boss socially. It makes me feel like he'd know all about me."*

> *"I learned early on—never tell someone something you don't want thrown back in your face in a fight."*

You tend to reject people before they have a chance to reject you, or you proceed so cautiously when getting to know someone that he or she experiences your caution as rejection. Sometimes you suffer for being left out, when you unwittingly pushed the person away in the first place.

People experience you as defensive, but you don't agree. It's true that you will vigorously defend your opinions. But that's because your independence makes you suspicious of anyone's point of view but your own. People say you have "a chip on your shoulder," referring to the automatic way you bristle at small comments you don't like. Veiled criticism, minor errors in interpretation of your behavior all feel like assaults, because even a microscopic injustice makes you mad. You won't let things slide—because you can't. Other people describe you as "difficult" though you feel strongly that you wouldn't be difficult if they would be fair.

Your vigilance and independence are not compatible with free and easy friendship. In order to like people and connect with them readily, one has to be able to overlook a lot. You can overlook nothing. You not only notice, you keep score. In the end, your independence leaves you lonely because when caution and defensiveness keep you apart, other people go right on without you.

Common Battlegrounds

Almost any relationship can become an arena for ongoing fury, depending on what goes wrong in the interaction. Sadly, the most likely tend to be the relationships closest to your heart or most central to your day-to-day life. It only makes sense that these would be the people with whom you would be angriest. After all, you are most vulnerable to them, so a disappointment, a harsh remark, a loss, cuts the deepest.

If you are carrying around a load of angry baggage, you most likely have a troubled relationship with one or more of the following:

▪ Your parents—who can't be pleased, or can't be left, or can't be loving, at least not the way you need them to be. (And you can't stop being furious about it.)

▪ Your ex-spouse—whose specific crimes are catalogued in a laundry list written in blood. These crimes center on sexual and financial betrayal, inequities of responsibilities, slander of your character, lies, broken agreements, verbal or physical abuse, theft of the hearts of your children and friends, and other great and small spiritual gashes common to divorce.

▪ Your in-laws—who never welcomed you into the family properly (you know, because you recall every detail of the early days, however many years ago), who never supported the creation of your new family but rather, threatened your marital bond. They committed these crimes against you, all the while denying they ever did any such thing and blaming you for new family tension.

▪ Bosses, colleagues, or employees—whose relationships with you echo your family structure. If you have a repeated pattern of conflict with any or all of the groups in the professional hierarchy, you are probably carrying a lot of angry baggage toward authority figures or sibling figures. Your baggage can destroy a productive work life.

▪ Men or women, as a group—because you've suffered the scars of serial monogamy, which left the tracks of so much disappointment, so much duplicity. It's hard not to be angry with the next man when the two who came before him took advantage of you. It's difficult not to feel fury with the next woman when the last one left with half your assets.

If any of these battlegrounds is present in your life, that is, if you are in an ongoing angry struggle with your parents, your ex, your in-laws, your boss or co-workers, or new romantic relationships in general—*you have angry baggage.*

It doesn't matter that it's not your fault. It doesn't matter that they started it, that you are the victim, that you can't just let someone walk all over you. The anger is yours, and you and the people you love suffer because of it.

Your Marriage

She: "You have no idea. He fights with everybody. And I'm never allowed to disagree with him, because then he's furious with me for not taking his side."

He: "If we're supposed to be a couple, we should stand together. Believe me, if anyone is rude to her, I never forget it. But she just won't do the same for me."

Angry warrior marries peacemaker. Together they lock into an endless negotiation over how much injury is too much to forgive.

You can see how it might easily happen. As we said earlier, marriage is motivated in part by the desire to marry someone who is not burdened by the baggage you yourself struggle with. Having chosen someone free of your baggage, you naturally resent them sometimes because they don't share your burden.

When we are easily roused to anger, we marry a peacemaker; it's a bit like keeping the fire extinguisher close by if you do a lot of deep-frying. The greater the chance of fire, the greater the need for the extinguisher. Conversely, the peacemaker marries us so we can flare up on his or her behalf. Then he can remain in his stable, comfortable, familiar role of peacemaker and still have fury pour forth on those who abuse him. All in all, it's a good system but for its one overwhelming weakness: the marriage can become a battleground over where and how it is O.K. to be angry.

You see—as the warrior, we are angry. That's our baggage. We get angry; we feel entitled to our anger. Like most feelings, when we feel it, it feels right, justified, inevitable. We warriors wish that our (wimpy) partners would get as angry as we get. But we understand that s/he is more naive, more unsuspecting, more forgiving than we could ever be. We accept that. But we don't want to be told that our anger is wrong, or that we shouldn't be angry in the first place. And we certainly don't appreciate having our mates stick up for the person who injured us: "All I want her to do is to say she's mad too. Or she hates the son of a bitch too. But no. She's always telling me why what he did wasn't so bad!"

Why does she do that? Why does the peacemaker make things worse by apparently siding against the warrior? Why can't she just say, "You're right, honey, my mother is a horrible nag." Instead, she'll say, "Now remember, honey, Mom does an awful lot for us . . ." The peacemaker won't give the warrior what he wants, for three reasons:

▪ Because his rage makes her so anxious, she is afraid to add fuel to the fire: "I'd love to complain about my mother, but he's on such a rampage I'm afraid my complaints would be permission to do something really awful!"

▪ Because she disagrees. The peacemaker does not assume her role just because anger and confrontation make her nervous, though that is one motivation. She's also a peacemaker because she sees things from many points of view. Maybe she was less deprived as a child than her warrior mate, so she is therefore capable of a more generous spirit. (When you've been given more, you have more to give away.) She sees what made him angry, but she also sees what is provoking her mother to nag. When you can appreciate the other point of view, it is difficult to be single-mindedly angry.

▪ She might not endorse his righteous anger, because she is angry with him herself. It's a tremendous emotional burden for peace-makers to live with warriors. No matter who is the actual object of the warrior's outrage, the peacemaker is his constant audience. She is the one who receives his frequent angry outbursts, even though they come labeled with someone else's name. (When the driver of a car curses another driver, the person who receives those curses is the passenger—a passenger who did nothing more to deserve the curses than have the misfortune of sitting beside an angry driver.)

When you are the recipient of so much rage, you can get angry yourself. Peacemakers have difficulty expressing that anger directly. So they express it indirectly by refusing to support the warrior's righteous indignation.

THE INNER PORTRAIT

It may be true that when you hunt for injury, you are better prepared to defend against it. But it's also true that you find it more often, feel hurt more often, suffer more often. What could prompt you to construct your life around this tension-filled hunt?

We begin with your theme song.

Your Theme Song: "How Dare . . ." "I Wish . . ."

It plays over and over in your brain: "How dare my sister ignore my promotion." "How dare my friend not include me at the party." "How dare my ex show up at the school play on my weekend."

"I wish my father treated me the way he treats my brother." "I wish my wife would stick up for me when her dad starts making his mean remarks." "I wish that bimbo would be in a car accident."

"How dare . . ." is the voice of your fury. It rivets your attention to a past insult, ripping off the psychic scab, reminding you of your mistreatment at someone else's hands.

"I wish . . ." is the voice of your sense of deprivation. It too turns your attention to an injury, though in this case, it is the pain of omission you are reminding yourself of. "I wish . . ." is every piece of love, support, compassion, favoritism, understanding, indulgence that did not come your way. "How dare . . ." is every slight that did.

Together these two become a chorus of passionate complaint that can drown out your life. It might preoccupy you on a daily basis, turning your attention to some negative experience during otherwise unoccupied mental time, like when you are driving a car, walking to work, or doing the dishes. If the wound is new, or deep, or you are very vulnerable, "How dare . . ." or "I wish . . ." might interrupt your sleep, make concentration on work impossible, consume your sexual energy, your loves, your tenderness in one uncontrollable storm of fury.

No matter how lovely the outside scenery, you are caught in some nightmare inner landscape where injustice is committed against you, over and over. Your unconscious attention is focused on these experiences, filtering through life's rewards until you come up with an injury.

Why? What purpose does it serve to keep reminding yourself of every unfair thing that ever happened to you, or every terrific thing that didn't? Why can't you quiet that inner voice?

Remember, each theme song serves the needs of your ruling passion. People who need to be right hear "I should . . . I should" because it helps them to retain control. People who need to feel superior remind themselves "I am . . . I am" because it reassures them of their self-worth. If you dread risk and rejection, you will concentrate on "What if . . . What if" so you can protect yourself best and feel most secure.

And if you create drama, you will always have a voice in your head reminding you "I feel . . . I feel . . . ," because your feelings let you connect deeply with the rest of us.

All these theme songs put a person in the best position to satisfy his or her ruling passion. The same is true of "How dare . . ." and "I wish . . ." Yes, they focus on the negative, and that hurts. But there is a payoff: You focus on the negative *so you can undo it*. You right the wrongs that were done to you, in your own mind.

If you examine "I wish . . ." or "How dare . . ." this process of mentally righting the wrong will become clear to you. You don't just focus on the insult or the injury when you remind yourself over and over of a negative event. You take it one step farther. In your mind, you retaliate, in the way you either didn't, couldn't, or wouldn't in real life.

You say the devastating thing you hadn't dared to say. You attack, shame, humiliate, devastate, inflict dreadful pain on the person who injured you so deeply. You tell your mother-in-law she's a witch, and your husband stands by your side and cheers. You envision a selfish friend apologizing, a backstabbing colleague confessing. In your imagination, you are no longer their victim. In some chorus of your theme song, they are yours.

Over and over, you play out this unconscious ritual: Find the inequity. Mentally right the inequity. Find the wound. Mentally injure the perpetrator. In this way, you are mentally dramatizing your deepest craving: a passion for justice.

Your Ruling Passion: Justice

The central force that drives you on and stokes your fury is your drive for justice. All your strengths—your independent judgment, your willingness to fight for a better world, your capacity to look below the surface of social interaction—are fueled by a passion to identify wrongs, so that you can fight to right them. Sometimes your fights are extremely effective and sometimes they degenerate into the mire of a feud. Whether you live out your passion actively or not, your inner life is usually tied up with some ongoing battle for justice.

I've never worked with someone whose personality fit the profile just painted who was not in a white fury with one or both parents. The person who is angry and mistrustful of the world today is almost always the person who felt unfairly deprived as a child, and is still furious about it. The fury revolves around the same themes that today make this person quick to be angry with the world—namely, being treated unfairly, being denied something crucial. Scratch a woman who feels her boss is unfair, her sister-in-law is mean-spirited, and her acquaintances are out to use her, and you will find a woman still furious over a parent's abuse or neglect. Talk probingly with a man who prides himself on his canny distrust, who cannot marry because he has yet to meet a woman who is not just looking for a free ride, and you will find a man still steaming over a sibling who was favored or a mother's lack of love.

Deprivation is not an objective phenomenon. It is possible to see the with fury over deprivation in the midst of material plenty, just as it is possible for some people to get emotional nurturing in the most psychologically and physically abusive environments.

If you are one of those who was cut to the core by emotional deprivation, it really doesn't matter that others who had as little were wounded less. It is only relevant that *you* felt wounded. And you have spent the rest of your life guarding against the possibility of another such wound—seeing malevolence where other people see misfortune, retaliating against insults that to a less deprived person were mere lapses of tact; identifying inequity as your due and injustice as your inevitable reward.

As a child, you felt that you got less than your share of the good stuff, or you got much more than your fair share of the bad, or most painful of all, both. As a consequence of this, you are still furious with *them* (your parents or grandparents, more favored siblings), and you expect the same unfair treatment from people now. You just know that a boss will be more critical of you, a colleague will be sneaky and unkind, a friend only wants something from you. After all, you learned this firsthand at home. This time though, you are ready to fight back. You couldn't right the wrongs in childhood. You were too weak. Now things are different. Now you aren't going to take things lying down. Now you will fight for justice.

You satisfy your driving internal need for justice in two ways. The first is by mentally undoing your injuries through your theme song, which we've discussed. The second is that in your adult life, you have a pattern of fighting battles in self-defense. Here is how your pattern unfolds:

First, you identify someone as your attacker. That someone qualifies by virtue of being critical, unfair, depriving, judgmental, sarcastic, unappreciative, hostile, controlling. Then, having identified him as someone who has abused you—in effect, pulling the scab off your own psychic wound of childhood injury—you do what you could never do as a child: You fight back. You fight uncontrollably and interminably. You must see justice done.

Sometimes you identify one person in your adult life—say a brother-in-law—and you fight him for decades. The battle rages, creating tension at every holiday, every celebration. It becomes a family focal point, but you are unable to stem your flood of fury. This relationship bears the weight of all your childhood rage over being treated badly. No amount of family intervention, no pleading, no confrontation satisfies your need to do battle.

Sometimes we focus not on one attacker but on a series of people. Last year, you were in a bitter battle with a depriving boss, but this year, you've switched jobs. Now you find yourself in a fury over a friend who used you badly. If you stop to reflect, you realize there is always someone, whether central to your life or at its periphery, who assumes the role of bad guy in your thoughts. You are always fighting this figure mentally, always wishing him harm, fantasizing revenge. Depending on how much control you have over your rage and how much permission you give yourself to act out, you might also fight him literally—either with nasty words, nasty deeds, or actual assault.

The whole process works—in a way. Your theme song focuses your attention on an injury. Then the battle you stage gives you a chance to fight back on behalf of that psychic wound. You fight back to satisfy the demands of your ruling passion—namely, the demand for justice and fair play. It works, but at a high price to you. You have to hold tight to your anger in order to have the fuel for battle. And that anger is, by and large, baggage.

WHAT'S THE BAGGAGE?
YOU CHERISH YOUR RAGE

You can see from this overview that anyone might hold on to a pet hate: some one person who hurt you, cheated you, or stole something or someone you cherish. At the same time, though any of us could hold on to anger, some of us are most likely to. We are the hypersensitive, hypervigilant souls who are always on the lookout for assault— so we can defend against it, and so we can wreak vengeance on our attackers.

Whichever the source of your rage, you are hungry to right the wrongs done to you. That passion for justice stokes a fury that can burn for a lifetime. You'll cling to the fury because, in many ways, fury makes you strong.

Some abused mates will clean up after an assault, so that neither they nor their attacker will have to look at evidence of what occurred. Your long-lived fury is exactly the opposite of this approach. The wounds may have been inflicted years ago—the sexual abuse over, the divorce behind you, the family business sold. Everyone who participated in this painful episode shows signs of moving on, of burying the past. Only one thing makes that impossible, only one thing stands as testament to the injustice that was done to you. You may feel that only one thing makes retribution likely, and restores your dignity. That one thing is your rage.

Rage makes you strong in a second way, too. As long as you are angry, you don't have to wrestle with guilt. If, for example, you initiated a divorce, you might fall into this trap. No matter how valid the reasons, the person who leaves a marriage usually feels a measure of guilt or shame, especially when he notices his children bearing the cost of his abandonment. Rather than squirm under the burden of guilt, which erodes self-esteem and clouds certainty about our decisions, he converts the guilt to anger: "How could she make that remark!" "I'll never forgive how she turned the kids against me."

Guilt leaves us confused, makes us question our own judgment. Rage is clear light, outlining right and wrong in bold, heavy strokes. After guilt, rage makes us feel better about ourselves.

Finally, we sometimes hold on to rage because it is the only emotional tie we have to someone from whom we are loath to part. One woman explains wearily why she won't stop battling her spouse, despite the misery the marriage is for both of them: *"I'm afraid if I stop being angry, I'll have no feelings. I'm afraid there's nothing left but the anger. It would be like having a lobotomy."*

Your passion for justice makes you stronger. It gives you a long memory and a clear-eyed vision of the underbelly of human nature. It frees you from guilt because it helps you see right and wrong in black and white. Unfortunately, the strength you get from your crusade for justice can also be a measure of its poison. Justice makes you strong. But the anger it stirs can make you sick.

THE STRENGTH: By Cherishing Your Rage, You Are More
Likely to Hurt the People Who Hurt You.
BUT
THE BAGGAGE: You'll Hurt the People Who Haven't Hurt
You Even More.

Nowhere are we so blind as we are to the damage our rage inflicts on the people we love. We can't see it because the only victim we notice is ourselves.

You are the one who was betrayed, cheated, or abused. You are the one whose parents could do nothing but criticize, whose best friend stole the job you wanted, whose brother stripped the family home of possessions before the will was even probated. The people closest to you were not able to protect you from being victimized. You understand that. But surely they won't ask that you protect them from your anger.

In fact, far from protecting them from your anger, you half expect them to share your rage. They love you. Won't they therefore hate the person who inflicted such an injury on you?

Well, sometimes they will. Your mom might obligingly hate your ex with you, or even hate him more than you do if she identifies closely with you and your life. Your son might willingly detest your boss or the colleague who stabbed you in the back and cost your family a promotion. Your mate is quite often willing to take on your rage at your mom or dad, reacting vigorously to slights you'd learned to ignore by the time you were seven. There are any number of instances where your baggage can be partly carried by the people you love.

But sometimes it weighs too heavily on them.

Most typically, someone close to you cannot fully support your anger when the person who hurt you is also someone he or she loves. This is the situation for the child caught between divorcing or long-divorced, still-enraged parents, the mate left in the crossfire between parents and spouse, the close friend forced to choose sides when a couple dissolves, and most bitter of all, the mother pressed to pick either father or son in a fight to the death for the family business.

Don't kid yourself. Every single one of these persons is being pressured to choose sides. As long as you are in a rage, you will always pressure the people closest to you into supporting you against your enemy. You will say all the right things. You'll say, "Darling, he's still your father. I understand why a relationship with him is important." You'll say, "I can't expect my mom to side with me against Dad. After all, she lives with him." Or, "I'd never ask my friends to pick sides."

You'll say all these perfectly rational, reasonable things, but you won't mean them. You'd like to, but you can't—because your fury burns too bright and your hurt goes too deep. So you'll end up staging small and large loyalty tests. You watch and you measure: Which of two feuding siblings gets the more thoughtful birthday gift from Mom? With which parent does the child of divorce choose to spend a birthday? Which of the two of us still gets an invite to the Fourth of July bash? Always weighing, evaluating. When you carry angry baggage, you test everyone in the network of relationships against one central concern: Whose side are you on? All the while, you deny the struggle by insisting that you wouldn't/couldn't and clearly appreciate that you shouldn't ask anyone to take sides in the first place.

Your rage forces people to choose. It becomes baggage because it wounds the people you love far more deeply than it hurts the person you are angry with. Sometimes the wound is so great they have to pull away and leave you in order to save themselves from your fury. Then you've doubled your losses.

> **THE STRENGTH:** You See and Remember
> What Others Deny or Forget.
> Seeing Helps You Defend Yourself.
> Remembering Makes Justice More Likely.
> BUT
> **THE BAGGAGE:** The Seeing and the Remembering
> Make You Sick.

Rage erodes your body, your spirit, and your thinking. When you hold on to rage, you do more damage to yourself than your enemies might have ever envisioned. In essence, your baggage finishes whatever it was they started.

Rage makes you physically sick. You know it and I know it and I can't believe you really need a catalogue of its malignant possibilities. But as a reminder, when you indulge in long-term fury, you may give yourself a better shot at cancer, heart disease, ulcers, hives, colitis, hypertension, headaches—oh, a host of miseries that you might have otherwise avoided.

Sadly, your fury will also make you emotionally sick. We pay for our ability to maintain anger directly out of our capacity to love. "Angry" is something you feel instead of "happy," or "pleased" or "relaxed" or "content." The feeling of hatred is toxic in and of itself. In fact, the only thing that happens to that sick feeling over time is that you get used to it. It doesn't get better or nicer or easier. But you've been angry so long you forget how it feels to feel good. That makes it easier to bear.

Finally—most corrosive of all its deadly costs—rage spreads. At first, it focuses on the person who wounded you so deeply. You would be pained enough if that rage simply festered, causing you to cringe each time you were reminded of it. But a rage unspent does not just fester. It grows.

Mary, for example, is unable to visit her adult daughter, the only truly cherished person in her life. What prevents comfortable visits is the presence of the daughter's boyfriend, an attractive, marginally employed charmer who is dependent on her daughter for structure and stability. The relationship between these two—the nurturing daughter and her needy lover—floods Mary with an uncontrollable hatred. It is a hatred whose original source is the daughter's father, a needy ex-husband whom Mary nurtured for years, just as her daughter is doing now. That marriage deteriorated into a decades-long battle for alimony, child support, visitation. Now, twenty years after the event, Mary is physically incapable of being in her daughter's home, because the boyfriend triggers her fury. "I want to cook for my daughter but I don't want to see him eating it." So she stays home alone, missing the daughter she loves, because rage spreads.

Rage spreads. It begins with the daughter-in-law who criticized you and spreads to the granddaughter who is most like her. It originates with the friend who made love to your wife, but it spreads to everyone else who refused to disown the friend for his crime. In every instance where you carry rage as baggage, you increase the possibility of sucking another relationship into its vortex.

The price you pay for cherishing your rage is exceptionally high. It makes you physically and emotionally sick, dimming your possibility for love or peace of mind. And it threatens every new relationship because they are all targets for your old baggage.

Rx: FORGIVE: A PEACE PROGRAM

In a sense, the medicine for hatred is the simplest of any instance of excess baggage. All you have to do is forgive.

Forgive, and you can heal, move on, reduce your health risks, lighten your spirit.

Forgive, and you can overcome your central sense of deprivation, because forgiveness opens up a world of possibilities to satisfy your needs.

Forgive, and you restore a harmony to your family, restore to these relationships a joy that you had forgotten was even possible. Forgive your ex-spouse, and you erase the tension that contaminated your daughter's joy on her wedding day. Forgive rude and critical in-laws, and your forgiveness makes Christmas possible again for your wife. Forgive your sister her mean-spirited abuse, and your mother can sleep through the night again.

Forgive, and you free all the energy you are currently using in reviewing old injuries, fantasizing revenge, craving justice. Forgive, and the piece of you that was tied up with rage is free to be much, much more.

Ah, but forgive, and you eliminate any possibility of justice being done. Forgive, and the person who injured you goes unpunished. Forgive, and you are stripped of the soothing ointment of your rage and left to confront your wounds.

Forgive, but how?

How do you bring yourself to the point where you *want* to forgive? And then, even at that point, how do you learn to let go of an anger that feels uncontrollable? Remember, unloading the baggage of rage is not the same as managing your temper. There are a variety of techniques, including delay tactics, planning, key words, aggression diaries, and so on that can make your day-to-day anger less of a problem for you. (See the notes on this chapter for references about these techniques.) Forgiveness is not about controlling anger, or venting it more productively. Forgiveness is about letting go of hate.

It is so important to understand that forgiving is something you do for your own sake. It is not a gift to an undeserving foe. Forgiveness is not approval. It is not your way of saying, "Oh, never mind. It doesn't really matter." Forgiveness does not mean that what the other person did was acceptable or even tolerable. Quite the contrary. Forgiveness says, "What you did hurt me deeply and you were wrong to do it. I have hated you for what you did long enough. Now I want to let go of my hatred. I forgive you."

Forgiveness is not forgetting. The idea that you would forget a life event of such significance, one that evoked such pain, is naive. For-giveness is remembering, but remembering without rage.

I can and will suggest techniques that might set you on the path to a more tranquil spirit. The rage you bear is a terrible psychological burden, a burden that these techniques might help you to lighten. The burden is psychological; however, the cure is really spiritual.

The body of knowledge with the greatest amount to teach us about forgiveness is not psychology but religion. It is religion, of whatever variety, that teaches us how to be strong again when great and incom-prehensible wounds have been inflicted on us. It is religion that helps us find a path toward inner peace when some heinous betrayal makes all that is beautiful seem trivial by comparison. In a way, it is between you and your God whether you will cling to a justifiable hatred, or find the strength to let it go. The courage and capacity to forgive, as well as the motivation to bother to try, are reflections of our spiritual power more than of our psychological strengths. In this sense, religion—in whatever form it operates in your life, through which-ever spiritual leader takes you farther on the path—should be your guide.

The following forgiveness strategies describe what a psychologist can offer to assist you in letting go of this very painful baggage.

Identify the Battle

Begin by confronting the fact that you are carrying this baggage. For most of us, forgiveness needs to be directed toward the person in adult life who hurts us—whether that is an ex-friend, a disloyal sibling, a drunken driver, whoever attacked our safety and satisfaction.

But those of us who are prone to rage because of our personality style have the double burden of forgiveness. We need to struggle to forgive those people in our present life who are currently identified as attackers. But we will also have the burden of forgiving the original injustice, the one that sliced us when we were too young to protect ourselves, the one that cut to the core. We will have to forgive our parents.

We begin by identifying a relationship that is disturbed, an old attachment that was poisoned:

▪ It doesn't matter how long ago the event occurred. This person may be long out of your life (the stepmother who kept all your own mother's things when your father died, the envious college roommate who spread lies about you). What is important is self-examination. Are you still angry?

▪ It doesn't matter if you "understand" why it happened. ("I know my father didn't choose to leave me when he left my mom." "I know my mother drank because she was sick.") Forgiveness is necessary if you are still angry. The fact that you don't think you "should" be angry is irrelevant.

▪ It doesn't matter if you try to trivialize or belittle the relationship. ("My neighbor was horrible to me when we first met. But we really don't socialize, so I don't care." "When I think of how my brother took advantage of me, it infuriates me. But we were never close.") Angry is angry. Old anger is baggage, and you'll still need to forgive.

▪ It doesn't matter if the surface has healed. Yes, it probably is a step forward if you can now be in the same room with the colleague who almost got you fired or the daughter who lied to you. But surface healing is just a step along the way. Rage is no longer baggage when your spirit is no longer carrying it around.

So make your list, mentally or on paper, of all the places where your relationships are disturbed because you are holding on to angry baggage. And begin to imagine an internal step where you say, in your heart, "You hurt me. I forgive you."

Call a Cease-Fire

It is difficult to attempt to forgive while the battle is being waged. True, to some degree, time heals. But if the battle never quiets, you never get to test those healing properties.

If you are able to remove yourself from the person who hurt you, you have an easier chance for forgiveness. (It's easier to forgive the lover who went back to his wife if you don't work with him every day.) On the other hand, when you are no longer coping with the person, you may have less motivation to forgive. You might carry old baggage that would be easy to drop but for the fact that no one is pressing you to drop it.

The most stressful objects of our rage and the people hardest to forgive are those who must remain a part of our lives. With them, we have the most reason to work on forgiveness, because we are aware of the crippling impact of our anger, sometimes on a daily basis. But they are the hardest to forgive, because each new interaction threatens the possibility of new insult. The fighting father and son try to reconcile, but once again, the son finds the father to be controlling and the father finds the son to be cruel. Now they have fresh reasons to be enraged. Ex-spouses who share the tie of children have every motivation to move toward forgiveness. Unfortunately, they also both have ever new instances of betrayal to fuel their anger. It's a deadlock.

If the objects of your rage are part of your present life—call a cease-fire. This might mean:

Telling the person directly that you believe the two of you shouldn't meet for a specific period of time. That's right. You call your ex, your father, your stepson, and you say, "There is so much anger between us I think we need to take a break. Let's not meet or talk for six months [or whatever time period feels right], and then we can talk and see if we can work things out better."

Going out of town, or physically removing yourself permanently from an ongoing feud. It's not always practical to leave town. But even when it is feasible, it is an option often overlooked. We have a prejudice in our society against leaving a difficult situation. We call it "running away" and tend to withhold our support from friends or family who have a impulse to do just that. In general, it's probably a good bias because it encourages people to face life and cope with difficulty. But sometimes, in the face of ongoing rage, betrayal, and tit-for-tat abuse, physical distance is the best medicine. When your husband leaves you for a new love and the two of them dine around town at your preferred social spots, you don't have to stay and face it. It's O.K. to take an extended vacation, let the dust settle, heal in private, and search your heart for a way to forgive away from the heat of the injury. When your mom who adores you demeans and belittles your wife because no woman is good enough, it's O.K. for you to move your family outside weekly visit range. You can give your wife some breathing space while she struggles to forgive your mom.

Ending any legal proceedings, no matter who is winning at the moment. Forgiveness is not possible while lawsuits are pending. So if you are still suing, countersuing, going back to court to pay less, to get more, to enforce a judgment, to reduce an obligation, you are still in the heat of battle. You pay for every dime you get with its weight in the venom you stirred to get it. Make sure the money is worth it.

Ending the conversation. Some hatred gets directly expressed over and over. Some ex-spouses stage dramatic eruptions of rage every time they transfer the care of their six-year-old. Some family dinners are rife with sarcastic jabs, vicious digs, hostile comments, because no angry family member is willing to let the enemy get the last word.

In other ongoing battles, there is little or no communication between the warring parties. Two ex-spouses often fight bitterly by communicating their hatred for each other only to their children. Two friends pass their poison through a third. An in-law battle might be waged only by dumping on or ripping apart the person to whom you are both related.

Whichever mode of expression you use to vent your hatred, whether third-person or direct assault, a cease-fire would be simple: You've said it all before. Don't say it anymore. For some predetermined period of time, don't vent your anger. Don't confide your feelings if solicited. Don't communicate them if provoked. Keep silent, because silence is a step to a cease-fire. And a cease-fire is a step toward forgiveness.

Label Your Fear

Forgiveness is a complicated, difficult task. But even if you knew how to forgive, there is no certainty that you would do it. First you'd need to overcome the fears forgiveness rouses.

We talked earlier about the payoffs of anger, about how it helps us to punish wrongdoers, how it protects us from facing other, more difficult emotions like guilt. Whether consciously or unconsciously, most of us fear that if we let go of anger, we'd have to deal with these underlying issues. But we have other, related fears as well. And they interfere with our capacity to forgive:

"If I forgive, s/he will abuse me! Only my anger stands between me and that selfish, aggressive person. I know my ex (my sister, my son-in-law). Give an inch and he'll run over you like a steamroller."

Sometimes it seems as if only anger makes us strong enough to fight. We fear that if we forgive, the other person will take advantage. This is partly true, which is why a cease-fire is often necessary before you can forgive. You need to forgive from a safe distance.

But partly this is only fear talking, a fear shared by your enemy. If neither person takes a first step because each needs his or her anger as a defensive shield against further injury, the cycle of fear and rage just continues. And your baggage festers, spreads, and shadows more of your life.

"If I forgive, he gets away with what he did." Since rage is part of how we punish those who hurt us, forgiveness feels like we're letting someone off the hook. But the problem is, sometimes we stay angry forever. That means we punish forever, which is usually way out of proportion to the crime.

Besides, our rage is a relatively ineffective punishment. We usually keep it to ourselves or share it with people we feel good about. But even if you do vent it from time to time at the true object of your anger, the whole outburst lasts only seconds or minutes. Meanwhile, you've been carrying the baggage, living with the anger, rehearsing the monologue for days, months, even years.

You are the one most punished by your anger, because you are the one who experiences it most intensely. When you are able to forgive, the person you let off the hook is yourself.

"If I forgive, it means I'm weak." Often angry baggage is the inevitable by-product of a bitter power struggle. The first person who blinks loses. To forgive is to blink.

It's hard to understand how we get ourselves into power struggles, harder still to identify it once we're in one, and very, very difficult to dig ourselves out of one once it gets going. Forgiveness is the way out, but it's a way that stirs a lot of fear.

You are probably in a power struggle if you find yourself constantly arguing with someone with whom you have an ongoing relationship. You and your mate bicker endlessly over chicken or fish, what time to leave, which street to drive on, was the color navy or black? Or you and your has-to-have-it-his-way parent can't sit at the dinner table without getting into a barbed discussion on anything from politics to the proper way to shell peas.

It's unlikely that you will readily identify your own role in this struggle. Instead, you will feel victimized, provoked, and the notion that you should turn the other cheek, forgive your provoker, will feel very uncomfortable. Forgiveness is not weakness, but it is a way to bow out of the battle. You can deepen your understanding of a troubled relationship by recognizing that ongoing bickering is usually a struggle for dominance. Then you can make a conscious decision: Is it important for me to struggle for dominance in this relationship? If the answer is yes, bicker away until you can find a more satisfactory way to work it out. But if the victory is not as important to you as it once was, don't take the angry route. Forgive instead.

Decide to Forgive

O.K., you've done the first three steps: you identified your angry baggage; called a cease-fire in the relationship if one was necessary; you've confronted your fears that forgiveness would make you a loser in some way. You've decided to proceed. You want to get the anger out of your way. You are willing to work on forgiving, but you can't imagine how to begin.

Begin by making a decision. I will forgive _____. Do something concrete to represent the seriousness of the decision:

■ Write down your intention to forgive on a piece of paper.

■ Throw away something that represents your anger. It might be pictures of the two of you, or old letters, or some article of clothing or souvenir—anything that stirs the anger when you look at it. Throw it away ceremoniously, telling yourself you are throwing away the anger.

■ Announce your decision to forgive to people close to you.

■ Tell the person who injured you that you've made a decision to forgive him.

■ Write a letter pouring out your rage. Write down exactly what happened to you. Start at the beginning; don't leave anything out. When you are done, reread the letter. Then burn it.

■ Have a healing visualization. Picture yourself confronting the person who hurt you. See yourself telling him or her exactly what he or she did to cause you pain. Then see the pain and anger leave your body. You might put it in a mental box, gift-wrap it, and hand it back to the person who gave it to you. Or you might envision a light healing your emotional scars.

▪ Pray. Go wherever it is that you feel closest to God and announce that you have made a decision to forgive. Then pray for the strength you will need to carry out the decision. Remember, whomever else you may be talking to when you pray, you are first talking to yourself.

The decision to forgive is not an end point but rather a step in the process of letting go of your anger.

Appreciate Your Struggle

Forgiveness is unburdening your spirit of a load of anger you've been toting. Because the load of anger and pain runs so deep, this unburdening is an internal struggle. If you can appreciate the struggle, you can push yourself farther along the path.

There are steps along the way, any one of which could be enormously difficult for you. First of all, you have to acknowledge to yourself how deeply you've been hurt. It would seem that having identified the anger, you would be past this step. But that is not always the case. Anger can be a mask for pain. You can be so outraged at a spouse's custody maneuverings during a divorce that you never have to acknowledge how much you lost when you lost her. When you are furious with a best friend who talked behind your back, you never have to face the wound to your self-esteem over what she had to say.

Next, you have to admit you feel hatred. You can't struggle to forgive unless you admit how malignant is the feeling you are holding inside. You are not mad, irritated, annoyed, pissed off, or any of the other acceptable forms of anger. The form of anger you feel is hatred, and hatred can eat your spirit alive. Hatred is what you let go of when you forgive.

You will also have to see what is happening through different eyes.

This is the most difficult step in forgiveness. It is utterly necessary that you reprocess the events from another point of view. In order to forgive, you must work to redefine the intention of the person who wounded you. Yes, you were deeply hurt. But it does not necessarily follow that the original intention was to hurt you. This shift of focus is crucial for your healing. Most people who hurt and disappoint us are acting less *against us* than they are acting *for themselves.* The spouse who cheats, the child who lies, the business partner who steals, the brother who abandons your aging parents—each of these people may have wounded you profoundly, and your anger is certainly justified. To forgive, you need to see that each acted according to his or her own interests. These conflicted with yours and caused you pain. But they did not act *in order to* cause you pain.

You might need to get an idea of how you contributed to the miserable outcome over which you are now suffering so deeply. This does not mean that whatever occurred was your fault. Whatever occurred was probably less a question of fault than of two people acting according to their own conflicting needs, or of one person acting out of a weakness that deeply intruded on the other. "Different eyes" means that you see painful events less through the eyes of a victim and more through the eyes of an adult realist.

For example, one woman holds a lifetime grudge against parents who pressured her into an unhappy marriage because they were embarrassed to have their unmarried daughter living with a man. The adult realist sees that her parents, albeit conservative, clumsy, and interfering, were trying their best to guide her. She also sees that, while she was pressured, she was not forced into her choice. She herself was also responsible for the decision to marry. These different eyes help her to forgive her parents and heal herself.

Another man clouded all his relationships with women because of his fury at a mother who left his dad for her younger, handsomer boss. This man remained loyally at his wounded dad's side, refusing contact with his mom for years and resenting her deeply because he felt deprived of her love. In order to establish a loving relationship with a woman, he had to find a way to stop being so deeply angry with his mother. Eventually, he came to view her betrayal differently. The adult realist saw that, while his father was a great dad, he was a poor husband. When Mom left her marriage, she was saving her own life. She tried to take him with her, but he refused to go. With this different perspective, he has tentatively begun to build a relationship with his mother. And he has begun to heal.

Finally, you try for closure and/or a reconciliation. The last step in forgiving is to communicate your anger, your pain, and your forgiveness to the person who hurt you. Then you take him or her back in your life and close the circle broken by rage.

This step is not always possible. Sometimes you can't take it because the person is dead, though there are symbolic ways in which you might speak to this person and make him or her a part of your life again.

More often, we can't take this step because the other person is not willing to hear us, because he or she is still unwilling to be responsible for hurting us in the first place. The point is not for you to accept a blame that your wrongdoer wishes to pass on to you. The point is for you to say you were hurt and enraged over this hurt, for him to be able to acknowledge that yes, he did hurt you—whether deliberately, inadvertently, unconsciously, it doesn't matter—he hurt you deeply. And then you let him know you forgive him, and you build a new relationship from there.

This final step in forgiveness depends largely on the other person's capacity to hear the truth and to be responsible for his actions. If he hasn't matured to the point where he is capable of this level of self-awareness, don't let it stand in your way. Remember, you struggle with forgiveness to free yourself from the pain and poison of rage. It is true that forgiveness is easier if your persecutor can acknowledge and be responsible for the injury he caused. Give him the opportunity to do so. If he can't or won't take it, let it go.

The real-life complication comes because, most often, the two of you have hurt each other. She left, but she's angry because he drove her to it. But he's still furious because she left. It's quite possible that the person toward whom you carry such rage carries every bit as much toward you. Then you have a double duty. You have to forgive how you were hurt *and* you have to acknowledge how much hurt you inflicted. Double duty naturally means a double struggle with forgiveness.

You might stumble over any or all of these points. Forgiveness is a long road. It's a lonely one, too. It all happens inside of you. You get few points for your progress. You might not even be cheered along the way, since those close to you are just as likely to stoke your anger as to support your capacity to forgive.

Still, in the end, your capacity to forgive—whether a minor lapse or a major betrayal—is the one medicine that can lighten your load of angry baggage. If you are one of those tired spirits carrying around a load of rage, you know how you get in your way. If you are one of those whose rage starts with the core feeling of deprivation, you know how hungry you are, how much it would take to even things up, to make you feel on a par with the world. Whatever the source of this angry baggage, forgiveness is the cure.

In essence, forgiveness is about letting go, and letting go is the primary antidote to each of our inner obstacles. The problem is not so much that we have baggage but that we cling to it so tightly. We need to let go of the reassurance of being right, let go of the heady sensation of being superior. We hold so tenaciously to our dread of rejection, to our desire for drama. We need to let them go.

It's hard, though. We hold on to them because they're familiar, because they soothe our anxieties. In the end, we hold on because our baggage is so closely identified with our strengths that we confuse the two. We worry:

How can I insist on justice for others if I forgive an inequity done to myself?

How can I stay deeply attached to people if I no longer need them to rescue me, to think for me?

How can I feel secure if I expose myself to risk over and over?

How can I feel valuable if I'm not the very best?

And how can I take charge of all that I handle if I'm not sure I'm doing the job right?

It's easy to feel that your baggage is such an integral part of your power that if you give up one, you give up both. But I think you'll find that that's a distortion.

Your baggage is your strength taken to an extreme. When you go to extremes, when you always *have to* respond one way, you are turning your own strength against yourself. Free yourself of your baggage and you free your strengths to work for you.

Free yourself of your baggage and you lose none of your personal power. You just bring yourself back into a healthy balance, a balance that will prove to you: You don't have to be the smartest, the best, the safest, the sexiest, the fairest. You don't have to be the most *anything* to be happy. As you'll see in the final chapter of this book, you just have to be enough.

Chapter Eight

ENOUGH

Even this book has baggage. It can't get around these contradictions:

Baggage is a blind spot. Yet we have moments of blinding clarity, moments where we see ourselves be ourselves—and we realize how much we allow to get in our way.

Baggage is an inevitable side effect of personality. Yet it seems also to be an inevitable side effect of life. That is, it seems impossible to avoid the barnacles on our spirit, or the demons we gather with experience.

Baggage is the part of ourselves that gets in the way. And yet who could deny that other people go a long way toward weighing us down too? Your sarcastic ex, your impossible-to-please dad, your vindictive neighbor, insecure boss, demanding in-law—all those people impossible to escape, yet impossible to enjoy—are a part of what gets in our way.

Baggage is something you don't know about yourself. But at times, it is so intrusive that it seems difficult to know anything else. It is the enormous distraction of unresolved emotion or unfinished business. It is the friend with whom you can't patch it up, the lover you never left in your heart, the fatal personal weakness you thought you'd overcome only to have it resurface. On the one hand, we are unaware of our baggage. On the other, it is impossible to ignore.

These contradictions are an inherent part of the now-you-see-it-now-you-don't nature of excess baggage. After all, baggage is part of human nature. And what could be more contradictory than human nature's eternally conflicting needs?—the hunger for security that lives with our passion for risk, the deep wish to be closely attached to another person that vies with our equally deep craving for freedom, our impulse toward change and stimulation and our contrary attachment to the stable and familiar. Happiness is most accessible when we are able to strike a balance between these longings.

Self-defeat occurs when we tilt to an extreme in one or another direction. Excess baggage is what tilts us.

None of us can avoid tilting a bit because, as we've discussed, we all have baggage. We have baggage because we have strengths, and we take these strengths to the extreme. The result is predictable: we end up standing in the way of our own possibilities.

We are all on the same psychological path, moving slowly toward being more than we already are—more loving, more generous, more at peace with one another. We are hoping to be wiser than we were yesterday, more realistic about our own weaknesses, and more tolerant of the weaknesses we see around us. We are hoping to be stronger, too, to contribute more to the rest of the world.

It would be an easier path, a breeze really, but for the obstacles in our way. Yes, life imposes many of these. It gives us financial problems, career complications, health crises. Our circumstances limit our opportunities and frustrate our best intentions to grow. And other people often stand squarely in our path too, disappointing us, disturbing us, burdening us, and ultimately setting us back instead of moving us forward down the road toward who we might be.

Through no fault of our own, life presents us with these unpleasant hurdles on a regular basis. But *we* are responsible for whether we crash into them. The truth is that most of us are smart enough, strong enough, and spirited enough to navigate life's hurdles buoyantly.

But our baggage drags us down.

Baggage makes life into work in two ways: it makes life's inevitable obstacles harder to handle, and it creates obstacles of its own, problems you would never have to face but for your excess baggage. But if you are willing to tolerate some anxiety, you can push past your own baggage and have a clearer path before you.

Not to say that this is easy. You have to see yourself in a realistic way, and that is always momentarily disturbing. And then you have to change.

Ah, but if you do, it will all get so much better, so much easier. You'll *feel* better. Baggage is an inner load. You have to tense your emotional muscles to carry it around. Drop your baggage—your sense of superiority, for example—and it's like taking off a pair of gorgeous shoes two sizes too small. You thought they made you look good when you put them on, but now you long to go blissfully barefoot.

But your reward for change is more than feeling better. If you shed your baggage, your relationships with the rest of us will sweeten too. Fear and anger are so much a part of each variety of baggage. When you are less afraid of the people around you, less concerned about their critical judgments or possible rejection, you'll feel much more comfortable. The barriers you automatically put up dissolve. Since you no longer have to avoid potential pain, you are more available for pleasure.

When you let go of your baggage, you lose some of the anger it packs. Other people are happier to be with you, because you aren't so harsh with them for doing what they shouldn't or for failing to do what they should, you aren't so critical of their flaws, and you harbor fewer grudges over past inequities. It's hard for other people to get close to an angry person. But a peaceful, confident person is a magnet—and that's who you'll be closer to being when you get your baggage out of your way.

When the problem is a question of extremes, the solution involves balance. Balance means finding a middle ground, a compromise. It means moving an inch off your position, taking a step closer to the middle and therefore closer to where someone else is standing.

No matter what the baggage that throws you off balance, there is one guiding principle you could introduce to restore your equilibrium. Just remind yourself of "*enough.*"

"Enough" means, "I'm good enough. I own enough. I've spent enough. I know enough. I'm smart enough, pretty enough. My husband is strong enough. My wife is exciting enough. My child is exceptional enough. I ate enough, drank enough, exercised enough. Stop. It's enough. The house is clean enough. My thighs are thin enough. I've proved enough. I am important enough."

"Enough" is a catchphrase that recollects an old fashioned virtue—satisfaction. It reminds you that wherever you are, whatever you have lost or accumulated, learned or forgotten, you can consider yourself, at any given moment, enough.

"Enough" encourages an inner feeling of peace, an acceptance. It acknowledges that, indeed, there is more out there to have, to be, to own, to achieve, and you are allowed to feel happy and satisfied without having it, being it, owning it, or achieving it.

Don't confuse satisfaction with settling. "Enough" is not permission to avoid risk or resist change. On the contrary, satisfied people can be very brave, exploring their limits and accomplishing great things. They do so less out of an inner gnawing and more out of the natural progress of an uncluttered human spirit. "Enough" does not mean, "Give up." It means, "Savor what you've got."

It is the sense of satisfaction that can restore balance when your baggage pushes you to extremes. It is satisfaction that allows you to work to a level of excellence without wasting your efforts on the pursuit of perfection. It is satisfaction that will help you to cultivate relationships that pay off rather than those you pay for.

And it is satisfaction that presents a direct challenge to your excess baggage. "Enough" speaks to each of us:

If you need to be right, you let go of your excesses by reminding yourself that you've worked enough, you've done enough, and you know enough. When you believe "I know enough," you don't have to know it all.

If you feel superior, you could call the contest when you are convinced that you are worth enough. You aren't the best, you aren't the least, but "I'm important enough."

If you dread rejection, you could brave the world if you were shielded by the belief "I'm strong enough." And you would not need to avoid every risk, be protected from every danger, if you could focus your attention on this truth: "I'm safe enough."

If you create drama, it's easier to curb your excesses when you believe "I am loved enough." You have enough support, enough attention. You don't need to create a crisis in order to attract more.

Finally, *if you cherish rage,* you could lighten your emotional burdens by accepting the idea of "enough." It goes beyond the reminder that you've been carrying your anger long enough and it's time to let it go. It goes to all the inequities we experience, all the ways we have been hurt, abused, or disappointed. Because no matter how much we got, there is something we didn't get. Which means that we all have reason to be angry, and clearly some of us have more reason than others. For those people who, reason or not, got their spirits stuck in this anger, it helps to remind yourself: "I didn't get it all. I didn't even get my fair share. But I got *enough.*"

Enough. I know enough. I'm loved enough. I'm worth enough. I'm safe enough. I'm strong enough. I got enough.

"Enough" reminds us that satisfaction comes from balance. Balance means that you see the world as it is and see yourself as you are. And realize that both offer the basic elements you need to be happy. Everything else is excess baggage.

THE ANXIETY OF CHANGE

The great temptation is to delay change until it doesn't make you anxious. It's a lovely thought and many people enter psychotherapy with this very wish: "I'll change when it doesn't scare me, when it doesn't make me uncomfortable. Please make it not scare me."

It's sobering to realize that only by confronting the anxiety can you overcome it. You face the anxiety and wade straight through it because it's the only path to change. It's the only way to discover that the worst usually doesn't happen, and when it does, you live. Besides, not changing makes us anxious too—but in a far less productive way. The freedom you get from this lesson is incalculable. The price of tuition is anxiety.

You have to pay up, but you can use some techniques that will lower the cost. Don't bear the weight of your tension without support. When you feel uncomfortable attempting a new behavior, try one of the following time-honored anxiety-reduction techniques:

Call someone—as long as it's not someone who will give you permission to quit trying to change.

Write about how awful it is in a letter, a journal, on a scrap of paper you're free to burn.

Tire your body. Exercise, that great cure-all of the eighties, continues to be the number-one weapon against anxiety. It's hard to worry on a Stairmaster.

Break the new behavior into bite-size bits. You can't bear to let your wife plan the family vacation because she's sickeningly extravagant. Then let her run the show for just one day. Her way could turn out to be fun, too. Is the idea of showing up at a party where you know no one but the host just too overwhelming? O.K. But force yourself to talk to two strangers at the next familiar gathering. Push yourself against your own current, but just enough that you can stand it.

Pray, meditate, do deep-muscle relaxation, give yourself a pep talk, read a list of positive affirmations, practice yoga. Read Herbert Benson's books for relaxation training and mind control; Zig Ziglar for upbeat motivation; Tim Gallwey, Shakti Gawain, and Adelaide Bry for positive mental imagery; and Lawrence LeShan for a good introduction to meditation techniques. (Complete references are in the Bibliography.)

Review your use of caffeine and food. If you put too much of the wrong thing in your body, it can make you jittery, restless, or just generally uncomfortable. When you are making a change, try not to compound your stressors.

There are some excellent antianxiety medications which, when properly monitored, might reduce some of the more intolerable physical side effects of anxiety. If you are burdened with the belief that medication is "bad" or that strong people should face things "on their own," you have some belief baggage in your way. We all face life on our own, using a series of tools for coping and succeeding. Properly used anxiety medication is just one of those tools.

On the other hand, every tool has its risks.

Beware the standard anxiety escapes. Self-medication, with drugs, alcohol, food, and television, is the standard anxiety solution in our society. It's probably unavoidable that we use them to some degree, but monitor them carefully. It's true that these tools often work with miraculous efficiency to reduce anxiety. But it's also true that they sedate your spirit. When you reduce your anxiety in one of these four ways, you are highly unlikely to take the risks necessary to change. Most often, you just end up spacing out until you fall asleep.

For a more thorough review of techniques to reduce your anxiety, see *Anxiety and Its Treatment* by John Greist et al. And for a more thorough and motivating discussion of why you can and must face anxiety in order to change, read Susan Jeffers's *Feel the Fear and Do It Anyway*.

I don't know which of these techniques will help you reduce your anxiety sufficiently to make room for change. One person is soothed by a renewed faith in God and the comforts of religion. Another is inspired by an energetic, optimistic motivational tape. Remember, if you persevere in the face of anxiety, *it will get better*. And when your anxiety gets better, you'll get better—freer, lighter, happier. After all, you will have freed yourself from some baggage.

Acknowledgments

■

Pamela Dorman edited this book. Then she reedited it. Then she did it again. And every time she did it, she improved it. Pamela Dorman is everything an editor is supposed to be, and I am very grateful to her.

Susan Schulman has been my literary agent for nine years. If you know anything about writers and their agents, you'll know that speaks for itself.

Denise Logan is my link to the computer age, a completely reliable, unfailingly sweet-tempered, and very smart link. Thank you.

In addition, the following people contributed substantially to this project and/or to me personally: Brett Bender, Mary D'Anella, Denise Drummond, Jane Glassman, Spencer Henderson, Spencer Hoffman, Pamela Kerr, Sherry Lefevre, Harry Logan, Rick Mitz, Nancy Nowacek, Larry Rinehart, and Gerry and Harold Sills. Thank you.

In my private practice, I work with an outstanding group of people. I am proud that these are the people who've chosen me as their therapist, and very grateful for the contributions they have made to *Excess Baggage*.

Finally, although I am the sole author of this book, my life is largely a joint venture. Therefore, I thank my husband, Lynn Hoffman. It's not just that he does the usual—the spouse-supports-the-author deeds that would earn him the customary "without whom." It's that he does the unusual. And he does it with style, and it made this book better, and it makes my life better, and I'm lucky to live with him.

Author's Note

■

Research, observation, theory, and opinion in the social sciences are shared freely among professionals. We all read each other, repeat each other, quote each other in every new doctoral thesis, journal, article, and book. Eventually, a body of information takes on the shape of conventional wisdom, and it becomes impossible to determine which scholar made the original contribution or even which unique source is being cited.

Excess Baggage draws on much of the conventional wisdom of personality theory over the last fifty years.

I have included citations wherever a particular text is quoted, and an extensive bibliography of resources used to write this book follows. Many sources, however, repeat or restate the same information. Also, as I have been reading and studying personality theory for some twenty years, it is possible that I may have omitted citing some early sources for the thinking in *Excess Baggage*. If I left anyone out, I'm sorry.

Notes

■

Below are comments, sources, supporting documentation, and additions to the text. Published references include title and author; full citation is listed in the bibliography. Quotations not cited come from personal conversations, many of which were confidential.

CHAPTER ONE

Page 6
About two years after *Excess Baggage* was conceived, I came across Daniel Goleman's use of the metaphor "blind spots" to describe the way we selectively focus our attention to avoid the pain of anxiety. In his book *Vital Lies, Simple Truths*, Goleman presents his full argument. Of particular relevance to *Excess Baggage* is the chapter "Cognition Creates Character."

CHAPTER TWO

Page 12
For a deeper discussion of the role of anxiety in personality formation, see the classic work on the subject, *The Neurotic Personality of Our Time* by Karen Horney.

Page 15
The five ruling passions described here are in no way an all-encompassing list of the inner drives that shape personality. They represent my own

clinical observation. The idea of core motivation and/or a hierarchy of needs at the center of a personality formation is prominent in the works of many personality theorists. The five ruling passions I describe do not duplicate any of these lists, though there are many overlaps. You might also want to refer to *The Sane Society* by Erich Fromm or *Toward a Psychology of Being* by Abraham Maslow.

Page 16
The heredity/environment pendulum is lately swinging strongly back toward heredity as an explanation for human behavior. Carl Degler's book *In Search of Human Nature* contains a good discussion of this recent trend.

Page 23
The personality portraits in each chapter are drawn from my own clinical observation, and from several general references: the American Psychiatric Association's *Diagnostic and Statistical Manual of Mental Disorders* (third edition, revised); John Oldham and Lois Morris's *Personality Self-portrait*; David Shapiro's *Neurotic Styles*; Don Richard Riso's *Personality Types*; and Mardi Horowitz's *Personality Styles and Brief Psychotherapy*. In addition, each chapter draws on works that specifically address the personality issues covered in the chapter. Those references are included in the notes for each chapter.

CHAPTER THREE

Page 36
Leon Salzman confirms these observations of the likely sexual problems of someone with an obsessive personality in *Treatment of the Obsessive Personality*, page 20.

Page 42
A very interesting discussion of the dynamics of this common marital pattern can be found in "Narcissism and Dependency in the Obsessional-Hysteric Marriage" by Joseph Barnett.

Page 44
See Karen Horney's description of "The Tyranny of the Should" in *Neurosis and Human Growth*.

Page 45

In *Neurotic Styles*, David Shapiro uses the term "dogma" to describe the rigid perceptions of the obsessive. He then includes a vivid description of the ways in which "should" is imposed by the perceived requirements of a situation. The description of the theme song is basically a restatement of Shapiro's observation.

Page 51

See *Type A Personality and Your Heart* by Friedman and Rosenman. See also "Type A on Trial," the *Psychology Today* article by John Fischman.

Page 54

See *The Second Shift* by Arlie Hochschild.

Page 70

The suggestion for a list of "things you are not going to do today" came from *Overcoming Perfectionism* by Ann Smith, page 116.

Page 73

See Postscript, "The Anxiety of Change," for a more complete discussion of techniques that quiet anxiety.

CHAPTER FOUR

Page 83

Dr. Otto Kernberg, one of the most renowned thinkers on the subject of narcissism, refers to this tendency toward self-criticism as a "crushing self-judgment" in *Borderline Conditions and Pathological Narcissism*, page 335.

Page 97

For a rich discussion of the influence of contemporary culture on superiority, see *The Culture of Narcissism* by Christopher Lasch.

Page 98

Some typical patterns of family dynamics appear to contribute to a lifelong preoccupation with self and self-worth. Probably, in our earliest years, we were either way too important or not nearly valued enough. If you grew up at either end of this emotional spectrum, or if, as is true for some people, your value in the family swung from one end to the other depending on the whim of volatile parents, you are likely to develop superior baggage.

Those of us who were the "special child" of the family know the sweet inflation and awful burden of the role. We are the Daddy's girls who were closer to Dad than Mom ever was, sitting on the couch with him watching football while Mom and the others were off somewhere else, doing something else not nearly as interesting or important. Or we are Mommy's little man, the one for whom she saved the best cut of roast beef, the one she always protected, the one she believed in long after she stopped believing in Daddy.

Or we are the treasured only child, focus of the love and hopes and dreams of two generations of adults. We are the children who could silence a roomful of grown-ups at a holiday dinner with an off-key rendition of almost anything.

Or we are simply the favored child because we were born first, or last, or because we were the long-awaited daughter after several sons, or vice versa, or because we were born at a happy time in our parents' marriage, which made us dear to them, or born at a bad time in their marriage, which made them refocus the love they once had for each other on us. Whichever set of circumstances made us the lucky pick, the psychological effect is the same: in life's first great competition—the one that rages between siblings for the love and attention of parents—we have somehow managed to win hands down. It must be a reflection of our superiority. We must be superior, because look how much we are valued. At the same time, we feel we must remain superior, in order to be loved.

The role of the "special child" is discussed in depth in *The Emotional Incest Syndrome* by Patricia Love and Ashner and Meyerson's *When Parents Love Too Much*.

The opposite can be true too. Sometimes a sense of superiority develops instead of self-esteem because your early experiences blew the chance for true self-esteem to develop. Victims of physical or mental abuse are often so wounded at the core that they spend a lifetime constructing a superior shell to mask the damaged inner spirit. The children of parents who need to be right, or parents toting their own load of superiority, can come to feel so frightened of criticism that only the feeling of being better than all the rest of us can ward off its dangers. And quite often, the child of a parent with poor self-esteem will identify with Mom's weakness or Dad's inadequate self-image.

Page 102

In *The Snow White Syndrome*, Betsy Cohen makes this observation about the relationship between envy and self-esteem.

CHAPTER FIVE

Page 118
Harriet Goldhor Lerner's book *The Dance of Anger* is full of examples of the way fear of rejection helps us hold on to familiar anger rather than risking change. We are moved to fury by a husband relaxing in front of the TV while we are in a housework frenzy. We complain about this for a decade and make it the focal point of a perennial marital battle. But we'd never risk changing ourselves—deciding on our own to hire help, refusing pleasantly to do laundry, ordering in. Changing ourselves risks serious disruption. Familiar go-nowhere quarrels are safer.

Page 128
In *The Pleasers*, Kevin Leman describes the guilt and self-esteem problems of women who dread rejection. Also, somewhere at the height of the feminist movement, it became very clear that you couldn't free people economically and politically if they were trapped in a psychological prison of fear. Therefore, a great deal of time and attention went into identifying this baggage and devising techniques to help overcome it. Collectively, they became known as "assertiveness training." While it is less fashionable and therefore less widely available today, assertiveness training is still one of the most effective behavioral strategies for overcoming the passivity created by this kind of baggage. For self-instruction, you might look at the classic popular assertiveness book, *When I Say No, I Feel Guilty* by Manuel Smith, or at *How to Be an Assertive (Not Aggressive) Woman in Life, in Love, and on the Job* by Jean Baer. As you'll see, both these books were written in the mid-seventies when the movement was very popular.

Page 132
Here are warning signs of an abusive relationship:

- If you are hit. Period. At all. Even "just a little." Even "just a few times." Even if you "provoked" it. Even if you "aren't really hurt." The same holds true if you are male and your female partner hits you. Even if "it never bothers" you.

- If you are verbally abused—criticized, reviewed, screamed at, humiliated, "teased," called names.

- If you need your partner's permission to go places without him, to see friends or family.

- If you are afraid of making your partner angry, afraid to disagree with him, afraid to leave him, afraid to say no. Fear has no place in a loving relationship. No place at all.

Many women report finding Robin Norwood's *Women Who Love Too Much* very helpful on this subject.

Page 138

T. D. Borkovec, "What's the Use of Worrying?" and *How to Reduce Worrying*. Dr. Borkovec of Penn State University has successfully applied the various techniques of cognitive psychology to the self-control of worry. An application of these techniques of interest to the mental health professional is in Costello and Borkovec's "Lost in What-Ifs: Treatment of a Case of Generalized Anxiety Disorder."

Page 139

Psychiatrists Alexander Thomas and Stella Chess have identified fifteen percent of babies who are "slow to warm up" who appear to have a temperamental need for the secure and the familiar. Their cautious conclusions are detailed in *Temperament and Development*.

Page 142

Even if you are not depressed, either chronically or occasionally, your avoidance can cost you your health. For example, your passivity and reluctance to handle anger in a straightforward manner have been directly linked to a "cancer-prone" personality in research by psychologist Ronald Grossarth-Maticek. (See references to his work in B. Wein, "Heart Trouble," *New Woman*, August 1990, p. 62.)

Page 148

"Affirming," or affirmations, are positive thoughts you deliberately put in your mind to counteract the automatic negative reactions to which worriers are prone (e.g., "I am sexy" or "My work is excellent" to substitute for the "What if . . ." worries under discussion). Affirmations have a more powerful impact on your thinking than you might suppose. But they must be written and repeated on a several-times-daily basis to be effective.

CHAPTER SIX

Page 159
Dr. Brian Gould, at the time a resident in psychiatry at Pacific Presbyterian Hospital in San Francisco, used this nursery rhyme to introduce a case presentation.

Page 181
The metaphor of a car with a high idle was first presented to me by senior psychoanalyst Dr. Robert Rubinstein of San Francisco.

Page 182
In *The Soap Opera Syndrome*, Joy Davidson offers biological explanation for drama seeking, based on the sensation-seeker research of Dr. Marvin Zuckerman of the University of Delaware. Zuckerman accounts for the behavior of sensation seekers (high-risk takers, sexually and socially uninhibited people, people drawn to variety, change, stimulation of all kinds) by positing a brain chemistry level of the substances that control arousal. In effect, sensation seekers have a sluggish level of significant neurotransmitters and they seek sensation to jolt themselves to a more comfortable arousal level. Davidson uses this theory of sensation seeking as a possible biological basis for the drama seeking of women, arguing that women who seek sensation are not encouraged to have productive outlets for their needs and so turn to creating conflict or challenge in their relationships. It's an interesting idea, though Dr. Zuckerman does not necessarily agree with it (private conversation). He sees emotionality and sensation seeking as two different phenomena, though they may show some of the same traits. If you are interested in deciding for yourself, or in learning more about sensation seeking in case it does apply to you, see the references to Dr. Zuckerman's work in the bibliography.

Page 183
A "still point of the turning world . . ." from T. S. Eliot's "Four Quartets."

Page 188
The idea that we make mistakes in our thinking because of our emotional distortions is a central principle of all of cognitive psychotherapy. Cognitive therapists are the ones who have developed most of the techniques for changing our distorted interpretations.

CHAPTER SEVEN

Page 207
This distinction between anger and rage is from Neil Clark Warren's book *Make Anger Work for You*.

Page 211
Willard Gaylin's *The Rage Within*, page 111. This book contains a full discussion of Gaylin's concept of "grievance collecting."

Page 228
Refinements of the "Type A" research of the early sixties point out that the significant personality factors in heart disease are a tendency toward anger, hostility, and aggression. See Fischman's article, "Type A on Trial" in the February 1987 *Psychology Today*, Eysenck's "Health's Character" in the December 1988 *Psychology Today*, as well as the original book, *Type A Personality and Your Heart* by Friedman and Rosenman.

Page 230
Neil Clark Warren's book *Make Anger Work for You* includes a wide range of techniques for managing your temper. And *Anger* by Carol Tavris is an outstanding discussion of a variety of theories and perspectives on anger.

Page 231
These suggestions are drawn partly from what has been useful in my clinical practice and partly from suggestions made by Lewis B. Smedes in *Forgive and Forget*. Also, while I did not include it, you might find helpful the description of the stages of forgiveness in *Forgiveness* by Sidney and Suzanne Simon. And Marianne Williamson's synopsis of the Course of Miracles in her book *A Return to Love* presents a powerful argument for the price of rage and the rewards of forgiveness.

Page 237
In *The Achilles Syndrome*, Harold Bloomfield describes a healing visualization in detail.

CHAPTER EIGHT

Page 243

For an inspiring discussion on increased access to happiness, see Mihaly Csikszentmihalyi's *Flow*. The ideas presented there are a natural extension of the philosophy behind *Excess Baggage*. When we do get out of our own way, flow is the happy result.

Bibliography

■

Ashner, L., and M. Meyerson. *When Parents Love Too Much*. New York: William Morrow, 1990.

Baer, J. *How to Be an Assertive (Not Aggressive) Woman in Life, in Love, and on the Job*. New York: New American Library, 1976.

Barnett, J. "Narcissism and Dependency in the Obsessional-Hysteric Marriage." *Family Process,* 1971, 10:75–83.

Benson, H. *The Relaxation Response*. New York: William Morrow, 1975.

Benson, H., and William Proctor. *Your Maximum Mind*. New York: Times Books, 1987.

Bloomfield, H. *The Achilles Syndrome*. New York: Random House, 1985.

Borkovec, T. D. "What's the Use of Worrying?" *Psychology Today,* December 1985, 59–64.
———. *How to Reduce Worrying*. Rev. ed. Health Information Network, January 1990.

Bry, A. *Visualization*. New York: Harper & Row, 1978.

Chodoff, P., and H. Lyons. "Hysteria, the Hysterical Personality and Hysterical Conversion." *American Journal of Psychiatry,* 1985, 14:734–40.

Cleghorn, R. A. "Hysterical Personality and Conversion: Theoretical Aspects." *Canadian Psychiatric Association Journal,* 1969, 14(6):553–64.

Cohen, B. *The Snow White Syndrome*. New York: Macmillan, 1986.

Costello, E., and T. D. Borkovec. "Lost in What-Ifs: Treatment of a Case of Generalized Anxiety Disorders." In A. Freeman, F. M. Dattilo, eds., *Casebook in Cognitive Behavior Therapy*. New York: Plenum, in press.

Csikszentmihalyi, Mihaly. *Flow*. New York: HarperCollins, 1990.

Davidson, J. *The Soap Opera Syndrome*. New York: Berkley Books, 1988.

Degler, C. *In Search of Human Nature*. New York: Oxford University Press, 1991.

Diagnostic and Statistical Manual of Mental Disorders (Third Edition—Revised). Washington, D.C.: American Psychiatric Association, 1987.

Dowling, C. *The Cinderella Complex*. New York: Pocket Books, 1981.

Easser, S., and B. Lesser. "Hysterical Personality: A Re-evaluation." *Psychoanalytic Quarterly*, 1965, 34:390–405.

Eysenck, H. J. "Health's Character." *Psychology Today*, December 1988, 28–35.

Fischman, J. "Type A on Trial." *Psychology Today*, February 1987, 42–50.

Friday, N. *Jealousy*. New York: William Morrow, 1985.

Friedman, M., and R. H. Rosenman. *Type A Personality and Your Heart*. New York: Knopf, 1974.

Fromm, E. *The Sane Society*. New York: Rinehart, 1955.

Gallwey, T. W. *The Inner Game of Tennis*. New York: Random House, 1974.

Gawain, S. *Creative Visualization*. New York: Bantam, 1978.

Gaylin, W. *The Rage Within*. New York: Penguin, 1989.

Gendlin, E. T. *Focusing*. New York: Everest House, 1978.

Goleman, D. *Vital Lies, Simple Truths*. New York: Simon and Schuster, 1985.

Greist, J. H., J. W. Jefferson, and I. M. Marks. *Anxiety and Its Treatment*. New York: Warner, 1986.

Gunderson, J. G. "Personality Disorders." In Armand Nicholi, ed., *The New Harvard Guide to Psychiatry*. Cambridge: Belknap Press, 1988.

Hall, C. S., and G. Lindzey. *Theories of Personality*. 3d ed. New York: Wiley, 1978.

Hochschild, A. *The Second Shift*. New York: Viking, 1989.

Horney, K. *The Neurotic Personality of Our Time*. New York: W. W. Norton, 1964.
———. *Neurosis and Human Growth*. New York: W. W. Norton, 1950.

Horowitz, M. *Hysterical Personality*. New York: Jason Aronson, 1977.

————. "Self-Righteous Rage and the Attribution of Blame." *Archives of General Psychiatry*, November 1981, 38:1233–38.

Horowitz, M., et al. *Personality Styles and Brief Psychotherapy*. New York: Basic Books, 1984.

Jeffers, S. *Feel the Fear and Do It Anyway*. New York: Fawcett Columbine, 1987.

Kernberg, O. *Borderline Conditions and Pathological Narcissism*. New York: Jason Aronson, 1978.

Krohn, A. J., ed. *Hysteria: The Elusive Neurosis*. New York: International Universities Press, 1978.

Lasch, C. *The Culture of Narcissism: American Life in an Age of Diminishing Expectations*. New York: W. W. Norton, 1991.

Leman, K. *The Pleasers*. New York: Dell, 1987.

Lerner, H. G. *The Dance of Anger*. New York: Harper & Row, 1985.

LeShan, L. *How to Meditate*. New York: Bantam, 1974.

Lindzey, G., and C. S. Hall. *Theories of Personality*. 3d ed. New York: John Wiley, 1978.

Love, P. *The Emotional Incest Syndrome*. New York: Bantam, 1990.

Mackinnon, R. "The Hysterical Patient." *The Psychiatric Interview*, 1972.

Maslow, A. H. *Toward a Psychology of Being*. 2d ed. Princeton: Van Nostrand, 1968.

McKay, M., P. D. Rogers, and J. McKay. *When Anger Hurts*. California: New Harbinger, 1989.

Newman, J. "Forgive Him." *Self*, March 1991, 154.

Norwood, R. *Women Who Love Too Much*. New York: Pocket Books, 1985.

Oldham, J., and L. B. Morris. *Personality Self-portrait*. New York: Bantam, 1990.

Peele, S., and A. Brodsky. *Love and Addiction*. New York: Signet, 1976.

Peletier, K. *Mind as Healer, Mind as Slayer*. New York: Dell, 1977.

Riso, D. R. *Personality Types*. Boston: Houghton MIfflin, 1987.

Salzman, L. *Obsessive Personality: Origins, Dynamics and Therapy*. New York: Science House, 1968.
————. *Treatment of the Obsessive Personality*. New York: Jason Aronson, 1983.

Segal, Erich. *Love Story*. New York: Bantam, 1970.

Shain, M. *Some Men Are More Perfect Than Others*. New York: Charter House, 1973.

Shapiro, D. *Neurotic Styles*. New York: Basic Books, 1965.

Simon, S. B., and S. Simon. *Forgiveness*. New York: Warner, 1990.

Smedes, L. *Forgive and Forget*. New York: Pocket Books, 1984.

Smith, A. W. *Overcoming Perfectionism*. Deerfield Beach, Florida: Health Communications, 1990.

Smith, M. *When I Say No, I Feel Guilty*. New York: Bantam, 1975.

Tavris, C. *Anger*. New York: Simon and Schuster, 1982.

Thomas, A., and S. Chess. *Temperament and Development*. New York: Brunner/Mazel, 1977.

Ulanov, A., and B. Ulanov. *Cinderella and Her Sisters*. Philadelphia: Westminster Press, 1983.

Warren, N. C. *Make Anger Work for You*. New York: Doubleday, 1983.

Wein, B. "Heart Trouble." *New Woman,* August 1990, 62–66.

Widiger, T. A., and A. J. Frances. "Personality Disorders." In J. A. Talbott, R. E. Hales, and S. C. Yudofsky, eds., *Textbook of Psychiatry*. Washington, D.C.: American Psychiatric Press, 1988.

Williamson, Marianne. *A Return to Love*. New York: HarperCollins, 1992.

Zetzel, E. "The So Called Good Hysteric." *International Journal of Psychoanalysis,* 1968, 49:256–60.

Ziglar, Z. *Top Performance: How to Develop Excellence in Yourself and Others*. New York: Berkley Books, 1987.

Zuckerman, M. *"Sensation-Seeking: Beyond the Optimum Level of Arousal*. Hillsdale, New Jersey: Lawrence Erlbaum, 1979.
———. "Sensation-Seeking Trait." In *Encyclopedia of Human Biology,* vol. 6. New York: Academic Press, 1991.

Index

■

abusive relationships, 131–32, 258n, 259n–260n
Achilles Syndrome, The (Bloomfield), 262n
acting out behavior, 190–91
addictions, 51, 142, 153, 180, 187
affirmations, as self-help technique, 260n
alone, fear of being, 174
ambiguity, 56, 57–58
ambivalence, decisions and, 7, 40, 56–57
anger, 7, 38, 42, 43, 44, 260n, 262n
   drama creators and, 165–66, 174–75, 204–5
   management of, 262n
   and need to be right, 52–53, 66, 68
   rage vs., 207, 262n
   rejection fears and, 124–25, 133, 134–35, 142
   as safety, 211, 225–26, 235, 236, 241–42, 259n
   see also rage, cherishing of
Anger (Tavris), 262n
anxiety, 18
   blind spots and, 5, 255n
   change and, 22, 107, 245, 249–51
   control of, 12, 22–23, 241, 249–51, 257n
   of drama creators, 174, 176, 188–90
   and need to be right, 45, 59, 73
   rejection fears and, 116–17, 118, 123, 127, 142, 153
   see also fear; worries
Anxiety and Its Treatment (Greist et al.), 251
apathy, 7, 142, 158
apologies, 38, 71–73, 129
appreciation, criticism and, 87
approval, 99–101, 142, 158

arguing, arguments, 38–39
   see also family; marriage
Ashner, L., 258n
assertiveness, 126, 259n
attachment, need for, 35, 159–205
   aspects of (chart), 26–27
   baggage identified with, 184–91
   exercises to cope with, 192–205
   as ruling passion, 15, 26, 182–84
   see also drama, creation of
attention, need for, 160–61, 168–69, 172–178, 182, 183, 185, 197–99
audiences, independence from, 197–200
authority figures, 170–71, 213–14, 218
avoidance behavior, 119, 125, 127, 141–43, 145
avoidant personality, 122

Baer, Jean, 259n
baggage:
   aspects of (chart), 26–27
   balance and, 245–47
   as blind spot, 4, 6
   in characteristic themes, 5–6
   described, 2–4, 7–10, 243–44
   excess (chart), 26–27
   identification of, *see* identification of baggage
   strength-weakness connection in, 12–14, 15, 16, 244
   see also self-defeating traits
balance, satisfaction and, 245–47
Barnett, Joseph, 256n
belief baggage, 9, 24
Benson, Herbert, 250
"best" mantra, 77, 86, 89, 98, 105–7

"be yourself," as formula for happiness, 8

blame, blaming, 132, 230, 239, 240
  of others, 2, 3, 15, 37, 41, 42, 96
  see also criticisms; self-criticisms

blind spots, 5, 255*n*
  excess baggage as, 4, 6, 7–9, 10, 12–14, 19, 243–44

Bloomfield, Harold, 262*n*

Borderline Conditions and Pathological Narcissism (Kernberg), 257*n*

boredom, 7

Borkovec, Thomas, 138, 150–51, 260*n*

bragging, marketing as, 91

Bry, Adelaide, 250

careers, *see* professions

catastrophizing, 166–68

catcher-flier marriages, 95, 131, 132–33

ceremoniousness, 41

change:
  anxiety and, *see* anxiety
  meaningful, 66–69
  resistance to, 17–23, 259*n*
  rewards of, 21–22, 245, 251, 263*n*
  small shifts and, 18–19, 21, 28, 61–66, 145, 154, 155, 192, 201, 250
  stifling vs., 136–37, 141, 158
  therapy and, 157
  three-step process for, 19–23
  see also fear; risks

Chess, Stella, 260*n*

choices, forced, 226–28

closure, forgiveness as, 240

codependency, in marriage, 132–33

cognitive patterns, excess baggage in, 9

Cohen, Betsy, 258*n*

commitment, 94, 96, 97

communication, withdrawal of, 234–35

competitiveness, 92–93, 98, 102

complaining, 125, 221

computers, personal, 33

consistency, of personality style, 9, 10

consumer culture, 97

contradictions, excess baggage and, 243–44

control, need for, 29–75
  aspects of (chart), 26–27
  baggage identified with, 49–61
  exercises to cope with, 61–74
  as ruling passion, 15, 16, 26, 46–48
  see also right, need to be

Costello, E., 260*n*

creativity, 178

criticisms, 100, 140, 216, 258*n*
  acceptance vs., 85, 143–44
  avoidance of, 86–87, 127–29
  excellence vs., 83
  expertise as, 91–92

responsibility vs., 63, 67, 69

crusaders, in social causes, 214

Culture of Narcissism, The (Lasch), 257*n*

cummings, e. e., 167

Czikszentmihalyi, Mihaly, 263*n*

Dance of Anger, The (Lerner), 259*n*

Davidson, Joy, 261*n*

daydreams, *see* fantasies and daydreams

deadlines, as drama, 186–87

decisions, decision making:
  ambivalence about, 7, 16, 40, 55–59, 129
  emotional basis of, 168, 169–70
  others charged with, 62–64, 67–69
  ruling passions and, 20–23
  see also change; self-help

defeat, surrender to, 7

defenses, 12, 17–18
  attachment needs and, 165–66
  baggage as, 22
  control needs and, 40–42
  justice needs and, 211, 212, 213, 222, 224–26, 235
  in personality portraits (chart), 26–27
  security needs and, 130–31
  self-esteem needs and, 84

defensiveness, 216–17

Degler, Carl, 256*n*

delays, in self-help strategies, 152–53, 154–156

dependency, 132–33
  emotional extravagance and, 171–72, 173–74, 177, 179–80, 183, 192, 193–202
  on "homeandfamily," 120–22, 146–47

depression, 125, 142

deprivation, sense of, 211, 214–16, 221, 223

diet, anxiety and, 250

disappointment, 7, 76, 102, 105–7, 144, 162

disapproval, sense of, 41, 45, 106, 128–29

domination, 46–48, 89, 92–93, 100, 236–237

drama, creation of, 3, 28, 126, 159–205, 212, 261*n*
  aspects of (chart), 26–27
  baggage identified with, 184–91
  portraits of, 160–84
  rage and, 204–5, 207
  remedies for, 192–205, 247
  see also attachment, need for

easing up, of controlling behavior, 61–74

efficiency, 30–32

effort, change and, 21–23

Eliot, T. S., 261*n*

embarrassment, 82, 85–86

Emotional Incest Syndrome, The (Love), 258*n*

emotional patterns, excess baggage in, 10
emotional reserve, 260n
  lack of, 159–205
  and need to be right, 35–38
  rage and, 209–11, 216–20
  rejection fears and, 123
  superiority feelings and, 82
energy, saving of, 65
"enough," satisfaction in, 246–47
envy, 102–3, 177, 206, 211, 258n
excess baggage, see baggage
exercise, physical, as self-help technique, 73, 250
exercises, self-help:
  in anxiety control, 249–51
  in attachment problems, 192–205
  in control reduction, 61–74
  in rage reduction, 229–42
  in rejection fear reduction, 147–58
  rewards of, 74
  in superiority-fantasy reduction, 107–15
ex-spouses, 217, 225–26, 234

failure, fear of, 4, 79, 91, 93, 98–99, 103, 115, 119, 158
family, 10, 257n–58n
  drama creators and, 163, 170, 171
  and need to be right, 38–39, 52–53, 258n
  rage cherishers and, 217, 218, 223–24, 229, 231–32, 234, 239–40
  rejection fears and, 119–22, 140, 144
  superiority feelings and, 78, 85–86, 88, 98, 112–13, 257n–58n
fantasies and daydreams, 7
  of drama creators, 173, 176, 177, 180
  and need to be right, 24, 58
  in personality portraits (chart), 26–27
  of rage cherishers, 212–13, 222, 224
  rejection fears and, 117, 123–24, 128, 155
  security needs and, 157–58
  superiority feelings and, 77, 79–80, 93, 107–15
  see also "what if" concerns
fear:
  in abusive relationships, 260n
  as baggage, 4, 20, 245
  of being alone, 174
  of being ordinary, 84, 94
  blind spots and, 5
  of failure, 4, 79, 91, 93, 98–99, 103, 119, 154
  labeling of, 235–37
  of losing all feelings, 226
  of rejection, see rejection, dread of
  of risks, 67–70, 118–28, 137–39, 145–46, 149, 152–58, 222

Feel the Fear and Do It Anyway (Jeffers), 251
finances:
  of drama creators, 161, 178–80, 194
  and need to be right, 39–40, 56
  of rage cherishers, 213–16
  rejection fears and, 129–30
  superiority feelings and, 81–82, 87–89
finish, need to, 6, 34–35
Fischman, John, 257n, 262n
Flow (Czikszentmihalyi), 263n
Forgive and Forget (Smedes), 262n
forgiveness, 97
  rage and, 206, 212, 229–42, 262n
Forgiveness (Simon), 262n
Friedman, M., 257n, 262n
friendships, 41, 53, 86, 107, 112–13, 114–115, 169–70, 172, 195, 216–17
Fromm, Erich, 256n
frustration, 51, 52–54, 144

Gallwey, Tim, 250
gambling, 180
Gawain, Shakti, 250
Gaylin, Willard, 211, 262n
giving, receiving vs., 7, 130, 133, 134, 135, 142, 143–45, 214
Goethe, Johann Wolfgang von, 107
Goleman, Daniel, 255n
Gould, Brian, 261n
grandiosity, see superiority, feelings of
gratification, 9, 16
Greist, John, 251
grievance collection, 211–12, 262n
Grossarth-Maticek, Ronald, 260n
grudges, holding of, 209, 221, 225, 236
guilt, sense of, 45, 128–29, 213, 225–26, 259n

habits, baggage as, 7, 9
  see also routine and ritual
hardest things to do:
  attachment needs and, 162–63
  control needs and, 61–62
  justice needs and, 212
  in personality portraits (chart), 26–27
  security needs and, 127–28
  self-esteem needs and, 82
hate, letting go of, 230–42
heredity/environment pendulum, 256n
histrionic personality, 163
Hochschild, Arlie, 257n
"home," as sanctuary, 119–22, 140
Horney, Karen, 255n, 256n
Horowitz, Mardi, 256n
How to Be an Assertive (Not Aggressive) Woman in Life, in Love, and on the Job (Baer), 259n

How to Reduce Worrying (Borkovec), 260n
humor, sense of, 82, 87, 92, 163
hyperbole, 161, 165
hypersensitivity, hypervigilance, 208–11

identification of baggage, 4–7, 19
  of drama creators, 161, 162, 165–67,
    171–77, 180–81, 183–93
  in need to be right, 32, 34, 36, 37–39,
    40–41, 42, 43, 45–46, 48–62
  of rage cherishers, 206–8, 210–12, 213–
    220, 223–29, 231–32
  in rejection fears, 116–19, 122–23, 124–
    125, 127–30, 132–35, 136, 138–46,
    148
  in superiority feelings, 79, 83–84, 86–
    87, 88, 95, 101–8
identity, development of, 111, 142, 192
illness, 257n, 260n, 262n
  drama creators and, 161–62
  of rage cherishers, 228–29
  stress-related, 51, 73, 228
image-consciousness, 81, 88–89, 97–98
impulsiveness, 57, 59
  of drama creators, 165–66, 169, 190–91,
    192–93, 200
"I'm wrong," as tactic, 71–72
independence, 216–17
  exercises in, 193–202
inferiority, sense of, superiority feelings
  and, 99, 102–3, 107
infidelity, 96, 177
information junkies, 32–33
in-laws, 217
inner portraits, 19
  of drama creators, 181–84
  of need to be right, 44–48
  of rage cherishers, 220–25
  rejection fears and, 137–40
  of superiority feelings, 97–101
In Search of Human Nature (Degler),
  256n
integrity, 40–41
intimacy, 53–54
  being there and, 52
intuitiveness, 164, 178, 188–90

jealousy, *see* envy
Jeffers, Susan, 251
judgment, fear of, 86–87, 127–28, 143–44
justice, need for, 206–42
  aspects of (chart), 26–27
  baggage identified with, 206–8, 225–29
  exercises to cope with, 229–42
  as ruling passion, 15, 26, 221, 222–25
  see also rage, cherishing of

Kernberg, Otto, 83, 257n

Lasch, Christopher, 257n
leadership, 90–91, 196
Leman, Kevin, 259n
Lerner, Harriet Goldhor, 259n
LeShan, Lawrence, 250
lies, 24
  and need to be right, 34, 71, 72
  rejection fears and, 124
  superiority feelings and, 85, 93, 113–15
listening, 80, 96, 164–65
lists, listing, 31–32, 81, 110–11, 202–4
Longfellow, Henry Wadsworth, 159
love, loving:
  barriers to, 8–9
  criticism as expression of, 85
  drama creators and, 161, 163, 172–73,
    178, 182, 187–88
  and need to be right, 35–37, 43, 52, 54,
    56–57
  rage cherishers and, 218, 226–29, 234
  rejection fears and, 130–37, 144–45, 158
  superiority feelings and, 95–96, 98–101,
    103, 107
Love, Patricia, 258n
Love Story (Segal), 95

Make Anger Work for You (Warren), 262n
marriage, 3–4, 256n
  abuse in, 131–32, 259n–60n
  conflict in, 41, 43, 54, 66–67, 68–69, 95–
    97, 105, 133, 135, 137, 174–75, 176–
    177, 215, 218–20, 226, 259n
  drama creators and, 174–77, 178, 182
  and need to be right, 42–44, 49–50, 52,
    53–54, 56–57
  of rage cherishers, 215, 218–20, 226, 234
  rejection fears and, 117, 131–37, 144
  superiority feelings and, 86, 90, 93–97
  see also love, loving; spouses
martyrdom, 130
Marx, Groucho, 95
Maslow, Abraham, 256n
materialism, image-consciousness vs., 81,
  88–89, 97–98
medications, anti-anxiety, 250
meditation, 73–74, 151, 250
memory capacity, 33, 37
men:
  baggage associated with, 25
  in catcher-flier marriages, 132–33
  spouse choice of, 42, 44, 53
Meyerson, M., 258n
mind-quieting techniques, 73–74, 151, 250
money, *see* finances
morality, need to be right and, 40–41
Morris, Lois, 256n
mottoes, personal:
  as cognitive baggage, 9, 24

of drama creators, 172
and need to be right, 34–35
in personality portraits (chart), 26–27
of rage cherishers, 213
rejection fears and, 126
superiority feelings and, 78–79
mystical beliefs, 78

nagging, 144
narcissistic personality, 78, 257n
Neurosis and Human Growth (Horney), 256n
Neurotic Personality of Our Time, The (Horney), 255n
Neurotic Styles (Shapiro), 256n, 257n
"no" response, 126, 155, 169, 259n
Norwood, Robin, 260n
numbness, worry and, 51
nurse-stray puppy marriage, 134–35

obsessive personality, 32, 44, 256n, 257n
obstacles, inner, *see* self-defeating traits
office, as "home," 121
Oldham, John, 256n
out-of-control behavior, 151
outrage, *see* anger; justice, need for
overreactions, 188–90

paralysis, sense of, 3–4, 51, 136–37, 141, 142, 158
in decision making, 7, 40, 55–59, 129
paranoid personality, 211
party invitations, reactions to:
attachment problems and, 162, 168–69
control problems and, 41–42
justice problems and, 216–17
in personality portraits (chart), 26–27
security problems and, 122, 127–28
self-esteem problems and, 84, 89–90
passion, cravings for, 159–60
passive-aggressive personality, obsessive mate and, 44
peacemakers, 219–20
People, 161
perceptions, changes in, 19, 60–61, 260n
see also thinking
perfectionism, 57–58, 257n
personality portraits, 256n
aspects of (chart), 26–27
description of, 23–25
of drama creators, 160–84
of need to be right, 30–44
of rage cherishers, 208–25
of rejection fears, 119–40
of superiority feelings, 77–97
see also inner portraits
Personality Self-Portrait (Morris), 256n
personality styles, 255n

baggage associated with, 25
dominant drives in, 15, 16
psychiatric labels and, 32, 78, 122, 163, 211
surprises in, 65
see also strengths; weaknesses
Personality Styles and Brief Psychotherapy (Horowitz), 256n
Personality Types (Riso), 256n
perspective, forgiveness and, 238–41
phobias, 122
phobic personality, 122
pickiness, superior standards and, 108–9, 110, 111, 114
planning, in self-help strategies, 154–56, 196, 200–202
power, 46–48, 100, 236–37
see also control, need for; self-esteem, need for
praise, 84–85, 101
prayer, as self-help technique, 238, 250
premature ejaculation, 36
priorities, setting of, 65
privacy, need for, 216
procrastination, 55, 57, 58–59, 186–87
productivity, 55, 218
being vs., 52
as dogma, 30, 31–32, 45, 51
dramatic tension and, 186–87
professions:
of drama creators, 178, 187, 195
and need to be right, 39
rage cherishers and, 213–14, 217–18
rejection fears and, 129, 145
superiority feelings and, 87–88, 97
projections, as defense, 169, 212
psychiatric labels, 32, 78, 122, 163, 211
put-downs, 143–44

rage, cherishing of, 6, 28, 204–5, 206–42, 262n
aspects of (chart), 26–27
baggage identified with, 206–8, 225–29
personality types and, 207–8
portraits of, 208–25
remedies for, 229–42, 247
see also justice, need for
Rage Within, The (Gaylin), 262n
rationalizations, 114, 127–28
reactive behavior, 145–46, 188–90
Reagan, Ronald, 90
reality, 128, 157–58
self-esteem and, 107–15
reconciliation, forgiveness and, 240
rejection, dread of, 4, 28, 86–87, 107, 115, 116–58, 188, 212, 259n
aspects of (chart), 26–27
baggage identified with, 141–46

rejection (cont.)
  portraits of, 119–40
  rage and, 208
  remedies for, 146–58, 247
  see also security, need for
relationships:
  of drama creators, 160–62, 163–64, 165,
    167, 168–77, 182–84, 185, 187–88,
    192, 261n
  and need to be right, 41–44, 49–50, 52–
    54, 56–57
  of rage cherishers, 209–11, 213, 216–20,
    226–29, 231–37, 238–42
  rejection fears and, 120–21, 123–28,
    130–37, 141–47, 148–49, 152–57, 158
  superiority feelings and, 76, 80, 81, 82,
    84–86, 89–91, 93–97, 101, 105, 107,
    112–13, 114–15
  see also family; friendships; love, loving;
    marriage; social behavior
relaxation, deep muscle, 73–74, 151, 250
religion, forgiveness and, 231, 238
resentment, 124–25, 130, 133–34, 146–47
responses, slow, 139
responsibility:
  control vs., 16, 46–48
  to cope with baggage, 244–45
  lack of, 163, 169–70, 186–87, 191
  shifted to others, 62–63, 65, 66–69, 179
retaliation, 212–13, 222, 223–24, 225, 236
Return to Love, A (Williamson), 262n
right, need to be, 2–3, 25–28, 29–75, 212
  aspects of (chart), 26–27
  baggage identified with, 48–61
  portraits of, 30–48
  rage and, 207
  remedies for, 61–74, 246
  see also control, need for
risks, 259n
  emotional basis of, 164, 180, 181, 185
  fear of, 67–70, 118–28, 137–39, 145–46,
    149, 152–58, 222
  grandiosity and, 79, 103
  rituals vs., 121–22
  of self-medication, 250–51
  surrender of control and, 62–69, 72
Riso, Don Richard, 256n
romance, 35–36, 176
Rosenman, R. H., 257n, 262n
routine and ritual, 7, 9
  drama creators and, 162–63, 185–88
  as "home," 121–22, 147
  unconscious, 222
Rubinstein, Robert, 261n
rules, 61, 172–73
  breaking of, 69–70, 171
  obedience to, 40, 45, 59–60

superiority feelings and, 78, 88, 96
ruling passions, 24, 255n–56n
  attachment as, 15, 26, 182–84
  baggage created by, 16–18
  change and, 18–23
  control as, 15, 16, 26, 46–48
  defined, 15–16
  justice as, 15, 26, 221, 222–25
  in personality portraits (chart), 26–27
  resistance to, 18–23, 61–62, 108
  security as, 15, 16, 26, 139–40
  self-esteem as, 15, 16, 26, 76, 99–101
running, long-distance, 73

sacrifice, 130–31, 143
saint-sinner relationships, 41
Salzman, Leon, 256n
Sane Society, The (Fromm), 256n
satisfaction, 8
  change and, 20, 21–22
  "enough" concept and, 246–47
  ruling passions and, 15–16
schedules, making of, 31–32
scorn, superiority feelings and, 76, 98–99
"second best," dissatisfaction with, 7
Second Shift (Hochschild), 257n
secret brag, 24
  of drama creators, 165–66
  in need to be right, 32
  in personality portraits (chart), 26–27
  of rage cherishers, 211
  rejection fears and, 131
  superiority feelings and, 77–78, 110–11
secrets, as baggage, 10
security, need for, 116–58, 260n
  aspects of (chart), 26–27
  baggage identified with, 141–46
  exercises to cope with, 146–58
  as ruling passion, 15, 16, 20, 26, 139–40
  see also rejection, dread of
Segal, Erich, 95
self-acceptance, 8, 112, 114, 115, 246
self-awareness, 10–11, 131, 184
  anxiety and, 5, 18
  self-consciousness vs., 80
self-consciousness, superiority feelings and,
  80–83, 98–99, 112–13
self-criticisms, 257n
  and need to be right, 32
  rejection fears and, 127–28, 132, 137,
    140, 142–43
  superiority feelings and, 80–81, 83–84,
    87, 97, 98–99, 103, 112
self-defeating traits, 4, 5, 24, 244
  causes of, 15–17, 49
  clues to, 6–7
  combinations of, 25

consistency of, 9
described, 2–4, 7–10
of males vs. females, 25
in normal lives, 14
self-awareness vs., 10–11
see also identification of baggage
self-defenses, *see* defenses
self-doubt, 129
self-esteem, need for, 76–115
aspects of (chart), 26–27
baggage identified with, 101–7
exercises to cope with, 107–15
as ruling passion, 15, 16, 26, 76, 99–101,
258n
see also superiority, feelings of
self-evaluation, 66–68, 109–12
self-help, 10–11, 18–23
for drama creators, 192–205
for need to be right, 61–74
for rage cherishers, 229–42
for rejection fears, 146–58
small steps in, 18–19, 21, 28, 61–66, 145,
154, 155, 192, 201, 250
for superiority feelings, 107–15
self-hypnosis, 151
self-image, rejection fears and, 116–17, 142
self-interest, 130
self-loathing, 125, 127, 129, 143
self-love, 204
self-medication, risks of, 250–51
self-pity, 211, 212, 213, 214–16, 217–18,
221, 226
self-recrimination, 142
self-regard, self-esteem vs., 100–101
self-reliance, 193–202
self-respect, 131, 196, 204
self-righteousness, 29, 41, 219–20
self-serving reflections, 112
self-worth, 138, 142, 188, 257n–58n
sensation-seekers, 261n
separation pain, 183
sexual behavior, 7, 256n
of drama creators, 176–77, 187–88
and need to be right, 35, 36, 43
of rage cherishers, 210, 218, 221
rejection fears and, 117, 139
superiority feelings and, 83, 96
Shain, Merle, 159
Shapiro, David, 256n, 257n
shopping, attitudes toward:
attachment needs and, 179–80
control needs and, 39–40
justice needs and, 214–15
in personality portraits (chart), 26–27
security needs and, 128, 130
self-esteem needs and, 81–82, 87–89
"should" dogma, 256n, 257n

liberation from, 65–66, 68–69, 73
and need to be right, 45–46, 50, 51, 54,
56, 60
Simon, Sidney and Susan, 262n
smart vs. likeable behavior, 42, 60–61, 72,
91
Smedes, Lewis B., 262n
Smith, Ann, 257n
Smith, Manuel, 259n
Snow White Syndrome, The (Cohen), 258n
Soap Opera Syndrome, The (Davidson),
261n
social behavior:
of drama creators, 162, 164–67, 168–74,
198–99
and need to be right, 40–42, 53–54
of rage cherishers, 210–11, 214, 216–18
rejection fears and, 116–19, 122–29, 142,
143, 145, 146, 152–57
superiority feelings and, 80–81, 85, 86–
87, 89–93, 101, 113–14
see also relationships
Some Men Are More Perfect Than Others
(Shain), 159
"special child," 257n–58n
spontaneity:
"should" dogma vs., 51
thinking vs., 190–91
see also impulsiveness
spouses:
choice of, 24, 28, 42, 43–44, 53, 57, 86,
94–95, 117, 131–32, 134, 135–36, 174,
175, 218–19
as delegate, 90–91
emotional baggage and, 10
see also marriage
status, signs of, 81, 85, 88–91, 94, 97–98,
104
stifling, sense of, 136–37, 141, 158
strengths:
of drama creators, 160–64, 168, 178,
183–84, 184–91, 204
and need to be right, 30, 33, 39, 40–41,
46, 48, 49, 51, 52, 55, 59, 61, 74
in personality portraits, 24
of rage cherishers, 206, 209–10, 225–29,
241–42
rejection fears and, 137, 140, 141, 142,
143, 145
superiority feelings and, 77, 78–79, 84,
90, 91–92, 101–7
weaknesses related to, 12–14, 15, 16, 244
stress:
drama creators and, 161–62
and need to be right, 51, 61, 65, 66, 67,
73
rage and, 208–11, 220, 228–29

success:
    and need to be right, 39, 56
    nonachievement of, 8, 16
    rejection fear and, 119, 129, 146–47,
        149–50, 156
    superiority feelings and, 20, 78–79, 84,
        87–88, 97
    see also failure, fear of; risks
superiority, feelings of, 2, 16, 28, 75, 76–
        115, 127, 212, 257n–58n, 259n
    aspects of (chart), 26–27
    baggage identified with, 101–7
    portraits of, 77–101
    rage and, 208
    remedies for, 107–15, 247
    see also self-esteem, need for
support, in self-help strategies, 157, 249
suspiciousness, 211, 212, 216–17
symbiotic couples, 135–37

Tavris, Carol, 262n
telephone, drama creators and, 199–200
television, rejection fears and, 122
Temperament and Development (Thomas
        and Chess), 260n
themes, baggage characterized in, 5–6, 26–
        27
theme songs, 24
    of drama creators, 181–82
    and need to be right, 44–46
    in personality portraits (chart), 26–27
    of rage cherishers, 221–22, 224
    rejection fears and, 137–39
    superiority feelings and, 98–99, 113
therapy, change and, 157
thinking, 9
    change and, 19–21, 260n
    feelings vs., 165–67, 178–79, 181–82,
        190–204, 261n
    projections in, 169, 212
    rationalizations and, 114, 127–28
    spontaneity vs., 190–91
Thomas, Alexander, 260n
toning down techniques, 192–93
Toward a Psychology of Being (Maslow),
        256n
Tracy Ullman Show, The, 76
travel, 120, 121
Treatment of the Obsessive Personality
        (Salzman), 256n
Type A Personality and Your Heart (Fried-
        man and Rosenman), 257n, 262n

uncertainty, 56, 76, 103

victim, role of, see self-pity
visualization, 73–74, 149–50, 156, 237–38,
        250, 262n
Vital Lies, Simple Truths (Goleman), 255n
vulnerability, to physical ailments, 51, 73,
        161–62, 228, 257n, 260n, 262n

Warren, Neil Clark, 262n
weaknesses:
    of drama creators, 160–62, 163, 165,
        166–67, 168, 169, 174–77, 181, 184–
        191, 204–5, 207
    and need to be right, 30–32, 36, 38, 41,
        42, 44, 45–46, 48–61, 207
    of rage cherishers, 206–9, 215–20, 225–
        229, 241–42
    rejection fears and, 116–19, 121–37,
        141–46, 208
    strength related to, 12–14, 15, 16
    superiority feelings and, 76–77, 79, 83–
        84, 87, 92–99, 101–7, 208
"what-if" concerns, 67–68, 137–39, 140,
        147, 260n
When I Say No, I Feel Guilty (Smith), 259n
When Parents Love Too Much (Meyerson),
        258n
Williamson, Marianne, 262n
withdrawal, from objects of rage, 233–35
women, 260n
    baggage associated with, 25
    in catcher-flier marriages, 132–33
    as drama seekers, 261n
    rejection fears of, 126, 139, 259n
    spouse choices of, 43–44, 131–32
Women Who Love Too Much (Norwood),
        260n
workaholics, 32
worries:
    management of, 147–52, 260n
    and need to be right, 51, 65
    of rage cherishers, 241–42
    rejection fears and, 128–29, 138, 143
    see also anxiety; fear
written notes, in self-help strategies, 148–
        149, 150, 151, 155, 156, 237, 250
wrong, being, 33–35, 38, 71–73, 129

yoga, 73, 250

Ziglar, Zig, 250
Zuckerman, Marvin, 261n

Read more from bestselling author
Judith Sills, Ph.D.

•

NEW FROM VIKING IN JANUARY 2004

The Comfort Trap
or What If You're Riding a Dead Horse?

We all have our comfort zones—*your* coffee bar, *your* pref-erence for half hazelnut/half decaf very light no sugar, *your* seat on the 8:24, *your* same old fight over the holidays with your parents. But the time comes when your comfort zone isn't so comfortable anymore—when it's keeping you from having a happier, more meaningful, and fulfilling life.

The Comfort Trap or What If You're Riding a Dead Horse? is for anyone whose life has temporarily run aground, whether you're stuck in a dead-end relationship, in a soul-killing job, or when your life just seems to have become one long summer rerun. The rewards for escaping your comfort zone are enormous. And Sills—who has helped thousands with her sage advice, dispensed in her signature go-get-'em style—has come up with a brilliant, excuse-busting seven-step plan that points a clear, inspiring way out.

ISBN 0-670-85847-1